Madison St. Station

Sam Fels

For Laughing Boy, Geezer, and Pias.

Epiphany
April 13, 2008
San Jose v. Calgary (Game Three)

      I know. It seems weird that a book about the Blackhawks and being a Hawks fan (at this point you're probably thinking "supposedly") starts off with a game between the Sharks and Flames. Well, it is weird. But this is the night that started this silly little journey of mine, that would give me a unique seat to the rise and conquering of the NHL by the Chicago Blackhawks. All of it viewed from my cold little post outside Gate three or from the empty-can-littered desk at which I'm writing whatever this is.

      I was living in Los Angeles at the time, half-heartedly claiming that I was there to do stand-up comedy but already figuring out that I didn't really have the stage chops to go anywhere with it. I had been out of work for a couple of months at this point, having decided that working overnights in various California casinos was taking too much of an emotional toll on me (that is if you gauge your emotional well-being by the regularity of crying in your car at dawn, which I think is a pretty handy way to do it). So needless to say, I was certainly at a prime point for a major pivot in my life and for whatever might cause it.

      And even from L.A., I had caught Hawks fever again. This was after Jonathan Toews and Patrick Kane's rookie season. It was a season that proved how futile our hopes had been in the seasons before, all of them bestowed on kids never worthy of it, such as Mark Bell or Tyler Arnason or whoever else was a synonym for "tomato can." This was after the season that Bill Wirtz had died and the shackles that held held the organization back for so long had come off. This was after the first season Rocky Wirtz and John McDonough took over and ran the Hawks like an actual organization in the twenty-first century (which is about the extent of what they did despite all the claims of geniusness coming from their own offices, but that's for much deeper into this book). This was after the season during which the Hawks ever so briefly flirted with actually making the playoffs, even if they would have gotten fustigated by the Red Wings in no more than five games that year. This was right after the season that Patrick Sharp netted thirty-six goals, the kind of total no Hawk ever dreamed of approaching for years even if they'd been allowed to shoot on their own goalies. This was after the season when a bevy of other young players came up for a look, and it was easy to see that something was bubbling here, like some witches brew from some Shakespeare play I wrote a middling paper about in high school.

      I'll remember the moment exactly for the rest of my life. I was walking back from the kitchen in our apartment where the carpet was dirty enough to create a new element or two and suddenly I froze, standing behind the couch, with the Sharks and Flames on the screen. I think the

Sharks had just scored to go up 3-0, a lead they would eventually blow to lose 4-3. Randy Hahn, the Sharks play-by-play man, was losing his mind on the call and perhaps it was the volume that snapped my mind into gear (for once). And suddenly it felt like something hit the natural frequency within me. You don't get a lot of these moments in your life, so you tend to notice when they happen. I couldn't move. My muscles basically froze. I'm guessing not a lot of people get such a clear vision of what they are supposed to do with their lives so immediately. Let me tell you something: it's better than coke.

I was going to bring back *The Blue Line.*

Well, that's not exactly how it went in my head. At such stupidly dramatic moments like as this, your thoughts don't spill out before you so well spelled out. It was more a bunch of words crashing into each other like souped-up bumper cars, but I was able to decipher what it all meant in the cavernous space between my ears. I saw the words "*Blue Line*" and "you" and "write" and "Hawks" and could put it together. Toss in a "fuckstick" because that word is generally always just below the surface in my mind. To the point that every phone I've ever had has memorized it within ten text messages written.

I had to sit down after a few moments, basically to come to terms with everything and in the hopes that the numbness within me would subside. Of course, being a Fels meant I had to see what could go wrong with this plan. Like, in painstaking fashion. Not just light musing or introspection, but a full out audit of all the ways I would fuck this up, even just mere minutes after thinking of it in the first place. The first challenge, of course, was finding the people who did the original program to see if they had any interest in doing it again. I don't know if I thought I would just write for them from Los Angeles or if I'd come home to take it over. I just knew I had to talk to them.

But what if I did have to do it on my own? Were there enough people like me who read *The Blue Line* who would want to read another version? Or had they all given up their Hawks fandom, never to return (like those on the Night Train)? Were they all Chicago Wolves fans now? Did they all die (if you spent any time in the standing room in the old Chicago Stadium, you know this was a reasonable question)?

I quickly began crunching numbers in my head, even though I had no concept of what the term "crunching numbers" actually meant and still don't, which is probably why I ended up making up a job instead of getting a real one. How many per night would I have to sell to make this work? How much were these to produce? It didn't seem like it took too many sales to at least break even. Even with all the different disasters I could conceive of, like dragon attack or bail money for when the Younger Wirtz would assuredly have me arrested, I couldn't find any angle that made it seem impossible or not worth going for.

The coming days included calls to my father and brother to see what they thought. I searched out Mark Weinberg, who wrote *The Blue Line,* through various message boards. It all eventually added up. That one night, watching the Flames and Sharks, sprang the next nine years that saw me standing in the snow selling my booze-addled thoughts on the Hawks to my fellow drunks. What follows is my story, their story, and maybe just a little bit of your story too, even if you're not a Hawks fan. All told through the fuzzy vision of your intrepid writer.

So with all apologies to Nick Hornby for parroting (or outright stealing) his *Fever Pitch* model, let's go for a ride, shall we?

Indoctrination
December 20, 1987
Bruins vs. Hawks

Of course, the seeds were planted much earlier than that spring day in 2008. Everyone has their first game. This was mine.

To be honest, I don't remember the details that well. I know my father came home from...well, I'd say work but I'm pretty sure it was the pool hall. I know he asked my brother Adam if he wanted to go to the Hawks game that night, and I'm fairly sure he did so because he'd found someone at said pool hall who wasn't skilled enough at the table to hold onto the contents of his wallet (point of order here: my father was a professional copywriter at several Chicago ad agencies throughout the years, he just liked to spend his free time playing pool, and playing for money is just more fun, isn't it?). The point is, my father had disposable income and wanted to use it to take Adam to a Hawks game.

What I do know is that I popped up unprompted to declare that I wanted to join in. This was received by my entire family as if I'd just said I'd discovered a weird growth on my body. They all had their reasons, I'm sure. I had shown mild interest in hockey before that, given that my brother was a fanatic and when you're five or six years old you will do anything and everything your older brother is doing. I have vague recollections of watching the Oilers win the Cup. It was this thing they did back then. A lot. I know my parents bought me a floor hockey stick with Wayne Gretzky's name on it, though I'm not sure if I asked for it.

My excitement about attending this game was solely about going with my brother Adam, and not reflective of a huge interest in the actual sport myself. Still, he was surprised at my sudden desire to go. Most older brothers would have dreaded watching over their shithead little brother at something like this. Adam was delighted that even at this fragile age I wanted to do something so...well, older.

My father probably just worried about having to spend the money on an unforeseen third ticket. My mother naturally feared for my life/future.

And if her little boy was so excited to go someplace like Chicago Stadium for a Hawks game at this tender age, was he already doomed? (Yes, he was.)

All of them had a common trepidation though, and that was the Chicago Stadium being somewhere you just did not take a small child, especially for a hockey game. My mother knew that the Stadium was on the west side, and this was a long time before the Mayor Daley Gentrification Plan started to crawl down Madison street. The neighborhood around the Old Stadium was, to put it mildly, colorful. I'm sure if my mother had had her way, none of her family would have stepped foot anywhere near it. My father, being unafraid of just about anything, knew that paying five dollars to a local resident to "watch the car" (i.e. make sure the other residents didn't smash it to bits or truck it off to your friendly neighborhood chop shop) was just about the only danger one would find on a game night.

My brother and father's hesitancy surely stemmed from what went on inside the arena, and that was mostly just the sheer noise. It remains a memory now, and a fading one, but the Old Stadium for Hawks games was considered something of an asylum. And that wasn't inaccurate. Much like the crowd you see at metal shows, you didn't see these people anywhere else but Hawks games. You didn't run into them at the grocery store or see them walking dogs in the park. It's like they were kept in a pen under the Stadium and let out about three hours before puck drop. And my brother and father were convinced that I would not be able to handle the noise.

However, wasn't the noise the point? Any hockey fan, or soccer fan for that matter, or wrestling fan even, will tell you that the first thing they noticed about watching these events, or back then listening to them on the radio, was the noise, the crowd. The sound of a crowd completely losing their collective minds seeping through the speakers on the TV or the radio is what drew us in. What was it about this thing that made people so excited that they made noise rivaling a jet engine five feet away? Surely this was worth an investigation at the very least. I had to know. Their fears only intrigued me more.

Besides, I may have only been six years old, but I knew I was a cool six-year-old (and thinking so shows just how out of it I was). I hung out in my brother's room while he blasted *Master of Puppets*; how many six-year-olds could claim that? My brother let me hang around when his friends were over, usually playing Strat-O-Matic hockey (and now you can see where my benchmark for "cool" became quite skewed). It didn't dawn on me that he was just being nice or trying to placate my mother. In my mind, Adam let me hang around because I was just that awesome of a kid. Here was this little brother that he just had to show off at Chicago Stadium? Pfft, I could handle that. I'd survived hanging out in my brother's bedroom after all, or even the halls of his high school once or twice. There was nothing I couldn't do.

It didn't take long for the rest of the family to see that any effort to keep me from this was

going to be futile. If it wasn't that night, it was going to be soon, so they might as well get it over with. Back then, it would have been a twenty-five or thirty minute drive from our apartment to the Stadium. That was long for a boy my age, because usually I was only in the car to go to school or the store. But this was somewhere NEW. My parents had no reason to take me in this direction before. Of course, when you're that age and you're told a neighborhood is bad, you're just about ready to see anything outside your car's windows. Would we be dodging gunfights on our way? Would there be fires? Roving packs of wolves? Perhaps for the first time, in my mind, I was headed somewhere I could seriously die (and no, not from the layers of secondhand smoke within the Stadium corridors, which probably will kill me sometime soon).

We arrived and my brother got out to find a scalper, which in those days didn't take long for a mediocre Hawks team in the middle of December. This was how we got tickets for the first several years of my fandom, because getting tickets from the box office at the Stadium was nigh-on impossible (remember, everyone else attending the games was kept under the ice, so their access to tickets was obviously that much easier). He quickly found three tickets, though what he didn't realize at the time was that they weren't together. I was told to get out of the car and go inside with my brother while Dad parked (perhaps to keep me from seeing where he might park and what he might have to do when he got there). So inside we went.

You've probably read countless stories of people's first baseball games: walking through the concourse and seeing glimpses of the sky through the gates before the splendor and the color and the vibrancy of the first viewing of the playing field hits you. The green of the grass, the beige of the dirt, the blue of the sky all making for a rich tableau that always brings us back no matter how old we get.

This was not how it worked at Chicago Stadium.

First off, the concourse at the Stadium was about four feet wide. I really don't have any idea how wide it was, because seeing any more than eight inches in front of you through the cigar and cigarette smoke would have been a minor miracle. Whatever glimpses you got from the concourse into the playing area were just more smoke-filled, dotted with very angry people in dingy lighting. Your shoes stuck to the floor, if said floor wasn't already flooded with what we only hoped was water. The smell of beer, or the beer-flavored water that Old Man Wirtz preferred, filled the air. That feeling that I could meet my doom on this night did not dissipate upon entering the gates.

I was home.

I don't remember much about the game. I do know that my father took the ticket that wasn't connected to the other two, and thus we didn't see him all game. You'd think this would have sent a small boy into utter panic, especially a boy who worshipped his father as I did and especially one whose day had been filled with terrors told of the surrounding neighborhood and didn't Dad go park in it and oh my god he's been eaten by those wolves while being shot by rats!

Actually, I didn't think about my father at all during the game. I was too transfixed. While the interior of the Stadium at first glance certainly would never match one's first glance of the field at Wrigley or Fenway or wherever else, the white of the ice was still mesmerizing. It didn't come through on our aging TV, and whatever iteration of SportsChannel the Hawks were on in those days wouldn't have had the production value to make it if we had a top-of-the-line one anyway. It just looked dull on TV. But in person? It nearly burned your retinas. It was so striking, and the lines so red. It was like the players were skating on a Vegas sign. As a small child you don't really watch the players at your first game, you kind of just stare at the ice.

But it wasn't just the ice. I couldn't help but have my eyes and (sadly for my mother) my ears scan the crowd. There were men (and really, only men) yelling things I'd never heard before with a fervor I could scarcely understand. Surely this must be the most important thing taking place on Earth if these people are getting this worked up about it. A fight broke out in the crowd every ten minutes it seemed, and it felt as if this was just part of the spectacle. People came either to fight with each other in the stands or at least to watch people fight with each other in the stands. And it never failed. And of course, the vocabulary expansion I was receiving that night would make me one of the more popular kids during recess at school the next few days.

But mostly, I sat in anticipation and fear of THE ROAR. No, not the marketed, slogan roar that the Hawks used in the arena's last year. No, this was THE ROAR that my brother and father were sure I was not ready for. Would it deafen me for life? Would it crush my head like I'd just heard the voice of God? (Yes, that's a half-reference to *Dogma*, a movie I've come to abhor as I've gotten older. We'll get through this together). I almost didn't want the Hawks to score, for fear of permanent injury from the wall of noise that I had no preparation for and that my still-developing ears would not be able to handle. And I also couldn't wait for the Hawks to score, because I had to know what they were so worried about and surely if I could survive this cacophony I was the coolest six-year-old boy in the history of time who would go on to slay his enemies and conquer the world.

Honestly, I couldn't tell you who scored. It was either Everett Sanipass or Denis Savard as I've looked this up. One obviously would have been cooler than the other (in case you're unlearned in the way of '80's Hawks hockey, as you probably should be, the latter would have been a cool moment for your first game where the former is just high comedy). I'm fairly sure it was only to tie the game at one or even just to pull the Hawks to within a goal. I know I didn't see it, because the people in front of me leapt up before the puck hit the net. But there it was. THE ROAR.

Yeah, it was loud. I know Adam immediately looked over to see if I was crying or scared or had, in fact, imploded. What he found was a gleaming smile on his younger brother. Usually boys my age only got this kind of smile from a new bike or Nintendo. I got it from a bellowing crowd of hockey fans that my parents didn't want me associating with.

Because how could one not smile when part of something like this? Something so raucous, so joyous, so COOL. And here I was, somewhere so dangerous, and what's better to any boy than to do what you're not supposed to do? And I BELONGED. I had to belong, because this noise did not kill me. I wasn't afraid of it. I could handle this. I'm sure it would have terrified all my friends, and this certainly wasn't a place for icky, scary girls (a main concern at six). This is where I wanted to be. I was one of these people, even at such a tender age when I shouldn't have been identifying with anyone.

I don't remember anything else about the rest of the game except for the empty-net goal that the Bruins scored to seal the game at 4-2. Someone slid it from center-ice, and I remember watching the puck streak unaccompanied all the way to the net. And as soon as it hit the back of the cage, fifteen-thousand people simultaneously stood up to leave. It looked like a comedy skit of some kind. It was sort of my first experience with this kind of groupthink, where a large group of people has the same collective impulse without ever communicating it to each other. At that age I didn't really know that an empty-net goal meant the game was over everywhere but on the clock. But they all did. It made me want to be part of this sort of hive mentality even more.

We found my father after the game, and I'm sure I was relieved to learn he hadn't been shot by rats. I was bouncing all over on the car ride home because the result doesn't really matter at your first game. I have no doubts my father was dreading all the extra money he knew he was going to have to spend to send me along with my brother to games now. He must've known, from the expression on his young son's face, that this was now a part of me. Most teenage boys, as Adam was at this point, wouldn't have been thrilled to know they were now going to have to bring their little brother along to a lot of games. But not him. I think he was jonesing at the chance to mold his brother into the person maybe he didn't think he could be himself. Or at least into a fun, cool younger brother. Whereas both he and my father weren't very popular or happy as children, perhaps he saw this as another chance to make me one who would be. And as the only kid in class who was taken to a hockey game at that point, I certainly was well on my path.

Poisoned

January 1, 1988

Capitals vs. Hawks

The next month was spent constantly pestering my brother and father, wondering when I would get to go back to the Stadium. When you're six, the concepts of income, employment, time, commitments, and whatever else older people worried about didn't matter to you if you could even conceive of what they were. At that point, the world simply revolved around when would I get taken back to a Hawks game. I thought it should be everyone in the family's first, second, and third priority. I didn't care that my father's employment status had become tenuous, or that my mother was making what money we had stretch barely over the educations for me and my brother, or that my brother was navigating his way through the college application process (and making a real hash of it as well).

I spent the intervening month regaling my school friends (ha, plural in hope only) with what I'd seen. I think most of them were completely unaware Chicago had a hockey team, and probably a fair few didn't even know what hockey was. Surely no one I went to school played the sport, and this was an age when some kids would have started.

I went to a private school. And this was my first indication of how being a hockey fan was going to make me a social or sporting "other." The parents of my schoolmates, if they were even sports fans at all, were Bulls fans. This was when Michael Jordan had basically taken over the world and with it the city's sporting attention (at least when the Bears weren't playing). And I was going to school with the offspring of the city's well-to-do and fresh crop of yuppies; all they knew was Michael Jordan. Yes, they all had the sweaters and collared shirts we've all associated with Bulls fans.

And I knew that was a group I wanted no part of. Did I have solid reasons? Assuredly no. George and Adam remained big Bulls fans, even after losing their season tickets to a price increase after Jordan arrived. I guess I just wanted to go full-bore into "outsider" territory.

But moreover, the Bulls and their fans didn't seem cool, at least not to me at that age. I knew better. I beseeched my friends to inform their parents that there was something better going on. There was something faster and brighter and kind of scary and loud and it's where the coolest people hung out. Of course, this being just about the first generation of parents that shielded their kids from anything scary and loud, you can see how futile my efforts would have been. And their dads weren't getting Hawks tickets from the boss, but they sure as hell were getting Bulls tickets. It wasn't long before I became known as "the hockey fan" in the class. In first grade, this was probably akin to having green hair in high school. This was stepping toward punk rock. If other parents found something dangerous about

Chicago Stadium and the Hawks, didn't that make me dangerous? I liked the sound of that (and with my sugar-bowl haircut, I'm sure I terrified everyone).

Make no mistake, at least back then the feel of separation comes early to any hockey fan. There is a special feeling thinking that you have something, or you know something, that almost everyone else doesn't. "Whatever," I thought, "I don't need them to join me on this. This is my thing." At the same time, no matter how old you are as a kid you don't want to be separated from the pack in any fashion. The worst thing you can be is different, after all. I may have talked big about prematurely adhering to a punk rock philosophy, but that didn't mean I had anywhere near the commitment to the bit. Especially at an age where I didn't know shit about punk rock.

While I've come to realize that the rivalry between Hawks fans and Bulls fans is silly (and possibly also racially tinged), you can certainly see how it might have started. After all, the Bulls had a genuine world star and were knocking on the door of a championship and were on TV and all of it. The Hawks? If anyone knew when and where they played they sure didn't talk about it much. The feeling of being left out in the cold snapped in pretty quickly.

It was also during this month that I became aware of the ham-fisted way the Hawks were being run. Before attending a game, I didn't really know that the home games were not on TV. I didn't have much interest in watching any game on TV before that anyway, but after the hockey fuse was lit I obviously wanted to stay in touch. I thought it was a bit peculiar that you couldn't see Hawks games on TV because I knew I could see Bulls and Cubs and Bears games on TV whenever they played. But thanks to six-year-old optimism and early bedtimes, I didn't kick up much of a fuss. After all, I didn't have a TV in my room but I could sneak a walkman in after bedtime to listen to Pat Foley describe the anarchy that was going on to the south and west of home. You could sense how ridiculous the adults thought it all was. While my passions and love for the game and team were planted very early, so too were my problems and suspicions with them.

Anyway, perhaps just to lessen their annoyance, my parents sanctioned this trip, and it was the first game of hundreds that only Adam and I attended. I couldn't have been happier. Other friends had older brothers, and all they did was kick the shit out of them and scowl. My brother certainly kicked the shit out of me often—it was his right after all—but then he was excited to do stuff like this with me. I don't know if it was the hockey I so craved, or time away from my parents with Adam. It was probably both.

Up Close
March 13, 1988
Flyers v. Hawks

  If there was any lingering doubt about my dive into the world of hockey, it was erased on this night. Any hockey fan or really anyone who has been to a game can tell you that it's a completely different sport when you get to sit up close. This was my first foray into the lower bowl of the Stadium.

  Judging by the time of year, it must've been a reward for my brother's birthday and/or finding a college that was willing to lower its standards and risk its reputation to let him in. Whatever it was, I didn't care.

  I knew this was an event because Adam made sure in the days preceding that it was. We acquired the season tickets from a father of one of his classmate's, and I was told it was around the tenth row. I knew it was the kind of seats we would never get or be able to afford, so this was going to be a big deal.

  Not only that, but this was the FLYERS. They were coming off playing in perhaps what is still the greatest Stanley Cup Final in history, losing in seven games to the Oilers the previous spring. While I knew the Oilers were the be-all and end-all of the league and sport, I also knew there was something different about the Flyers. The Flyers, and especially their fans, symbolized all of the elements that made going to a hockey game exciting and terrifying at the same time. While my brother would never admit to having any affection for them, looking back on it I know that he did. The Oilers were U2 or Bon Jovi. Yeah, they'd conquered the world and were the sport's "biggest band," but everyone knew who they were. They didn't speak for the real fans.

  The Flyers? They were Guns N' Roses. Volatile, violent, capable of brilliance and madness from one moment to the next. The stories of what went on at their home arena, The Spectrum (you can figure out what most called it. Hint: it rhymed) made it seem like Thunderdome was an actual place in our country. They wore orange and black, which just looked so threatening, and they were coached by perhaps the most unhinged guy in the organization, Mike Keenan. These were the Flyers of Rick Tocchet and Mark Howe and Peter Fucking Zezel and most infuriatingly, Ron Hextall. Even at that tender age, I knew about him and the rage he basically sent every opposing fanbase into. All you had to do was watch one Flyers game on TV, and it wouldn't be too long before you'd have to ask someone, "What is that noise?" The answer was invariably Hextall whacking his stick against both of his posts when the play was in the other end, mostly because it drove other fans nuts. He was known to be completely nuts as well, and one never knew when he'd simply Paul Bunyan anyone around him with his stick. This wasn't so much a hockey team coming to town but more of a biker gang that you hoped would leave town without spilling too much local blood.

We got to our seats and I sat in utter shock at how close we were. I tell most people that I've rarely enjoyed sitting very close at a baseball game, as I'm constantly attuned to not catching a foul ball in the teeth. That started early in my life. It was a similar fear sitting this close at a hockey game, but it wasn't a puck I worried about taking the full brunt of.

It's impossible to accurately describe the speed at which the game is played when you sit that close. You can't believe it. Things happen before you have time to focus on where they are, and then things pivot back the other way before you've fully comprehended what just happened. Whereas up top you can take it all in, this is pure adrenaline, especially in the '80's when the ice was a lot more open.

So considering the speed at which everything was happening, which my young eyes and nerves could barely handle, and knowing the reputation of the Flyers back then, I was more afraid of a human body (or just a severed head) flying through the boards and landing on me than I was about catching a wayward puck.

This was also the game at which some dickhead Flyers fan (redundant, I know) sent his two young daughters to carry a pro-Flyers sign down the aisle. Being young and being female almost certainly didn't shield them from hearing a few lord-knows-whats, such was the atmosphere. People in the section we were sitting in urged me, another child, to run up and take their sign away. To this day I still kind of regret that I didn't. I would have been a hero to the entire lower bowl of the Stadium, though I almost certainly would have earned an ass-kicking for my brother eight ways to Sunday from the girls' father. This was the Old Stadium, encouraging children to fight in the stands for their own entertainment.

Denis Savard netted the OT winner, giving the Hawks a 5-4 win. Savard was everyone's first Hawks hero, and he always scored when they needed. All kids were pushed to love Savard, and I did, but I knew that picking him as my favorite player would be uncreative or easy. Even then, even after going off the beaten path to be a hockey fan at all, I had to steer a wider path in choosing my idols. Savard existed on a different plane than every other player the Hawks had then, because he was just so much more skilled than any of his teammates. It didn't feel so much like he was a Hawk but a player bestowed upon the Hawks. It was such an odd dichotomy: within this barely standing building filled with smoke and stale beer, populated by an angry mob that couldn't resist fighting each other and that constantly bayed for blood, existed this artist who glided over the ice and around any opponent. He was a painter in an arena full of people working with a drill. He was the flower that springs out of the sidewalk. I'm still not sure how he wasn't killed.

First Heartbreak

December 26, 1988
Blues vs. Hawks

    I imagine being a parent to a sports-obsessed child comes with a lot of minefields that you never expected. You know that when you have a kid there are going to be hard, teachable moments that are simply torture to endure. The first time they hurt themselves. The first time they get bullied at school. The first time they strike out in little league. The first time their heart breaks. You should also prepare for the first time their favorite player on their favorite team gets traded, if they're so infected.

    I couldn't possibly tell you why Rick Vaive became my first favorite Hawk. He was in Chicago for barely a hundred games, arriving before the previous season along with Steve Thomas for Eddie Olczyk and Al Secord (and this was far before I would ever realize how great it would be to get Eddie O out of town). Secord was my brother's favorite player, and maybe I thought it was funny to pick the player they got in return and needle him that way. Yes, I was kind of a jerk at this young age, at least to my own family. Maybe I thought it was too easy to pick Savard or Larmer, because they were everyone else's and even at that age I had to be contrarian. More likely, I think I just liked the way the #27 looked (remember this, it comes back into play). Or maybe I liked that you could have two v's in one name. "Vaive" looked cool. It sounded cool. And for a good portion of his one full season in Chicago he had to wear a full visor thanks to a broken jaw. At seven, I probably thought that was cool too, because it was different. Rest assured, there was no rational reason.

    Not that Vaive wasn't a useful player. He was. He scored forty-three goals in his one full season as a Hawk, though in the '80s the list of players that scored forty-plus goals included numerous hobos and carnival folk. He piled up 441 career goals in thirteen years in the league, and 537 points. He had himself a career.

    Sadly, this was the day he was traded to Buffalo for a glorified obelisk in Adam Creighton. Rumors of the deal had popped up for a few days prior, as Mike Keenan, who had become the Hawks coach, craved a player you could park in front of the net and who couldn't be moved from there. Because in those days being able to stay anchored in that area required being able to survive assault with a deadly weapon. While Creighton couldn't actually do anything, he was big and hard to move simply by being big. Back then, this was a skill.

    Adam spent the days preparing and needling me about the impending move. I think he knew I would be upset, and wanted to prepare the ground while getting some revenge on my Secord-departure joy (and if you think exacting revenge on a seven-year-old boy is a sign of sickness, you're A) correct, B) never had a little brother, and C) are not of our family).

The day finally came, and even though I thought I was prepared, I was still flattened. They were taking my Vaive away. If it could happen to him, why would I bother giving my heart to another player if they could be so callously and viciously ripped out of my life? And to Buffalo? That might as well have been Mars. I vowed to never, ever warm up to Creighton, and thanks to his performance in a Hawks jersey that wasn't all that hard to do. My brother liked to tell a story that a couple months after the trade, while we were watching the sports segment on the local news (you did actually have to do this once upon a time to stay updated or to get Hawks highlights from home games), they played the highlights of Creighton scoring two goals (this apparently did actually happen once). As soon as it hit the screen I apparently stuck my fingers in my ears and shut my eyes, hoping to pretend that I didn't live in a world where Creighton was acquired for Vaive. As most Hawks fans will tell you, this is pretty much how we treated an overwhelming majority of trades and decisions they made during this time.

The first one is the hardest. You can pretty much deal with any player leaving town after the first one. It was not something I had ever dealt with before. My first favorite Cub was Ryne Sandberg, who didn't leave until I was a teenager. My first favorite Bear was Jim McMahon, who was barely there anyway. My Vaive scar still is there somewhere today, making all the ones that came after it that much more palatable.

Into The Lion's Den
December 28, 1988
North Stars v. Hawks
It was quite a wait for the next one. My brother had gone off to college, and my father hadn't entirely admitted to himself that he was going to have to regularly bring a second son to 1800 W. Madison to watch a sport he didn't much care for (as well as to ruin any chance of his kids being able to provide for him when he got older). Two and a half months might as well have been a century to my child mind. I did my best to stay in touch with the Hawks through radio and television, bending bedtime and homework around them as best I could (not that homework was much of a concern to me at that or any point really). There were many nights with a walkman in bed with me so I could listen to Pat Foley and Dale Tallon describe the action from the Stadium.

This was a pretty important season for the Hawks, though not record-wise because they didn't come close to .500 and they barely scraped into the playoffs only because pretty much everyone made the playoffs back then (sixteen of twenty-one teams, if you didn't know). They made something of a run, making it to the Conference Final before getting domed hardcore by the eventual champions, the Calgary Flames. This was the glass ceiling the Hawks always found in the '80's. They could muscle their way out of the

Norris Division every so often (emphasis on "muscle"), but they didn't have a prayer of beating Calgary or Edmonton. They did this five times in the decade, and it almost became Looney Tunes-esque in its repeated ruthless ending. This was Wile E. Coyote continually running into the boulder that was painted to look like a tunnel. The Hawks were usually similarly flattened. They had finally gotten Bob Pulford out of a position of power (temporarily, sadly, replacing him with Mike Keenan), and might, just might have a non-dinosaur making decisions on the roster.

For those who didn't grow up in Chicago or weren't familiar with the Hawks back then, Pulford was the undead drunk who everyone knew was a complete moron except for the owner Bill Wirtz, to whom he'd somehow become his most trusted confidant (or just drinking buddy, which was the same thing to him). For close to thirty years, whenever a coach or GM was fired, Pulford somehow floated back into the opening, like a soused piece of driftwood, firmly keeping the Hawks in neutral. As we came to find out, that was basically Wirtz's plan all along, and Pulford, who was barely aware of his surroundings most days, was the perfect patsy. Pulford was that guy at the office who you only see in the bathroom not particularly doing anything or even looking at anything, and you keep asking yourself what it is he does here and how he keeps his job. He just kind of stood in one place, when he was capable, and the team kept circling back to him.

Finally, he was punted into some closet at the Stadium (only to be unearthed again when Keenan bolted a few years later) and the Hawks looked like they might, just might, start taking some steps forward. Sure, Mike Keenan was completely unhinged and was on the verge of being murdered by any one of his players at any given moment. But he got results. This was the man who dragged the Flyers against the greatest collection of players of all-time in the Oilers twice, and went toe-to-toe with them twice with Peter Fucking Zezel. This was exactly what the Hawks needed. Keenan was one of the hottest coaching properties in the league, and he had somehow been convinced to work in Chicago for an owner known for not having a lot of desire to put a winner out there.

After what seemed like an interminable wait, my brother Adam finally came home for Christmas break. And the minute he stepped through the door, I made it very clear to the whole family what I was most looking forward to. No, it wasn't the presents at Christmas. No, it wasn't the rest of the family coming in from Michigan, whom I did love. Nope, it was that we were going to get back to the Stadium. That's all I had talked about for weeks before his return.

From the time it became clear, at my very first game, that this hockey thing wasn't just a bug but permanently in my bloodstream, my brother had been stoking the fire for us to take in a game in the standing room section of the Stadium. Looking back on it, his teenage desire to show his edge and dedication was at work here, but luckily for him he had an accomplice in me who felt the same things at way too early an age (or I just wanted to ape him. Either way, he got the desired result). He constantly told me how the "real fans" get there when the doors open to stake out their spot, watch the warm-ups, and go most wild for the anthem. Every time we talked about hockey, which was all the times we weren't talking about baseball, he would nudge me about watching a game there. So of course, by the time this date rolled around, my desire to be up there was basically ravenous. To watch a game anywhere else seemed like something on the level of eating Brussel sprouts.

However, telling your parents that you want to take your seven-year-old brother to the standing room of the Stadium was essentially saying you wanted to take him bear hunting, using him as bait. If the arena itself was an asylum, the standing room was where you needed security clearance to get into. This was where the fans who only had eleven bucks to their name spent it all so they could harangue (if not outright threaten) Dino Ciccarelli for three hours. This wasn't just a hobby for them. This was how they could function through the rest of their work week, by getting it all out during a game. The standing room was beyond the North Endzone at Soldier Field or the bleachers at Wrigley. This is where the patrons pounded the emergency exit doors to get the crowd going or to process some stuff going on within them, or both. This is where at least two fights started every game, before tumbling onto the seated fans below. This is where opposing fans were genuinely frightened to go. This was the enlarged version of the older boys' bathroom at school. You'd have to be nuts to go into it, and even more nuts to make it out of there. And much like said bathroom, it usually had cigarette smoke pouring out of it, even though smoking was supposedly banned.

Needless to say, my mother didn't approve. In fact, I'm kind of surprised she didn't bludgeon her eldest son for even suggesting it. I still had hope, after all. So we were told we could go to the game but under specific instruction that we would buy seats. Her baby boy was not going to be tossed to the wolves just yet.

Our father gave us a ride down, and he already knew how this was going to go and was resigned to it. He knew that as soon as we were let out of the car we were going to buy standing room tickets. There was no way he could stop it (I'm fairly sure this was the precedent my brother cited seven years later when I informed my father I wanted to see Megadeth at The Aragon Ballroom, which he greeted with as stern a "no" as I ever got from him about anything. Those of you who have been to the Aragon will understand completely). It was destiny. So my brother was given specific instructions that I was to come home with all ten fingers and ten toes, and if I had so much as a mark it wouldn't be him that Adam would have to deal with. The thought of being confronted by our furious mother was enough to keep both of us awake most nights, and her levels of apoplectic rage if her youngest was harmed in any way would have required an exorcist. My brother assured him I would be fine, though I'm not sure how much he actually believed it.

We procured our standing room tickets, and my brother instructed me that we had to rush upstairs so we could get a spot right on the railing. I was more than willing and more than a touch excited. Except he forgot to mention one thing. At the Stadium, to get to the top of the second deck where the standing room was, you had to ascend roughly 8,907 stairs. At least that's how it seemed. I know people complained upon their first look at the escalators when the United Center replaced the Stadium. I never did. Because I can still vividly remember the ache those stairs caused in my legs at a tender age. The burn turned into a rock-like feeling, where I thought my knees might never bend again and my leg muscles felt like they'd been filled with quick-drying plaster. When I finally stopped climbing, my legs screamed. Like, I was sure I could hear them crying. They throbbed for nearly half an hour after that first climb. And they did after every climb after that. But it had to be done. You also had to occasionally ignore or rationalize the sight of a sub sandwich-sized cockroach or dog-sized rat. And no, that's not a joke about the Hawks' blue line in those days, though it might as well be.

This was the first time I made the climb, and our location was set for the next ten years: right behind the net the Hawks attacked twice, and if that wasn't possible, then on the side right at the red line. The behind-the-net section was optimal, because in the Stadium the second deck dipped at the ends, meaning standing behind the net was basically akin to sitting in the seventh or eighth row. But that's why you had to be there early, and that's why you had to rush up that Everest of stairs to get a spot, no matter how jellied your legs might feel when it was finally ascended.

I remember Adam getting compliments on his little brother who thought he belonged in that spot. It wasn't something these people saw a lot of. My mimicking of their yelling at opponents only made them smile more, and their affirmation made it clear I would never spend another game anywhere else. I still wasn't "allowed" to swear, though whenever one of those words escaped my lips my brother couldn't do much more than laugh. After all, what chance was there I wasn't going to swear up there? It's like when you go to a concert of a band you don't know that well, but everyone around you singing the lyrics kind of makes you intuit the lyrics correctly anyway. And I'm sure the patrons found something rather adorable about this small child attempting to lasso the meaning and feeling of the word "motherfucker." The fact that we were all kept behind rails only further enhanced the feeling of a lock-up. This was where all the noise of the Stadium was generated and collected. It was like a metal concert every time.

There I was, in position, for the Anthem. You have to capitalize it around these parts. That's what it's come to mean. And through the years it's been dulled a bit, and the never-ending and unsolved debates over when and why it started and whether it's disrespectful or not have given it just a whiff of tedium. But on certain nights still to this day, it can be a near religious experience. And at the Stadium, it always was. This wasn't a crowd just carrying through with tradition simply because. This was eighteen-thousand lunatics trying to scare the living shit out of the opposing team by screaming as loud as they could for the entire duration of the national anthem. And some ex-players have admitted that standing on their blue line, their ears ringing and the building shaking and the faces of the crowd demanding their blood so clear in their vision that they felt like the loneliest people on Earth. There would be no shelter here.

For a young boy, this is probably the best time to be alive, these two minutes. Because where else are you allowed to make as much noise as you want for that duration of time? Certainly not school. Certainly not at home when all your parents want after a day at work is peace and quiet. This was catharsis. Maybe that's what it was for everyone else too. Can't yell at the boss, can't yell at the spouse, can't yell at the kids, so I'm just going to come here and do it. There certainly was an element of desperation to it. At that point, getting to experience the Anthem was enough to make for a good night. It was ok if the Hawks lost because I was a part of that.

They didn't lose on this night though. Savard and Larmer scored. The Hawks racked up twenty-nine minutes of penalties, which was just about the norm for Keenan's Hawks. And I had found where I truly belonged at far too young an age, and far too early to be saved later.

Gretzky
February 12, 1989
Kings vs. Hawks

After that first foray into the zoo of standing room, it wasn't too much longer before Adam had to return to college and I knew that by the time he got back for summer, hockey season would be over (no, I didn't hold out much hope of the Hawks playing late into the spring, and even if I did, procuring a playoff ticket then was akin to finding Incan treasure in the rain forest). Whenever I expressed this fear to my father, he probably sensed the panic and desperation in my voice, and he knew it was going to have to be him to keep his second son from the utter depression and hell that a Hawks-less life would be.

My father was not a hockey fan. The early wake-up calls and freezing at various suburban hockey rinks in service of my brother's playing career had clearly left him a bit jaded about the whole thing. He appreciated that both of his sons loved the game and did nothing to discourage it. But whereas hockey is the ultimate team sport—everyone gets a shift after all— my father desired performance and stardom.

This is partly why, I think, basketball was his first sports love. It is certainly why the Stones weren't just his favorite band but pretty much his raison d'etre. George craved the feeling one got from watching Jagger on stage. And basketball gives you that. Watching Dr. J or Michael or Magic on any given night, they weren't just playing. They were performing. They were captivating, as LeBron and Steph and Durant are now. They are stars, rock stars even, rising above and transcending all the other players around them. This is what my father sought in his entertainment, sports or otherwise. Yes, *The Fugitive* was one of his favorite films. So it was no surprise that the first game George decided he could bring me to and enjoy himself was a visit from Wayne Gretzky.

Even to the most neophyte fan, you watched Gretzky and the Oilers and you knew you were seeing something different. Hell, you didn't even really have to watch him play. You just had to read his stats every season to be entertained. Back then, during the intermission, the Stadium would run the leading scorers on the scoreboard over center ice. Gretzky was obviously always #1, and his numbers *looked* different. Not like, in another language, though they might as well have been. They just appeared to occupy the atmosphere differently. They had a lot more digits, let's say. It was as if he was playing a different sport, and in a lot of ways he really was.

My introduction to hockey was through the Oilers. My brother and father both sat and watched their Final appearances, because those were the out-of-market games that were always on. So I joined in. There was something about that blue and orange combination that captivates a kid. Also the fact that they won all the time, because every child is a front-runner at first. They were hockey, and Gretzky was the Oilers.

Until he wasn't. Once again, my age didn't let me fully comprehend the enormity of Gretzky being traded to Los Angeles. In hockey, this was akin to Massachusetts breaking off from the continental United States and floating to Iceland (and I'd really have no problem if Massachusetts adapted this strategy now). When you're that age you don't know anything about contracts or money or budgets or egos of players and owners alike—or that Gretzky had an actress wife that all of Canada was blaming for this. You know that players have contracts, but to you that's the same as them having helmets. To be fair, most of the hockey world was stunned that the greatest player of all time could be traded at the height of his power, and they understood all the parameters. To me, it made about as much sense as my parents dressing as clowns every day (side note: my parents did actually dress as clowns once).

And to Los Angeles? I barely knew the Kings existed. I knew they were always terrible, and they wore horrible uniforms (which I've now obviously come to adore. Is this growing up?). And when the Hawks played them out there the games started too late for me to watch all of before the cursed bedtime was enforced. It felt like Gretzky, the game's greatest jewel, was being sent to prison in Siberia.

Of course, Gretzky immediately made the Kings viable. He made hockey south of the Continental Divide viable. And in my mind, he was so powerful he changed the Kings' jerseys simply by showing up! Like he walked into the dressing room the first day, waved his hand, and the Kings went suddenly from yellow and purple to silver and black. And if I thought the Oilers' blue and orange was captivating, at seven-years-old, the silver and black was like witness God himself.

And my father was not going to miss it either. He knew exactly what Gretzky meant, and this was something to be planned for. Now he would surely get his "performance," because The Great One never missed. So not only did we go, but we acquired the Mora seats ten rows behind the penalty boxes. Dad and I were going to see this performer, and we were going to soak in it.

The first thing I noticed is that when the players took the ice for warm-ups, there were a lot more people in the building than normal and they all had cameras. Most games only saw a smattering of flash bulbs. This was a full-on assault of flashes. When he hit the ice there was basically a roar, partially in appreciation, partially in derision. This was still The Stadium after all.

Anyone who saw Gretzky back in his pomp knows that time basically stopped when he was on the ice. Whenever he came off the bench there was a heightened focus in the whole building. Because you might see *something*. Whatever was going to happen, it was going to revolve around him. Gretzky wasn't all that big or fast, but it was clear he was just playing a different game entirely than everyone else on the ice. Everything slowed down when he got the puck. It was as if his opponents were afraid to move for fear of opening up something for him that only he could see. They were the transfixed prey to his angler fish. His teammates moved as if by his volition entirely. It would drive the Stadium fans nuts, but almost every time Gretzky entered the offensive zone with the puck he would simply circle back toward the blue line, shaking the first wave of defenders and getting a look at the second, and then would almost telekinetically whip a pass across the ice to a streaking teammate for a chance. It happened every time, and though everyone in the stadium saw it coming, his opponents were helpless. It was Krusty yelling at a Washington General for not taking the ball a Globetrotter was just spinning on his finger. Except eleventy billion times more. Even when he wasn't doing that, Gretzky just always looked like he had more time and space than anyone I had ever seen. Because he did. Hockey, at its best, kind of feels like chaos. It moves so fast and players crash into each other and sometimes there doesn't seem to be a plan. And here was this guy simply rising above it, conducting a beautiful symphony in the midst of a riot.

He put up a hat trick on this particular afternoon. My father was beaming. He played the Hawks like they were marionettes that day, and most days really. This wasn't just Jagger on stage, this was Jagger shredding through "Brown Sugar." He might as well have been skating out there by himself, such were the Hawks' attempts to stop him (and given that they were attempting to counter him with such names like Bob Bassen, Keith Brown, Steve Konroyd, and Bob McGill, they might as well have let him skate by himself).

The downside to seeing a generational star like this was that you knew, or at least deeply suspected, that your team would never have anyone like him. There were only six or seven of these creatures in every sport, and they'd already been apportioned. We got Michael Jordan, and I was sentenced to never have anything like that in a sport or team I cared about. It was nothing I would ever know. But then, wasn't having a player like that cheating? That's why the Oilers won all the time, because they got to put out the ultimate cheat code.

But really, you feel cheated. Why didn't I get to have a player like that? One who would always come up with something to bring his team through and couldn't be stopped? One that they talked about throughout the league? It wasn't any different than complaining about the kid who got the Nintendo game you really wanted. It was juvenile jealously. It just lasted well into my twenties.

Bedlam
December 20 1989
Blues vs. Hawks

If there was any chance of my mother's hope that my fandom could be eroded eventually, it was erased in this week. It started with this game. Once again Adam had returned home for the holidays from college, and once again we immediately pivoted right back out of the house to standing room for a divisional game. I'm not even sure I let him unpack.

Hockey for at least the past decade has tried to trade on the passion and rivalry that existed during the '70s and '80s. It's a failed strategy, because the game isn't that way anymore and there are simply better ways to go about it. Back then there were only twenty-one teams, everyone made the playoffs, and you always ended up playing the same teams in the playoffs due to the divisional system and there only being five teams in said division. So there were always one or two teams that a given team would end up playing thirteen to fifteen times a season in multiple seasons. Do that enough, and you can see where familiarity bred contempt.

The NHL doubled up on this with its scheduling, as a lot of times the Hawks would play a division rival on the road on Saturday night, and then play the same team the very next night at home. Whatever "disagreements" there had been in the first game didn't get much time to subside by the time the players were lining up against each other again. I suppose the only indignity that was spared was making them all fly on the same plane between the two games, though if they had any sense of humor or adventure they would have.

The Norris Division, as it was known back then, was unquestionably the prison riot of all the NHL's divisions. I'm not sure how it came to be that way exactly. It was the only division to contain three of the Original Six, so the Hawks, Wings, and Leafs had been beating the shit out of each other for decades already. The North Stars and Blues probably figured they had to catch up. Whatever the cause, games between any two of these teams had a greater chance of turning into more of a Royal Rumble than a hockey game (as you'll see in the next chapter). You can see why the NHL is still trying to force feed its audience this kind of feel, because it really is unique to hockey. Or it was. No other sport can create the distaste for opponents that hockey can (football gives you a full week to wash it out). These teams genuinely hated each other. They all knew each other far too well. You can't replicate that now, given the spread of the player pool and the nature of the game changing.

You knew were in for something when you went to see the Hawks play a division rival. It had the same feel as walking into an illegal, underground boxing match or something. On this night, it was St. Louis. The Blues were just rounding back into relevance at this time. The Blues has made the Final in their first two years of existence, but that was more due to how the NHL aligned all expansion teams in one conference back then. Since those first two years, the Blues had never made it anywhere near there again. But now they had this brash young scorer in Brett Hull (he'd go on to have seventy-two goals in this season and to take a serious run at Gretzky's record the next with eighty-six). They had acquired Adam Oates to feed Hull. And of course, they had Peter Fucking Zezel. They were actually a real threat for once. They also still came with a cavalcade of jackasses that made any game something of a prostate exam: Tony Twist or Kelly Chase or the Cavallini brothers (how could one family create two fuckups like this?).

Generally speaking, Chicago and St. Louis already have a healthy distaste for each other due to proximity and of course to baseball. The Hawks and Blues were only too happy to add to it. This was the first time in a while that the Hawks were actually a contender. It was the first time in four seasons that the Hawks would go on to win the division, and at this point in the season it was all coming together. With Larmer, Savard, Steve Thomas, some kid named Jeremy Roenick, Troy Murray, Dirk Graham, and yes, even that construction horse Adam Creighton, they actually had depth at forward. Keenan had shaped the defense into a better unit, led by Doug Wilson (whom my father described as someone he could watch just skate for hours, but whom Keenan pretty much hated). Dave Manson was turning into an unhinged force, though he would miss a lot of the season with injury. And the Blues were looking like the main competitor, so this night certainly had a big-game feel to it, akin to what I'm told the air feels like on the night of a classic heavyweight boxing match.

Helping the cause was this taking place right before Christmas. In my brother's and my mind, and to a lot of hockey fans, hockey season doesn't really begin until there's snow on the ground. This usually happens around here in December, sometimes November. But Christmas is when it really kicks into gear. The early parts of the season are shrouded in pennant chases and football. It's not cold. It doesn't *feel* like hockey. The sun's still visible when you enter the arena. It feels like an out-of-town preview.

But at Christmas, baseball has faded and football is coming to an end (and here in Chicago, we rarely have to worry about playoff football). Daylight savings has made everything dark. It's cold, there's an edge to the air. Whereas baseball is literally your fair-weather friend, hockey is there to accompany you through the chill and the darkness. And given the clientele in those days, the chill and the darkness was an apt description and setting.

So everything added up to an occasion, and boy was it.

It certainly didn't start that way. The Blues jumped out to a 3-0 lead before the first period was even halfway over. The Hawks came roaring back with two goals in thirty seconds, but Brett Hull had an answer with his second goal before Adam Creighton responded to end the period at 4-3. That sounds ridiculous but just you wait.

From there it was a back-and-forth affair, with both teams flying at each other as if they'd had cayenne pepper spread on their scrotums right before puck drop (this actually used to happen in horse racing, and I must say that I know I'd run faster). Both teams racked up the goals, because it was the '80s and there were things like Vincent Riendeau and Jimmy Waite in net. Both teams racked up the penalties because there were things like Manson, Wayne Van Dorp, and Tony Twist running around. It was utter bedlam. Goes without saying that the standing room section was absolutely frothing the whole game. The Hawks took the lead in the second through Steven Thomas and Denis Savard to head into the second intermission up 5-4.

This was the game where I was introduced to a group called "The Fellas." These were a group of Adam's friends from lacrosse who attended more Hawks games than I could dream of (in retrospect, if I could go back in time to see my brother hanging out with a group that referred to itself as "The Fellas" and all played lacrosse I probably would have shot him dead on general principle). They were probably the metal kids my brother so desperately wanted to be. To put it in terms everyone can understand, every game before the third period—when beer sales were cut off then—one of this group would buy four beers and then try to sell the other three he wasn't drinking (maybe) for ten bucks. That would be about twenty-five dollars in today's beer dollars. It usually worked too, I have to say. Anyway, these guys were working on a different system.

Early in the third period, Hull completed his hat trick to tie the game. A few minutes later the Blues took the lead through Jeff Brown. There were nine minutes left. It was deflating. Here was the first big game I had seen live, the first time the Hawks were a *real* team, and their first test against a would-be competitor. And they were failing this test. Is this what it was going to be? When you're that age everything seems like a life sentence. Because they were losing this first, big game, the Hawks were going to lose every big game obviously. I just had to prepare for this to be my fate until the day of my death.

And then all the laws of logic and sense simply went out the window, and the day of my death looked like it was approaching awfully fast.

Dirk Graham tied the game with about eight minutes left. It renewed hope. There was electricity back in the building again. But before we had time to even build up expectation, Jeremy Roenick scored twenty-three seconds later to give the Hawks the lead. Now there was an ocean of noise. No way the Blues could stem this tide. And no, they couldn't, because thirty-six seconds later Dave Manson blasted one in from the blue line to put the Hawks up two. Everything was shaking from the noise, including my ribs against the rest of my organs. I can't fathom there's ever been a roar like that anywhere else in history. At least until fifty-seven seconds or so later when Creighton scored again and quite simply all eighteen-thousand became a different life form.

Four goals in a minute and fifty-six seconds. It was a team record. I only found that out later because there wasn't any chance of hearing that announcement over the PA. The place was up for grabs, and might literally have been off the ground at this point. Rapture would be a conservative description.

It was after that fourth goal in the sequence that one of "The Fellas" picked me up and lifted me over his head, such was the excitement he couldn't contain. I remember the look on my brother's face. It wasn't terror or worry so much. It was more quizzical as he mentally drafted the speech explaining to my mother that her second-born was tossed on the ice from the second deck and was now Hawks' property. Given the building, the atmosphere, and the individual lifting me over his head like some trophy, this seemed entirely possible. There was a moment when I thought I was going that way as well. And I think I was alright with it, because that's how everyone felt at that moment. Thankfully, he put me back down. The game ended with a 9-6 Hawks win. Imagine 9-6 now. It was so authoritative, so quick, so utterly over-the-top. It was like knocking someone out with something out of Punch-Out where you really got to wind up. It was perspective-shattering.

You couldn't have gotten the smile off of my face for days after that even if you showed me every horror film ever made on a loop. This is something only hockey is capable of. The speed, the emotion, the chaos, the noise, the RUSH. On games like this, it feels like anything and everything is possible and you really do have to sit down when it's all over. Hockey can swing you from one end of the spectrum to the other in a minute. Goals spring out of nowhere. It can happen so fast you feel like you're just hanging on to the bumper, scraping along the asphalt. The body and nerves simply can't take it. This is what video games try to capture, and they don't even come close to the real thing. My ears were ringing, my heart wouldn't slow down, I was sweating, I couldn't sit still. Don't let them tell you it's not a drug, and don't let them tell you it's not addictive. There was no coming back from this. I was then and forever strung out on hockey.

Even on a night where Adam Fucking Creighton scored twice. Life is strange.

Lunacy
December 28, 1989
North Stars v. Hawks

I don't know how we convinced my parents to not only let us, but sponsor us, to go to two games in a week on either side of Christmas. Looking back on it it seems Houdini-esque. There was no way this should have been possible, and I can't remember it ever happening again without some serious extenuating circumstances. Adam and I were likely so annoying over the holiday that they just had to get us out of the house in any way possible. This is a totally plausible explanation, and any parent reading this is probably nodding their head in agreement.

It was another divisional game, making this quite the week of anger, this time against the Minnesota North Stars. If the Norris Division had a child they kept in the basement and only fed fish heads, it was the North Stars. Until they moved to Dallas, they never really ever came close to winning the division and never, ever, did anything in the playoffs (oh just you wait). But they always came packed with a rare kind of asshole, making games with them utter torture. Basil McRae, Shane Churla (who I'm fairly sure actually ate fish heads), Mark Tinordi, Bob Rouse, and more and more names I could list but I don't want to lose my lunch while writing this. It was like the North Stars missed the whole point and were just going to exact their pound of flesh and call it a win before packing it back up to the hinterlands of Minneapolis.

Games between these two teams were always a bloodbath, and they'd already played three times that season with each game having no less than forty penalty minutes in it. It was curious, considering how cultured about the game Minnesotans like to see themselves, being the American home of hockey and all, and yet they had this professional team full of mutants and lab experiments gone wrong that they revered. The more I think about it, the more I'm glad they moved to Texas before they got any good. Exactly what those people deserved.

It was our normal routine, which involved watching the Bears and then immediately gearing up to head to down to the Stadium. We got our tickets, raced up the stairs (legs then paralyzed), secured our spots, and awaited warm-ups. The teams came out, and everything proceeded as normal.

I wasn't paying all that close attention about halfway through the warm-ups, as young minds tend to drift. Then I looked down at the ice, and all forty players were in a massive pile along the boards at center ice. It was just a huge throng, like they'd all become magnetized. And then everyone kind of paired off all over the North Stars' side of the ice. There were fights EVERYWHERE. Some were one-on-one, some were very much not. Jerseys and gloves and pads were strewn all over. It looked like a tornado had hit the ice. And there weren't any refs or anything on the ice to stop it. This went on for what seemed like forever. Some Star threw the net over on its side out of anger, drawing another ovation from a still half-full arena. It was insane. And you wondered just how far it would go, because who was going to prevent it from doing so?

I remember being pretty terrified. First off, no matter how tough you are as a kid, or think you are, and no matter how many video games you play and movies you watch, the sight of actual blood still takes you aback. Well, standing over the Hawks' tunnel to their dressing room behind the net, I could easily see each Hawk that was heading back bleeding pretty heavily. That's real. Live blood is a lot different than TV blood. Someone bleeding right in front of you is scary at the age of seven, because people aren't really supposed to bleed. Secondly, there was nothing to control these animals. It literally could have gone forever, and even if three refs had rushed onto the ice there were forty of these guys, all in some sort of psychotic rage. Where was it going to stop? How did people get like this before a game even starts? Aren't these supposed to be grown ups? What is wrong with these people? Even as a neophyte I could tell this was out of context.

Even the Stadium faithfuls that were there early, generally the hardest of the hardcore, were somewhat shocked. Yes, they spent most games baying for blood and loved a good fight or even a line-brawl. But even they couldn't really come to grips with this. It was madness. While the normal fight still tries to claim some connection to the actual game of hockey, this was just anarchy for the sake of anarchy. Supposedly, fighting during a game follows some sort of code. This had no code. This was out of bounds. There was nothing governing this, and everyone still had access to weapons if it got to that. And these two teams still had to play a full game against each other? I wondered if they still would, or if everyone would be sent home to get a grip. Maybe that would have been the proper tactic. My brother quipped, after it was all over, "Probably going to be a lot of slapshots tonight!"

I remember all the excited conversations between the end of the brawl and the start of the game, as everyone who had been there had to explain to those arriving after why there seemed to be an extra charge in the building for just the North Stars. "Wait, they did what? Why?" And then there were the explanations of who got hurt and who didn't and who started it and who didn't, as if we had any idea. It was one of the strangest atmospheres I can remember. Of course, no one really had an answer to the "Why?" other than, "Because hockey." Which as we've come to know, isn't really much of an answer at all.

Of course, it does rob hockey of some of the charm that brought us all there in the first place. Back then, there was still an element of danger in going to a hockey game. Some of it had to do with what was in the stands, some of it had to do with what was on the ice. It was still played in really dingy buildings, in front of scary people, by scary people. And that danger did somewhat spring from the idea that a pregame brawl like this, or similar, could happen. The rush was partially due to the idea that it could all go off the rails at any moment and you'd see something totally unhinged, either in the stands or on the ice. You might feel scared at some point. You don't get that now, and I don't know that anyone truly misses it, but I'm not sure that sort of uneasiness, that adrenaline, can ever be replaced. Maybe there was a way to market it to the masses that way, but the NHL sure missed the window if so.

Both my father and brother made it quite clear that my mother was in no way to know what had happened. The Tribune had the brawl in a huge picture on the front page of the sports section the next day though, so the jig was very much up quickly.

Of course, I didn't really mind so much when my classmates found out about it the next day thanks to that picture on the sports section and the awe they showed when I told them I was there. I didn't mention anything about being scared, of course. Hell, I probably made it seem like I was in the brawl. Again, that was part of hockey's charm back then. If you were a part of it, there was something scary and tough about you (even with your sugar-bowl haircut and glasses at that point). Is it any wonder I ended up in metal t-shirts before my tenth birthday?

J.R.
March 1, 1990
Blues vs. Hawks

My heart was still a little raw after Rick Vaive's trade (which is a fucking sentence and a half), and though my love for the team was now as strong as it would ever be, a child needs a certain player to channel it through. There has to be someone whose posters you put on the walls. The one you feel you identify with, the one who becomes something of a hero (and we won't have the discussion of having athletes as heroes and all the problems that entails. Let's just go with I was eight and this is what happens when you're eight). The one you look to when the team's down and sure that he'll bring his team back just because he's there.

Clearly, there was only ever going to be one choice.

Jeremy Roenick actually debuted with the Hawks the year before, taking Vaive's #27 jersey which was not something I was terribly happy about at the time. There can be only one, damn it! He was the first Hawks rookie in a few years that generated any kind of excitement. He put up eighteen points in just twenty games, though in the late 80's that wasn't quite the accomplishment it sounded like (if you could remain upright and breathe even remotely correctly, you were probably good for ten points in twenty games). He was certainly the best center prospect the Hawks had since Denis Savard, and he would actually grease the skids for Savard's exit soon after.

What was obvious to everyone immediately though, was that Roenick was completely out of his mind.

Roenick could score, and score a lot, but he didn't play like a scorer. Growing up with this era of Hawks hockey, my mind tended to break players down almost exactly like the original Nintendo "Ice Hockey" game (my brother and I were playing that constantly, until we moved on to "Blades Of Steel"). You had your skinny, fast, skilled scorers (Savard). You had your medium guys who could score but also be physical (Larmer, Graham, Thomas). And then you had your fat, go-nowhere bruisers (pretty much the rest of the roster). Roenick showed up and he scored like one of the skinny guys but played like one of the bruisers souped up on nitrous oxide. It looked a lot like Roenick either didn't know he could stop without crashing into something, or he didn't know how. While I had spent my previous years pining for our own Gretzky or Lemieux, what we got was something that had clearly been designed to be one of those with the same skill, but something went horribly awry in construction. There are lots of scorers now who also play very physically, but back then this was an anomaly. Roenick went flying into corners and the end boards and opposing defensemen like his nerve endings had all stopped working. And then he could dance around all of them with the puck when that was required too. He also fought, which was something prime scorers just didn't do, or at least I didn't know them to. Gretzky didn't fight. Lemieux didn't. Yzerman didn't. But ours? Yeah, that's just how things worked around here. There wasn't an aspect of the game that Roenick didn't fling himself into like a bowling ball.

A lot of nights, Mike Keenan would start games by throwing out a line with Roenick, Dirk Graham, and Jocelyn Lemieux (or some combination of the unhinged on the roster) and basically instruct them to play as if the puck didn't exist. Roenick would be so charged up every game that he would tear off from the blue line and start skating around before the anthem had reached, "land of the free..." Think about this atmosphere. The anthem has barely ended and the crowd is still jumping, and a minute later the puck is dropped and there are these three somewhat-guided missiles simply crashing into things and making loud noises all over the ice for forty-five seconds. It's a wonder most of the crowd wasn't slobbering by the time the first shift was over, and the building was simply acidic by the time they came off the ice. What did that feel like to opponents? Probably like it was time to get another job. Roenick's simply delirious style was the perfect mirror for the nutjobs in the stands of the Stadium. He played the game we all wished we could. He was completely wild but scored so much that you couldn't stop him from doing it. It justified all. If he wasn't playing, he'd probably be in the standing room on his third beer screaming the way we were.

It also didn't hurt that he wasn't unfathomably older than me. Roenick debuted at nineteen, which was the same age as my brother at the time. While all the other players seemed like grizzled grown-ups who were somewhat mythical to me, at least I could fathom Roenick. He wasn't that much older; I knew someone exactly that age. It was like he was possible. He was my hockey Batman.

He also celebrated his goals wildly, and wasn't afraid to say whatever was on his mind to the press. In hockey at this time, this was unheard of. It seemed like he was having the time of his life being an NHL player, mostly because he was. It'll shatter all the tenets of an eight-year-old's world the first time he hears a player have to have a portion of his postgame interview bleeped because he swore. Roenick was punk rock in a punk rock world. He didn't add up. He was dangerous, elegant, loud, and dominating all at the same time. He was everything at once.

The First
December 26, 1990
Blues v. Hawks

The game on this night wasn't important. I didn't even attend it. What was important was the day before. That was the day I received my first properly lettered, red Hawks jersey. And of course, it had #27 on the back.

I had one Hawks jersey before. It was white. It also had #27 on the back, but instead of "Roenick" it said "Vaive." And it wasn't properly lettered. Wherever my father got it just had the press-on lettering, and he probably thought I wouldn't know the difference. But even then, so young, I knew something was off about it. It didn't feel quite right. It didn't feel like what the older Hawks fans wore. It wasn't what the players wore. It felt like a half-measure. I didn't say anything of course, because I knew my parents didn't have that much disposable income and this still wasn't cheap. And I did love it, coming first and all. But let's say the love wasn't all encompassing.

That all changed on this particular Christmas morning. First off, this one was red. While the red Hawks jersey has now become ubiquitous in Chicago and other areas, this was most certainly not the case back then. First, the Hawks didn't wear them at home. You didn't ever see them live. It was just something on TV. So seeing one, in my very own home, in person, gave it a mythic quality. That blood red, the logo (and as a child I didn't know anything about the problems and connotations that came with that logo yet) with all its colors and details. It was almost like the man came alive against that red backdrop. I couldn't look away.

The black and white stripes at the bottom look not unlike a prison uniform from the days of yore. The stripes on the elbows. The shoulder patches. It all represented something which I was now officially a part of. When I first put it on I felt like I was seven feet tall.

And then I turned it over. First seeing the white numbers...it's piercing. It's SO white against that red. It pops. It pops from a distance, but when you're up close it's like the numbers are going to hit you in the face. People ask why 27 is my favorite number, and Roenick and my birthday are big reasons. But it's also the way 27 looks, especially on the back of a Hawks jersey. The rigidity of the 7, the curves of the 2, it's almost sexual. They just fit together while also being their own individuals (and this depth of description about numbers is scaring me as much as it is you). It's authoritative.

Then seeing the nameplate with "Roenick" on it. It was like I was in with the in-crowd. Sure, he was already the most popular player on the team but I knew before that.

This was before my friends and I got into band t-shirts. My first Metallica shirt was a couple years off yet. For us, sports jerseys were the holy grail to be attained. Your parents truly loved you if they gave you one. When you showed up to school in one you were the center of attention. And now I had the best one. Even if my friends didn't know hockey, they knew the jersey and they knew it was cool.

I threw it on and didn't take it off for weeks. The way the fabric felt against me, combined with the rigidity of the logo and numbers both back and front. The sleeves extending over my hands (my parents were going to make sure I didn't outgrow it for a long while). I could have run through a wall at this point. I was all-powerful, just like JR was on the ice.

I was that dedicated. I had the official uniform of a Hawks fanatic. No one could doubt my bonafides now. I kept that jersey for five years at least, far past outgrowing it. I couldn't let go. You never let go of your first, even if it's not really your first. I'll never forget it, wherever it ended up and in whatever state.

Perfect Flair
December 19, 1991
Canadiens v. Hawks

I have never seen video of it. I have never seen any record of it. From what I can tell, the memory exists in my mind alone, which is a weird place. But it would be a few years before I would dabble in hallucinogens, and unless I absorbed the ones my brother and father had previously done through osmosis, this happened.

For those who might not know, for as long as I can remember, between the second and third periods of every Hawks home game, they would do a shoot-the-puck competition for fans. Basically, three fans would get the chance to shoot the puck at a net that had been boarded up with a mini-golf-like three openings set up in said board along the ice. If they accomplished that, they would get a chance to shoot at the other one, which had been reduced to only one opening. If they hit that, they won free flights or money or something.

The pattern of the three contestants was always the same: one child, one clear-palooka in a Hawks jersey, and one very attractive woman who apparently couldn't be wearing anything less than four-inch heels. Let's just say this was not a feminist moment, because these contestants were clearly chosen to give the masses something to ogle. Even the organist would play "The Stripper" when she stepped up to take her shot. Considering the makeup of the crowd in those days, when the female contestant stepped up the reaction she got was...less than tasteful, let's say. Always the same pattern, and one the Hawks have only recently changed. And by "changed," I mean the organist has stopped playing "The Stripper" while the female contestant shoots. I suppose it's progress, but awfully slow.

However, on this night, the pattern was a little different. The kid still went first. But then the woman, whoever she was, went second. This was an obvious and mysterious breach of protocol. More strangely, there didn't appear to be a third shooter out there. No one in the crowd took much notice, just maybe a raised eyebrow.

Then two men emerged onto the ice from the penalty boxes. They were given a normal introduction. However, within seconds a murmur began from the crowd. A few seconds later, the murmur increased rapidly into a deafening roar. It was like a magic trick.

Ric Flair and Mr. Perfect were on the Stadium ice.

If you're not wrestling inclined, this was the time when Flair had first switched to the WWF (now WWE), which would have been equivalent to the speaker of the house switching political parties, and was becoming the counterpoint to Hulk Hogan. He was the biggest villain in the world, at least in my and every other kid's mind. Mr. Perfect was acting as his bodyguard then, but already had a distinguished wrestling career as well.

The thing was, they weren't introduced as "Ric Flair" or "Mr. Perfect." I'm positive they were introduced by their real names, Richard Fliehr and Curt Hennig. This would have been a breaking of the WWF protocol whereby character must be kept up in public at all times. This helped keep the mystery lasting for a few seconds.

But there was no mistaking Flair's piercing blond mane at the time. You could clearly see the shine from the balcony. Fuck, you could see it from a helicopter. It didn't take long for the Stadium crowd to identify him. I remember when the roar began to rise my brother saying, "Holy shit, IS THAT RIC FLAIR?! WHAT THE FUCK?!" This was the simultaneous reaction of about sixteen-thousand people.

It's still one of the biggest roars I've heard at the Stadium or the United Center. It was sheer surprise that created it, which probably wouldn't be possible now in the age of Twitter.

I don't know if it was staged or not, and it doesn't matter, but only a matter of moments after everyone figured out who they were, Mr. Perfect slipped and fell on the ice. Flair turned around, facing our side of the arena now, pointed at him, and his face basically exploded in a way only Flair's could. His eyes got wide and his mouth agape, so it looked like his face expanded to twice his size. The place lost it. He let out his patented "WOO!" right after, and even though he wasn't mic'd the crowd didn't need it to know to join in with one themselves.

I don't know if Flair scored or not. I know it doesn't matter. It remains one of the strangest moments in any sporting arena I can remember. As a kid, I HATED Ric Flair. He was the ultimate heel. He stood for everything wrong. He cheated, he backed out of fights, he let others do his fighting for him, and he always came out on top, preening all the way. I hated him when I was watching wrestling, I hated him when I talked about wrestling with my friends (and to this day it remains easier to find a fellow wrestling fan than a hockey fan). But it was contained in a certain frame. No wrestler ever infringed upon any other aspect of my life.

Yet here he was, basically breaking the fourth wall. And I loved it. Had it been a WWE event I was attending, I would have booed him until my lungs bled. Here? I cheered wildly like everyone else. That helped make it such an abstract memory.

It doesn't mean anything. It had no bearing on the Hawks. But it feels like one of those "Only In The Stadium At A Hawks Game" moment. You couldn't have trotted out Flair and Mr. Perfect at a Bulls game unannounced and have the entire crowd lose its collective mind. They wouldn't have been recognized by those squares and yuppies. You couldn't have done it at Wrigley Field either. Only out here on the edges would such an experience take place. And it was clear I was never leaving.

St. Patrick's Day Massacre
March 17, 1991
Blues v. Hawks

Every Hawks fan of the appropriate age will know this date. They will look at it and smile as if recalling the first time they cut class to get high behind the pet shop (that's where we did, anyway). It'll be with some cocktail of nostalgia, sinisterness, and menacing laughter. If you know a Hawks fan who remembers this the way we do, you'll probably want to take a step back when asking them about it.

This was the height of the Blues-Hawks rivalry. Ordinarily, these two teams were just blood rivals, only concerned with beating each other but not for real prizes. Now they were the two best teams in the league. The Hawks ended up beating out the Blues for the Presidents' Trophy (best regular season team) by one point that year. Only a handful of other teams were even close. This was no longer just squabbling family members at the children's table of the NHL (and given the nature of games in the Norris Division, this metaphor is especially apt). This was for the throne itself, at least during the season (which as we soon came to know, counted for horse and shit).

The added stakes to these games only contributed to the mayhem of encounters between the two teams. Just the night before this cage match back in St. Louis, the teams had combined for ninety-eight penalty minutes. Making them play one night later was an experiment in madness, which I'm sure had the league watching through their fingers, if not behind the couch. If there was such a mechanism in place, they probably would have moved or outright canceled this game. But there wasn't, and everyone headed to the Stadium not so much to see a hockey game but to see what would happen if a bunch of wild animals were let loose on each other having been freshly dipped in blood. If you were there or at any game like it, you no longer had to wonder what it was like to walk to the Coliseum during the height of the Roman Empire. We have seen the gladiators and lions.

What went on that night is hard to describe. It was the last scene of *Blazing Saddles* on ice. The first period alone featured thirty-one different penalties. It had ten misconducts, six of which were game misconducts. There were six fighting majors, and these clowns had forty more minutes against each other to go!

What took place in the second period is pretty much burned in the memory of every Hawks fan my age or older. Six minutes into the period, another line-brawl took place between the teams in the Blues zone. In the middle of it, Hawks defenseman Dave Manson called out Blues defenseman Scott Stevens. But they weren't going to be part of the muck. They both skated out to center ice for this confrontation. They weren't going to get tangled up by anyone.

This was when the two biggest kids in your grade school promise to meet each other by the flagpole after school, looking to prove who was the biggest badass in the sixth grade. You'd been waiting for it for months, and Manson and Stevens were just about the two biggest kids on either team. We'd known this was going to happen, but couldn't fathom what it would actually look like. In our minds, this was Joe Frazier and Muhammad Ali finally climbing into the ring at the Garden. As much anticipation and hype as there'd been, you couldn't quite fathom that they were actually going to tussle. It was too mythical.

You can find the video of this pretty easily on YouTube. It's important you take notice of the crowd even though the video isn't the best quality (again, wasn't on TV, though I'm sure the executives were thanking the Lord for that back then). It's not even a roar, or a crescendo. This is eighteen-thousand people reacting to their very basest urges all at once. This was as if a Ralph Steadman painting actually came to life. Reptiles eating each other everywhere, as was Steadman's style. When society collapses, all our gatherings will probably look and sound like this. Maybe they already do, thanks to Trump rallies. Whenever I wonder about the things people are capable of and what drives them to it, I remember this sound.

It was a fairly even fight until the end, when Manson landed all the big blows and ended Stevens' world. There was symbolism in it. Stevens was by far the Blues' best d-man, and also their dirtiest and most imposing player. Every forward in the league treaded cautiously when he was on the ice. Manson taking him down was essentially a microcosm of the Hawks taking the Blues down, as they wouldn't catch the Hawks after this. After all the things St. Louis threw at the Hawks in this game and during this season, the Hawks were last man standing. Just like Manson was over Stevens.

It is assumed that fans like me do not like fighting in hockey because we rail against the presence of goons and enforcers in the game. This is not so. Fights like this one are one of the more invigorating memories I have, and I only listened to it on radio. Ask anyone who was there and they can probably recall the details better than the birth of their own children. Manson and Stevens were far from useless players. Stevens went on to be a Hall-of-Famer and Manson had a decent enough career himself before being derailed by injuries. These weren't just two plugs who had nothing better to do.

It was such a moment because these two teams and these two players just hated each other so much that they couldn't stand it anymore. There were real stakes to it. There was real emotion. Not to be too in-character but just like wrestling, fighting in hockey is entertaining when it's telling a story. Here was the culmination of an entire rivalry, the epic battles between the two teams for the past two or three seasons, told by the fists of two players.

I still get a jump from watching it. It still feels genuine. It feels like hearing "Master of Puppets" for the first time. It is the embodiment of mayhem. If you have any primal urges within you, and we all do, they all get shocked, in a good way, watching it again.

The NHL has lost that, and sometimes I think that's good and sometimes bad. I don't know what the exact reason is. One is that real players, the ones that decide the games, don't want to fight anymore. Part of it is that they're now multi-million dollar assets, and no coach or GM is going to want to lose a player so important for six weeks after they break a hand needlessly. What we now know about damage to the brain is another piece. The league itself has tried to move away from and punish these things more heavily. They can't market players who are out hurt from a fight (that is if they knew how to market anything). Because in reality, it is stupid. We know now that fighting doesn't really have any effect on the outcome of games, and even less so when it's players who skate only a smattering of minutes partaking. Players don't really get intimidated and shrink because of fights anymore, nor do they find more space on the ice.

Now when we get fights, they're almost always between at least one and probably two goons who do it because they simply have nothing else to do. It's why they're on the team, or in the league, and they basically help each other out by engaging in this for half a minute. There are no stakes. There is no vitriol built up. It's the awkward conversation at a party between two people who don't know anyone else and just happen to be by the bar. It's passionless sex, basically. The emotion or the entertainment of it is basically forced. Hockey fights now are as fake, if not more so, than ones in the WWE.

Hockey will never look like it did on that March night in 1991. And nor should it, really. But that doesn't mean I don't miss it, even if I know better. Sometimes, I can't ignore that I am somewhat an animal. Maybe it was just a one-time thing, one fight symbolizing an entire relationship between two teams. What I do know is that it's gone now, and for the better, but it's still a little sad. The sport is less likely to make me physically tremble out of blood-lust and fear and violence and exhilaration.

The Hawks would of course take the biggest tumble possible when it really mattered. They lost in the first round to the lowly North Stars, taking 276 minutes in penalties in six games along the way. They thought they could either bash their way through Minnesota, or that the refs would simply tire of calling penalties, or both. They were simply too dumb to live.

At the age of ten though, you can't really register this kind of heartbreak. You just assume the Hawks will come back the next year and be just as good and get it right, because the boundless optimism of children can rarely be chained. If only my brother and father had been more willing to break my spirits, I might have grown up better adjusted. The Bulls would go on to win their first championship that June, and the Hawks were relegated to the depths and darkness for more than two decades. I enjoyed the Bulls, but as I watched their celebration I kept hope that soon I would have the party that really meant something to me. I was a witness to this one. I would be a part of the Hawks one. Just had to wait for it.

And wait for it. And wait for it.

Morons
March 22, 1992
Sabres v. Hawks

I don't know what the impetus was to go to this game. The Sabres weren't a terribly interesting bunch. They were below .500, going nowhere, and played in the other conference. The Hawks were pretty well entrenched in second place in the division and really didn't have much to play for before the playoffs. Maybe I knew the season was ending, and with the idea of getting playoff tickets a pipe dream, I viewed this as a last chance to get to the Stadium. I don't know what my brother was doing home on the last spring break he would have in his last year of college. Maybe my father's wonky employment status at the time made any trip for him other than coming home an impossibility. However, I'm sure glad I witnessed the madness that was to ensue.

I had seen the Hawks lose games before, but I had never seen them get truly labeled. It's a pretty deflating feeling for a child. When even the suggestion rises that you might go to a game on a Sunday night, as this one was, your mind is in a blender for the days preceding. Nothing else really matters, such is your excitement.

And then to have it all build up to watching your team get stuffed—it's like watching someone punch Santa and the Easter Bunny repeatedly in front of you. The fall is precipitous. I guess I never have to fear heroin withdrawal (note: I do not do heroin, but let's see how this book does before we say never). And worst of all, you had to go back to school in mere hours.

The Hawks did score first on this night, thirteen minutes in. It was Dan Vincelette, in case you were in need of a laugh. Then, from the last minute of the first period to the last minute of the second period, the Sabres scored six. This wasn't just a beating. This was aggressive throat-slashing.

Of course, these Hawks were not going to take a beating like this lying down without exacting a pound of flesh. Or six. We just couldn't quite anticipate where it would start.

With twelve minutes to go in the second period, and the Sabres just having scored three goals in thirty-nine seconds to go up 4-1, Eddie Belfour was in something of a mood. And when Eddie got in a mood, it wasn't too long before everyone in the arena knew it. Pat LaFontaine of the Sabres dumped a puck into the corner and went to chase it down. Eddie left his net. He might have glanced at the puck, he might not have; either way it was not his primary or secondary concern. His gaze was certainly transfixed on LaFontaine. The puck rimmed around the boards toward behind the net, but Belfour was still headed, at full speed, toward the corner. LaFontaine was still focused on the puck, so he never got wind of the freight train in goalie gear that then promptly plowed through him and nearly made him part of the Stadium boards (Eddie thus lived out the fantasy of many, many hockey fans around the world). It was the only roar the Stadium crowd generated that night, and it was thunderous. Obviously, a total melee ensued that Belfour was right in the middle of, being completely unhinged as he was. The brawl alone generated ten penalties, one of which was somehow LaFontaine getting ejected, but not Belfour (NHL officiating folks. You can't beat it with a stick). There were twenty-nine penalties in the period, including six ejections. All very grown up stuff here.

It was quite the juxtaposition to just a year earlier. On that night, the St. Patrick's Day Massacre, the fans, having just witnessed a fight-filled contest that the Hawks won, walked out of the building triumphant and cocky. No one could stand up to the Big, Bad Hawks.

Fast forward 370 days later and in the same building. We all witnessed the Hawks get thwacked in a fight-filled game to an unimpressive team, and no one walked out of the Stadium that night thinking this team was going anywhere. The petulant and boorish way they completed the game only convinced us more that the Hawks still hadn't learned any lessons, and forever would be too empty between the ears to make anything legendary happen. While drilling LaFontaine certainly was a rush for our more base impulses, we knew that the Hawks players, even the fucking goalie, consistently giving into those feelings would be the obstacle they could not clear when it mattered most.

Strike
April 12, 1992
Red Wings v. Hawks

The oddity about this one is that it wasn't supposed to be on April twelfth. It was supposed to be on April first. It's been lost in the subsequent work stoppages the NHL has infuriatingly engaged in, but this was my first experience with any sport I loved simply just stopping. The NHL players went on strike on April first, holding the playoffs hostage: just about the best leverage they could ever find. And it seemed as if the playoffs were under real threat for slightly over a week. My life, of course, was completely turned upside down.

But I didn't care about any of the issues or tactics at the age of ten. This was like watching your Christmas presents yanked away from you as punishment, except you know you didn't do anything wrong. The funny thing is that as a fan you don't really feel any differently about work stoppages in professional sports at the age of ten than you do at the age of thirty. While you might understand the actual issues a little better when you're older, it still seems like the dumbest thing on Earth. The only experience I had with anything like this was the 1987 NFL Players Strike. And at the age of six there was no way my father or brother could explain in any way that I would understand why the Bears were now losing to the sad-sack Saints. It was all beyond me then. The 1994 MLB strike and the following NHL lockout were still a couple years off. They might as well have come over and stomped on my Nintendo.

Of course, that feeling of being robbed is why fans keep coming back when these things end, because we don't really know what to do without it. If you're house gets robbed (and I've been through this), you don't decide you don't need a TV anymore. You just get a new TV. I used to blame them. I don't now.

I remember reading both major papers in Chicago every day during this awful week and a half. My parents got the Tribune and my fifth grade teacher, always had the Sun-Times in the classroom. I scoured them both for any hint of good news or hope. Considering the lack of coverage both had when the Hawks were playing, to call this search fruitless would be something of an understatement. This was a desert of misery.

I know I was miserable around the house. Instead of listening to games on the radio while pretending to do homework, I either had to actually do my homework (the horror) or watch basketball with my father (the horror) to avoid it. I distinctly remember sitting with my father watching a Bulls game a couple days after the strike started. During the broadcast, longtime TV analyst Red Kerr announced, "The NHL Lockout is over!... April Fool's!"

No father ever wants to see that look of heartbreak on their son or daughter. During the intervening seconds before Kerr revealed his "joke," I'm sure my Dad could see my chest fill with air and some semblance of color return to my face. And then to have it sucked out only seconds later...well, I doubt he laughed. If I could have, I would have reached through the screen and torn Kerr's larynx out (and by all accounts Kerr was a lovely man, giving you some idea of my rage). How dare he, from his lofty perch with the Bulls, mock those of us in purgatory?! It's so easy for you, isn't it Red?!! There was no bottom.

My father tried to counsel me about not taking sports so seriously. That this kind of thing could always happen and to invest so much emotion in things you had no control over was always going to end in despair. It's not that he was wrong, it's just that at ten I wasn't interested in logic. All I knew is that there wasn't hockey. And I was too young for a social life at night. I was too young for girls (now I'm just terrified of them). I didn't really have any hobbies. Little League was only just beginning its season. While the Cubs season was starting around then, the beginning of baseball season wasn't nearly as exciting as the NHL playoffs, and most Cubs games still took place in the day. I wanted the rush, the tension, the utter torture of the playoffs before I settled in for the summer of ethereal joy that baseball provides. And these people were stealing it from me. And there wasn't anyone around me who understood, with my brother off at school and my parents having other concerns and all my friends focused on the Bulls. I was adrift. I was an island. And it wasn't a tropical place.

A couple days before the strike actually ended, when I had assumed all was lost and was ready to turn myself over to the Cubs, the Sun-Times sports section ran a cartoon on the cover. It showed a grave digger rolling a coffin that was overstuffed with hockey players toward a grave. And someone was running after him exclaiming, "WAIT!!!!" This was before sports radio. This was before Twitter. Seeing this in the morning was the first sign of hope in what was one of the longest weeks of my life. That was one of the better school days of my life. I might have even paid attention in math, but doubtful.

I didn't know at the time what the sticking points were. They wouldn't have made sense to me at that point anyway. The fact that one of the biggest stumbling blocks was distribution of revenue from player cards now seems laughable. I didn't care that this agreement set the stage for another lockout. Hockey was coming back and that's all that mattered. It was the biggest relief of my young life to that point. I could go back to pretending to do my homework while listening to Pat Foley instead of just outright not doing it. It felt like I could breathe again.

The Best Day Ever (To That Point)
May 4, 1992
Hawks vs. Red Wings (Game Two)
Sometimes, it just all comes together.

The Hawks had squeezed by the Blues in the first round, the series turning on Jeremy Roenick getting high-sticked, handing his teeth to the ref, and the Hawks scoring on the ensuing power play in Game Six. Of course, that meant running into the Wings.

It already felt like the Wings were moving beyond the Hawks. After years of being the same knuckle-draggers the Hawks were, there had been a pivot. Sergei Fedorov and Nicklas Lidstrom arrived. They played actual hockey instead of the prison rugby the rest of the division had insisted upon for a decade or more. They had dusted the Hawks all season and finished eleven points ahead of them. The outlook was dark.

While we all expected the Hawks to be quickly returned to the dungeon they emerged from by the all-conquering Red Wings, they had somehow pulled out Game One through goals from Stephane Matteau and Jocelyn Lemieux (and no, I couldn't tell you how that happened). It seemed like a cheap thrill. Hey, we won't get completely embarrassed! Soon natural order would be restored but at least we inflicted a little anxiety into the Red Menace.

Game Two fell on a Saturday. The previous Tuesday was my birthday, though for some reason all celebrations were pushed to this day. It also saw a Little League game, and not just any Little League game. I would be playing the team of one of my best friends, and he would be pitching. For any young boy, you know what a momentous occasion this would be. The entire direction of the rest of the school year, and perhaps our entire lives, would hinge on how this encounter would go.

I walked and struck out in my first two at-bats, which seemed a draw to me and I would have been happy with that. But our team trailed heading into the bottom of the last inning by one run, and that meant my turn was going to come up again. I greeted this with fear. I just wanted my draw and to go home.

I was due to lead off the inning, and as I was on the on-deck circle waiting for my friend to finish his warmup pitches, he looked over to me. We had not actually spoken to each other during the game, only sharing a couple knowing looks. But the occasion got the best of him. Before his last warm-up pitch, I clearly heard him say, "You're mine." (this being the extent of trash talk two white kids at eleven years old could manage).

I don't remember if it was the first pitch or second pitch. I know it wasn't long. I cranked a ball out to right field and tore ass to first. In Little League you barely have a semblance of what's going on and are basically completely dependent on your coaches. But there was the first base coach telling me to head to second. Ok, cool, leadoff double. That was enough.

Except as I approached second and picked up the third base coach, I noticed that he and the entire team were going nuts, waving me around. Surely they didn't want me to head to third? That was madness! But I did. Hey, a triple. That would set us up nicely to tie the game and I don't think I'd ever actually managed a triple before.

But much to my amazement, it wasn't over. They didn't stop going nuts as I approached third. They couldn't possibly want me to keep going? What the hell was going on behind me? Did I really hit the ball that hard? Needless to say my angle rounding third wasn't exactly pristine and trying to turn for him I almost ended up in the dugout. A home run? Why not meet met there with a unicorn?

But as I approached the plate, the catcher didn't seem to be gearing up for any kind of throw. My teammates and their parents were still jumping up and down. They're really going to let me do this? I almost wanted to stop to see if it was a joke? Was this just for my birthday? Somebody was pulling something.

But no. I crossed the plate without a slide necessary. I had just cranked a game-tying homer in the last at-bat. Off one of my best friends! I had a trump card over him for life! This shit didn't happen to me! This happened to kids who weighed more than fifty pounds! What the hell just happened?!

(Ok, full disclosure: I had really only split the hole between first base and second base and then got a Chicago Park District homer when whatever goof was in right field let the ball roll past him as his glove was on his head or some such antic that the kid in right field always pulls. But it was a fucking bomb in the scorebook and that's how I'm going to remember it. Get fucked).

So, if nothing else, I have a game-tying homer to my name. Not bad for a birthday, right? I know after the game my father was gleaming. I suppose the joy a father gets from watching a child accomplish something like that can't be described. He talked about what a wonderful birthday present that must've been and how much fun we were going to have at dinner and then watch the Hawks. I told him it was nice but the Hawks were assuredly going to get smacked in Game Two. He said, "Hey, you never know. Maybe they'll win for your big day. They already won Game One."

And they did.

Clearly inspired by my baseball heroics, the Hawks returned home from Detroit and took a wild Game Three by a 5-4 score, blowing two separate two-goal leads before Dirk Graham netted the winner with five minutes to go. This set up the unthinkable potential for a four-game sweep two nights later. Most Hawks fans spent the time in an utter daze.

It remained scoreless until fifty-eight minutes of the scheduled sixty had been played. Then up stepped one Brent Sutter.

After a scramble in the corner, Greg Gilbert was able to squirt a puck into the slot from below the goal line. Sutter was in the right spot, as he seemingly was that entire spring, to slap a backhand past the sliding Cheveldae.

I've seen replays of this goal, and it makes me smile every time. But it's not the replay I remember. No, it's the sound. If I never saw the goal it would still hold the same place in my heart.

The roar that nearly broke my headphones. It permanently burned into my mind. It felt like the Stadium rose off the ground, and that was just through the radio. Foley's call could barely be heard over the din. I was bouncing on the couch in the same way all eighteen-thousand there were. It was if the entire city was shaking, even if only those in attendance and a smattering of those like me listening through the radio knew what was going on.

In the immediate aftermath, Foley delivered a line that every Hawks fan remembers: "AND THE BLACKHAWKS...ARE ON THE VERGE OF GETTING RID OF THE RED WINGS!!" In moments like this Foley never could hide where his loyalties were. He grew up here after all. He was and is one of us. It wasn't just that the Hawks were going to beat Detroit. It was getting rid of them, as if they were some plague that had to be eradicated.

They didn't just have to be beat, they had to be swept from the memory. This was good riddance.

That was the seventh win in a row in the playoffs for the Hawks. It was hard to come to grips with at the time. After sweeping The Menace, what couldn't be done?

It's All Possible
May 18, 1992
Oilers v. Hawks

We had to wait around for the Oilers and Canucks to decide who was next on the list, and sadly, by the time the Oilers decided it was going to be them, real life had gotten in my way. My brother had the temerity to graduate from college this weekend, which meant the day of Game One I was flying to Vermont with the rest of my family.

There was no Center Ice package then, obviously. Our crappy hotel in Vermont certainly wasn't going to have any channel that would have the game on. And we had to do some dinner with my brother anyway. My only hope was that somewhere, be it ESPN or CNN or something, would show the highlights.

When we arrived in Vermont, there was something of a mysterious call from my Adam. He asked me if I brought his Hawks hat that I had adopted, a black, corduroy one. I told him I did. Of course I did, I would be fucking naked without it. I was told in no uncertain terms that I had to bring that hat to his graduation ceremony, where he was somehow elected Senior Speaker. I took this order down dutifully.

We returned from dinner and I kept flipping between sports shows on two or three channels hoping for any word of a score. I'm sure I was awake far longer than my parents would have ever wanted. Finally, I think CNN quickly flashed the score. 8-2 Hawks.

Wait, what?

It couldn't have been 8-2. Sure, these were not the OILERS Oilers. Messier and Gretzky were gone. So were Anderson and Kurri. They had limped to third place in their division, but were able to upset Gretzky's Kings in the first round and then did the same to the Canucks in the second. Yes, they were led by Vincent Damphousse and Joe Murphy now (and I would learn what a curse the latter was in a few years), but they still donned the blue and orange that had tormented us the decade before. If nothing else, those colors were still to be feared.

8-2 across the screen. I couldn't believe it. They must've gotten confused. It must've been 3-2. And then I went to bed, still happy the Hawks had won.

The paper arrived in the morning, a USA Today as was the custom. I quickly raced for the sports section, looking for the score to confirm my suspicions that CNN had it wrong. It was only listed in the back of the section. But there it was.

"8-2."

I cursed my luck for being stuck in New England and not even getting to hear the roar that surely would have been emanating out of the Stadium. It wasn't my brother's fault. It was of course my mother's fault for making us come out here. So what if Adam had graduated? He had graduated from high school just four years earlier (in reality, both of these accomplishments were minor miracles). What was the big deal here? Clearly, I got to my punk, everything-is-your-mother's-fault age a little too early.

Anyway, I dutifully reported to my brother before the ceremony and he asked me what the Hawks did the night before. I was kind of shocked he didn't race for the result as quickly and as desperately as I did. At eleven, I didn't really conceptualize that this being his graduation weekend, he was assuredly drinking the night before, probably right up until this moment. When I told him it was 8-2, he yelled loud enough for at least half of the attendees to turn around.

"HOLY SHIT! SAM, WE'RE GOING TO WIN THE CUP!"

Here he was on the cusp of the biggest moment of his life to date, and what mattered more was the Hawks winning the Cup. At least that's how it seemed to me. He couldn't believe the score either. Soon graduation would be out of the way and he would return home for the moment he'd waited his whole life for. His excitement was palpable.

Anyway, I immediately turned over the hat he requested and asked why he needed it. He wouldn't tell but instructed me to wait and see. So we headed for our seats, and he headed for the stage. Not long after, he was introduced as Senior Speaker. He walked up to the podium, appeared hesitant at the start of his speech, and asked the audience for a moment. He then removed his graduation cap, and put on my Hawks hat. And then he turned it around backwards. Though he had been planning that for a while, I know it was done with a lot more pride with the Hawks on an eight-game winning streak in the playoffs. And it felt like I was up there too, just in hat form. He delivered his senior address with a backwards Hawks cap on. It's one of the more quintessential Fels moments.

Though I never got that hat back. Bastard.

Where Are You Going, Gramps?
May 26, 1992
Hawks v. Penguins

The Hawks easily sawed off the declining Oilers in the next three games. It was authoritative. It was efficient. It was far easier than it should have been, and the nature of that victory of course only built us up for an even bigger crash come the Final. We should have known, but we told ourselves different. Adding to my utter elation was my brother returning home after graduation, and the anticipation of enjoying the biggest moment any Hawks fan had seen in thirty years.

The Hawks being on this stage was hard to wrap one's head around, especially for those of us who had yet to see a World Series in town, were too young to really remember the '85 Bears, and didn't care about the Bulls. This was when you knew everyone was watching. This is when what had been personal to you, the characteristics and idiosyncrasies of your favorite players, were suddenly open to the world. It felt like some sort of coming out party. This was the showcase, and for the first time my Hawks were what the NHL would show to the sporting public in general.

When a team hits the Stanley Cup Final, they attach a badge to the front of each player's jersey. It goes up near the right shoulder. Seeing that on the red of the Hawks road jerseys that night almost made me dizzy. It's like we had finally made it, the feeling you get when you first arrive at college or at your first real job. It was a certification of being on the big stage.

I had never even thought of seeing the Hawks on this kind of platform. Even though they'd made the round previous a few times in my fandom's life, there was such little chance of winning those series that I didn't even consider what it would feel like to see the Hawks in the Final. Here they were, there was no farther to go. The finish line was there, and when it was done they could actually win the thing! It was a real possibility! This team of raging thugs who pounded teams into dust, all orchestrated by their nutjob of a coach and cheered on by people who belonged in a cage somewhere and let loose. This was the caddies taking over the pool in *Caddyshack*.

When they televised the players' introductions, every Hawk looked like he was about ready to shit himself. Perhaps they were just as mystified as their fans at just what they were doing there. Or maybe it had happened too fast. The Hawks had won eleven games in a row in the playoffs, which was a record. They had gotten so caught up in the run that maybe they just couldn't compute what it all meant. Or maybe they were just terrified of what sat across the ice from them.

The Penguins weren't a team so much as an army of super soldiers. This was Lemieux, Jagr, Francis, Murphy, Samuelsson, Tocchet, Stevens, Trottier. They were coached by Scotty Bowman, the greatest coach in hockey history. They had won the previous Cup, easily swatting aside the North Stars that had brought the world down around the Hawks' heads. They weren't nervous, they were supposed to be here. Looking back on it, it's a wonder I had convinced myself the Hawks wouldn't get blown out by twelve goals every game.

For just under forty minutes, this would be the best stretch in my young life.

Maybe the Penguins and their rep and pedigree took the Hawks a little lightly to start Game One. Maybe they weren't ready for just how physical the Hawks were going to play things. Maybe the Hawks were just too dumb to know any better before reality set in. But for the first period and more than half of the second, the Hawks were simply all over the Penguins. They were knocking them on their asses every chance. The Pens could only look wistfully to the ref for relief that never came. There was no room for them.

Chelios opened the scoring on the power play six minutes in. Michel Goulet and Dirk Graham scored thirty seconds apart with seven minutes left in the first. 3-0 to the Hawks. What was this? This wasn't hockey. This wasn't the Hawks. This was the Lord himself coming down and gracing my young life with a joy I couldn't possibly get my arms around. Euphoria wouldn't even be the right word. I kept looking to my brother to assure me that this was indeed possible and right. His face was even more frozen than mine. The Hawks couldn't possibly do this, could they? Show up to the highly celebrated and revered Penguins and simply put a glove in their face and smother them into oblivion?

Phil Bourque scored late in the first to get the Penguins on the board, but heading into the intermission up 3-1 was certainly beyond anything we had hoped for. The Hawks weren't going to get embarrassed. They could hang!

Brent Sutter scored halfway through the second period to restore the three-goal lead. He floated one in from a spot he should have never been able to score from. I'll forever remember the look on his face after he did. It was some combination of joy, shock, and giggling as he pumped his arms over his head and didn't glide over the ice so much as run above it. It was how we all felt at that moment. The Hawks, who had won eleven playoff games in a row, had saved their biggest punch for the biggest stage. Sure, it was only thirty minutes, but we could do this! My brother and I were literally running around our living room, and my father couldn't hide a smile at his boys soaking in so much joy.

Pride goeth before the fall.

We're a pretty fatalistic bunch here in Chicago. Maybe not more so than any other sports town, but this is the one I know. It probably stems from a lifetime of watching teams come up short. Until Michael Jordan taught us that things could be different (and much like Elvis to Chuck D, that didn't mean shit to me), this was a town that had two Bears championships in '64 and '85 and that's it. No Chicago baseball team had made a series at that point since 1959. Ours was a desert of sporting success. So naturally, we were usually inclined to expect everything to go wrong.

But a three-goal lead with Belfour in net? If there was ever a time to believe that maybe, just maybe, things could break our way, it was now wasn't it? The Hawks, having made the best team in their conference look silly two rounds before this one, were now doing it to the best team in the other one. It fit in with the roll they had been on. Surely it was ok to believe.

Tocchet scored a few minutes after Sutter did. It was still ok, we thought. A two-goal lead with twenty minutes to go, those didn't go away. It was a minute later when the winds began to howl.

Mario Lemieux came down with the puck through the center of the Hawks' zone, which is pretty much like watching the Grim Reaper stroll down the street and you're the last house on the block. But he couldn't get the puck under control and Chelios had cut off his path to the net. By the time he did have it under control, he was below the goal line, near the corner to Belfour's left. I know I thought it was ok to breathe at that moment, if only for a moment. Next thing I knew his arms were in the air. He had banked the puck off Belfour and into the net, a goal that should never have happened. Down came the guillotine.

Yeah, it was only 4-3. A lead heading into the third was still something to be valued. But we knew already. You could see it on the Hawks' faces. They were about to see a wave from the Penguins and they knew, deep down, they almost certainly couldn't turn back. We at home knew too. It wasn't about the two teams that were actually on the ice. It was more about fate. We weren't supposed to have nice things. The Penguins were what teams were supposed to be, and we were the dungeon dwellers. We knew that somewhere in the next twenty minutes, those annoying, do-gooder kids were coming to take our ill-gotten Trix away.

We just didn't know it was going to be in the most agonizing way possible.

The Hawks actually held on for fifteen minutes, which was just close enough to the finish line that we dared thought they might escape. Belfour had to make some incredible saves but seemed to have gotten over the Lemieux SNAFU. It was only five minutes. We could get there. It wouldn't be easy, but we could do it. There are so many ways to get through five minutes.

Then Jaromir Jagr, nineteen-year-old Jagr with his terrible fucking hair and his habit of slashing guys on his way to the bench and diving all over the fucking place and his dumb visor and his dumb Jofa helmet and his dumb celebrations, picked up the puck in the right corner of the Hawks' zone. He proceeded to dance around the entire team. It happened in slow motion. As soon as he escaped the first two Hawks, you knew what was going to happen but had to watch anyway. It's like when you slam the brakes in the snow but can see the car isn't stopping and that one in front of you gets closer and closer but you've done all you can. You just brace for impact, but when it comes it still shakes you to the core. Jagr made his way to the slot, and slid a backhand under Belfour. The Igloo erupted. The announcers lost their minds. We sat in silence.

This is what happens when an all-time great play happens against your team in the worst moment possible. You know in that moment that this goal will be replayed over and over. You know that everyone will remember it, which means every time it's mentioned, you will be returned to that feeling of your stomach falling into your ankles. Others will glean joy from that moment. You will only know pain. And you will know it over and over. There is no escape.

There was no mystery after that. While others may have told themselves that all they needed was a bounce or one great play, we knew the man in the black hood was on his way. We just didn't know the method of execution. And we didn't know exactly when.

With less than a minute to go, Steve Smith—brought from Edmonton for Dave Manson because he had been through this before and was supposed to be the steady head on the backend that the unhinged Manson could never be—took a penalty. Here it was, the axe to be swung through our necks, unveiled. Except we had to watch our own execution.

Face-off in the Hawks' zone to start the power play, to Belfour's left. Sutter loses it clean, and the puck makes its way to Larry Murphy at the point. Steve Larmer, in the middle of the zone, begins to drift toward the blue line, in something of a daze. While he's transfixed on Murphy, it's only Lemieux streaking by him toward the net. Murphy shoots, Belfour saves but kicks the rebound toward the middle of the ice. And there's Lemieux, with enough space to graze multiple head of cattle, couldn't possibly miss. He didn't.

I've seen this sequence in my head at least eight million times. Where was Larmer going? How could he let perhaps the most gifted player in the league at the time simply go by him? Why couldn't Belfour have put that rebound anywhere else?

It wasn't just that game that was over. We knew the series was over. In the immediate aftermath you try to tell yourself that it's just one game. The Hawks only need to get one in Pittsburgh. The Penguins couldn't handle the cauldron of the Stadium. They couldn't skate away from us on the smaller ice there. But you're just saying it, like talking while you're getting blood drawn at the doctor's to try to ignore the needle. It was over. No team, especially one as volatile and unstable as the Hawks, could recover from such a loss.

And they didn't. They lost meekly in Game Two. They put up a valiant fight in the return to Chicago in Game Three, but Barrasso was just a tiny bit better than Belfour, and Stevens's first period goal was enough. Game Four was a ridiculous affair that ended 6-5 and saw Dominik Hasek announce himself to the world. But the craziness or memorable nature of that didn't matter to me. The Cup was gone. Our dream was over long before Lemieux paraded it around the Stadium ice. It was over the moment he put that rebound away.

After Game three, which was the Hawks last stand, there was a picture of Roenick on the front of the Sun-Times sports section. He was simply looking down at his skates, looking lost at sea. And that's how I felt. It was so quick. We had dreamed so big and then it was gone in an instant. Even my friends at school, who never hesitated to point out the difference in success between the Bulls and Hawks, knew this was not a time to needle. They saw that front page, and even though at age eleven you don't really know how to extend condolences, they did what they could. Of course, that didn't matter a week or two later when the Bulls added championship #2, and I would once again watch a party from the sidelines I now had no hopes of ever enjoying myself. The reality was clear.

Seriously Larmer, where were you going?

Influence
November 8, 1992
Penguins v. Hawks

It had been such a strange offseason for the Hawks after that Final capitulation that the return visit of the Penguins felt less of an occasion than it should have. Let's see if I can get all of this in one go: the Hawks kicked Mike Keenan upstairs so they wouldn't lose Darryl Sutter as a coach to another team, then they nixed Keenan's agreed upon deal to bring Eric Lindros to Chicago, and because Eddie Belfour was in that trade they had to appease him by only trading Dominik Hasek for future dog-walker Christian Ruutu, all the while allowing Quebec to acquire the spine of the Colorado team that would then beat the Hawks over the head repeatedly years later, in a world where Gary Bettman had changed the division names and would soon go to conference playoffs instead of divisional. Phew.

Sure, this was the night the Hawks got a little something back on the team that broke our hearts the previous spring. Not that it mattered much. But that wasn't anywhere near the most important part of that game for me and for many other Hawks fans.

This night was the first time I got my hands on a copy of *The Blue Line*. For the uninitiated, *The Blue Line* was the unofficial gameday program for Hawks home games, written by fans like us. Little did I know on that night that my path in adulthood would follow the same route (after some wild meandering of course. And it strains credulity to call any of this "adulthood," but we'll get there). If you had told me that I would end up writing something just like it as a job one day in the future, you wouldn't have wiped the smile off of my face for decades.

Getting your hands on *The Blue Line* when you're in your adolescence is on the same plane as discovering The Spice Channel blurred on your cable a few years later (I can only imagine what happens for teenagers these days when they discover what the internet really holds. No wonder as a society we're fucked, if you'll pardon the loose double-entendre. And no, "Loose Double-Entendre" isn't an adult film star, before you go there. How many entendres are we up to?). *The Blue Line* was vulgar, it was angry, it was rebellious, and most of all it was utterly hilarious. One of the first issues I ever got had a front-page comic that depicted Pat Foley and Dale Tallon being "serviced" while broadcasting the game as the reason they were so energetic during their presentation. When you're twelve, this is like being handed "Appetite For Destruction" and a fair amount of speed and then being told to lock yourself alone in your room.

The Blue Line put into words what pretty much every Hawks fan felt. It loved hockey, it loved the Hawks, but it hated the way the Hawks were run and it hated the man responsible, Bill Wirtz. It was the pamphlet of the Resistance, even though we had no X-wings or lightsabers to fight the Dark Side (these references are only going to get more nerdy so if this is a problem, abort now). There wasn't anyone in the mainstream really even paying attention, much less pointing out what a sham the Hawks were under William Wirtz. Maybe every so often you'd get a column here or there from the Sun-Times or Herald or Tribune. But here was one publication that focused on nothing else. This was our voice, our thoughts, all told through the beer-soaked vision with which most Hawks fans saw the world.

The Blue Line was anarchy in a self-made publication. At that age and heading into teenage years, all we wanted to do was listen to the music we weren't supposed to, wear what we weren't supposed to, and consider ourselves somehow a threat to anything. *The Blue Line* was definitely not something the principal or any teacher would ever want to catch us with Sadly, it only made my mother laugh, so I would have to find other avenues to piss her off as any young boy is wont to do. Those all proved fruitless too, she was just far too cool to crack. Doesn't mean I didn't try. It had words we knew we shouldn't use and could only awkwardly muster when we found the courage to do so. It was dangerous. Needles to say, I was hooked, and forced my brother to get every copy he could from the bar down the street that sold it even when we weren't going to games.

It also became a staple of the Hawks experience. Get dropped off by Dad, pick up a personal Connie's Pizza from the truck outside, grab a *Blue Line*, head to the standing room for warm-ups, and then between warm-ups and the start of the game read your *Blue Line* and eat your pizza. I can't tell you how many times we went through this ritual, but it never disappointed.

Everyone's pregame routine for attending the game is sacred in some way. It's meeting at the same bar or restaurant or pounding High-Life in your car (don't do this, though). It's the bus or train you take, or both. The route you drive. The gate you enter. The beer vendor you first hit up. Ask most fans, and it's always the same way every time. It's part of the custom. Without it, it doesn't feel quite as special. There's a process to this. *The Blue Line* became part of mine, like so many other's, that night. Little did I know it was the start of me becoming part of other people's rituals for Hawks games some fifteen years later.

To quote Slim Charles, "Life's strange."

St. Valentine's Day Massacre...The Hockey Version
February 14, 1993
Red Wings vs. Hawks

After a bedding-in period under Darryl Sutter which saw the Hawks be pretty middling in the season's opening throes, things started to hum as the temperature started to drop. In December they'd put together an 8-1-1 stretch, and another of the same mark in January. All of it had positioned the Hawks at the top of the division and conference for another tango with the Red Wings. Having lost the previous encounter ten days earlier by five goals gave this one even more of a showpiece. Wrongs had to be righted, after all.

Though the Hawks sat in first when these two teams met on Madison St., and even though the Hawks had swept the Wings out of the playoffs the previous spring, there was still a feeling that the Hawks needed to measure up. It was obvious to all what Detroit was building, and any path out of the now-Western Conference was clearly going to involve trips to Joe Louis Arena (the horror, the horror...).

Ramping up the charge for this one, at least to me, is that I had made my first ever call to the sports-radio station in Chicago earlier in the week, The Score. And during that call I had told thousands of people that Bob Probert was a "jerko." I would end up being a regular caller on the station through my teenage years and into my 20s. When I look back, that probably robbed me of any fear of public speaking, which gave me the courage/lack of senses to start stand-up comedy, which led to me writing *TheCommitted Indian.* Strange how these things work.

The Hawks held a five-point lead for the division heading into this one, and a win felt like it would propel them out beyond where the Wings could catch. Though we know now there is no such thing as a "statement" regular season game, this was as close as you were going to get.

Then Steve Yzerman took the ice, and as Frank Zappa once said, "...and it was useless anymore."

This was one of Yzerman's signature performances, and perhaps one of his last before he ceded the stage to Fedorov and became something more of a two-way center. He terrorized the Hawks that night, putting up three goals and five points. The Hawks had actually crawled back into this one, coming back from 3-1 down to tie it midway through at 3. Yzerman then ended proceedings all by himself, as if he was just teasing us with a dollar on a string. It was cruel and...well, for the Hawks it was kind of usual.

His hat trick goal was a work of art. And he scored it right under where we were standing in the balcony. It felt like the ultimate raised middle finger, aimed right at all of us. He came down the right wing, facing Karl

Dykhuis. Merely mentioning that name should alert you, dear reader, to what would ensue. One inside-out move later and Dykhuis needed a raft and an oxygen tank.

After turning Dykhuis into pudding, Yzerman was clean through on Belfour, and he proceeded to roof one over his glove as if he were cracking his knuckles. I can still hear his joyus scream as he leapt into Yves Racine's arms, like he couldn't believe how thoroughly he'd dissected the Hawks all night. You could hear it throughout the entire building. It was giddy, bordering on laughter. On this night, there was no player in the world better than Stevie Y. He was involved on all five of their goals, sending us home with our figurative tail firmly placed between the arch of our legs.

Making it even more infuriating of course, is that no rational being could ever drum up any dislike of Yzerman. We may have hated every single other one of his teammates, but not him. He was just too good, just too graceful, just too skilled. Once again, we were left with a feeling that we'd never measure up, and even if we did they had a trump card we'd never possess in Yzerman. Sure, Roenick was really good but he'd never come up with anything like that in a game that we thought mattered so much. Savard was gone, Roenick just a half-step below the elite, and we'd remain star-poor. We wanted to be angry, but could only get angry that we had to admit we'd seen pure genius from one of the game's greats. Having to do that through gritted teeth only upped the frustration and depression. Anger can be sweet relief at times. When it's not available, there is no bottom.

Heading home that night, it felt like in some ways the season was already over. Sure, the Hawks might win the division, or they might not. Whatever they did, Detroit would be waiting. And Yzerman had just showed us what would be in store. What was the point?

My brother's and my mood wasn't helped on the trip home, as this was one of the rare times we had to make our own way instead of having our father pick us up. You could learn a lot taking the bus away from the Stadium those days. Most of it wasn't good, though it would all stick with you.

A couple stops after we got on heading toward downtown, a man got on the bus with a wad of crimson-colored paper towels pressed against his head, which was roughly the size of Mars. The amount of blood it must've taken to make that amount of paper towels that color left one wondering how exactly he was still standing and/or conscious. From then on my brother claimed that when the man briefly removed those paper towels, his brain was actually exposed. This was dismissed by my father time and time again, and my Adam's retort was always, "Fuck you. There was something red and squishy under there!"

I don't remember if we saw the dude's brain or not. All I know is that dude was in better condition than Karl Dykhuis that night.

Joe Murphy
February 28, 1993
Blues vs. Hawks

Joe Murphy will not go down as one of the greatest Hawks ever. He will probably not even be marked as "good" by most who watched him ply his trade here. At the time, he was something of a unicorn for Hawks fans.

Murphy was drafted by the Red Wings first overall in 1986 and made his first appearance in the league at nineteen. Clearly there was great promise, but it was never met in Detroit. After two seasons with the Wings where he was in and out of their lineup and bouncing between the minors and the NHL, the Wings cashed in on that still lingering promise, sending Murphy to Edmonton.

Murphy finally put something together in Alberta, scoring twenty-seven and thirty-five goals in his two full seasons there. This made Murphy and his agent pretty full of themselves. But as things worked in Edmonton under Peter Pocklington (the man who pretty much pocketed the ten-million he received in the Gretzky trade), when Murphy wanted to get paid he was told to sit on it and twirl. He held out all season in 92-'93, setting off quite the competition to complete a trade for him.

I didn't know much about Murphy, as this was before ESPN made it easier to watch other games besides the Hawks. The Oilers had slid out of relevance. What I did know is that my brother was very excited at the idea of Murphy as a Hawk. However, he had decamped to Minneapolis by this point to start his post-college life, and there was only one instrument of research available to me.

That would be Strat-O-Matic hockey. I couldn't even begin to count the number of afternoons my brother and I filled with that game. And when I wasn't playing him, he was playing it with a few friends from high school. For the uninitiated, Strat-O-Matic had different versions for each of the four major sports. It used real players and real rosters. And each player was represented by a card. Each card had four or five categories, and in those there were numbers one through twelve, and you would reference whatever number you had rolled on the dice. Through a combination of dice, play-cards, and a few other factors, you simulated a game. You made your own lines and pairings, you decided how you would forecheck and defend. This was well before any video game was anywhere near advanced enough to do these things. It was also clearly a bastion for the nerdy, before it was cool.

Of course, I didn't have the up-to-date version, but a couple-years-old one my brother had left behind. No matter, it was the year Murphy scored twenty-seven goals so it would do. So I took Murphy's card out of the Edmonton stack and placed it in the Hawks stack as soon as the rumors began to swirl. I played dozens of games, by myself mind you, with Murphy slotted in as Roenick's wing or Murray's wing or Sutter's wing. This was how I was going to determine if he was worth it. I can only imagine what my parents thought, watching their youngest son play this hockey simulation by himself for hours. The dream of grandkids probably evaporated right around this point in time.

Murphy passed my very scientific research, racking up enough goals in my simulations that I would be satisfied with his addition to the Hawks. Because clearly the Hawks needed my seal of approval before they could pull the trigger. Did I mention I didn't have a lot of friends?

Stealing
April 19, 1993
Blues vs. Hawks (Game One)

The Hawks entered the 1993 playoffs top of the division, conference, and were a lot of people's pick to be the last Campbell Conference representative in the Stanley Cup Final before it became the Western Conference. They ended the season on a 7-1-2 streak, Murphy had put up nearly a point per game since joining in midseason, and everything looked set for another long spring. Remember kids, never believe in anything.

The '93 playoffs also marked the NHL's return to network TV, which probably isn't something a league should have been "celebrating" at that point in time, but this was the NHL after all. ABC showed a game the last three Sundays of that season, and the playoffs kicked off on the weekend to be spotlighted on a major network.

We had only begun to hear the rumors a couple of weeks before, and I and a lot of others had no idea that Bill Wirtz's ban on televised home games did not and could not extend to network TV. He was powerless to stop it. So Game One against the Blues was going to be on TV from the Stadium, and be the first ever home game I got to watch from my couch. Well, not couch, because my usual position was on the floor in front of the couch and closer to the TV. While I'd like to blame my need for glasses (even post-LASIK) and questionable posture on faulty genes (those are responsible for more than enough), it was this habit that is almost certainly to blame.

This felt like stealing. Except more righteous than that. This was something we should have been able to do for ages before this, but were kept out by the evil grinch at the door. Now the gates to The Bastille were flung open, and we would be free. Even for one day, we got one over the rich owner. It was at this point in life, while jonesing on that feeling, that a communist really should have tried to indoctrinate me.

The pre-game build was something I actually tuned in for as well, wanting to soak up every possible bit. Local Chicago writer Steve Rosenbloom, one of about three writers in various sports sections around the city who knew anything about hockey, was a guest and proclaimed that everyone was playing for second place behind the Penguins (it really did look like that, just didn't work out like that). Of course, no major Chicago sporting event can ever take place without Jim Belushi inserting his unwelcome, bloated, and talentless mug into proceedings. You could see the Stadium stands filling in behind the set, the buzz getting a little louder with each segment.

Without a surround-sound setup, the anthem can't really translate through TV speakers. But it was still a charge to see it on screen for the first time. And maybe even a bit jarring? Is that what we really looked like? The building always looks so much larger on TV. The balcony was tucked away to the top of the screen, but I knew it to be hanging right over the ice. Even looking at how removed it seemed on TV made my legs ache thinking of those stairs. The only thing we needed now was a Hawks win, as everything was poised for a special occasion.

And then Curtis Joseph ruined it all .

The Hawks blew a 3-1 lead and then a 3-2 lead heading into the third. Joseph turned away thirteen third period shots, stifling the Hawks' comeback attempts. It didn't get any better as the series went on. Two nights later the Hawks threw forty-seven shots at him, and he swatted all forty-seven away. Here were the Hawks, division champ and conference leader, blowing the first two games at home to the fucking Blues. It couldn't be happening again, could it?

Oh yeah it could. Joseph didn't let anything by in Game Three either, stopping all thirty-four Hawks shots and effectively ending the series.

I didn't even watch Game Four. My father offered to take me to Wrigley instead. While some part of me hoped for a miracle, I knew the truth through and through. Maybe I thought if I didn't watch it, accepted our fate without the visual evidence, it would hurt less. Maybe I thought that if I didn't watch, that was the charm the Hawks needed to at least salvage some dignity. Most likely I just couldn't bring myself to watch another season end. So I was sitting in the Wrigley bleachers, watching Frank Castillo twirl a gem over the Reds for an actually passable Cubs team while Craig Janney put the Hawks to the sword in overtime. When I heard the score on the radio, there was some relief in not having seen it all end in OT or having to witness the end at all. It was like getting the call that a suffering relative had gone in their sleep at night. Everyone was better off this way.

For the second time in three seasons, the Hawks had taken one of the best teams in the league and driven it right into the dirt at first asking. Except unlike '91 against the Stars, they didn't even have the decency to win a game this time around. They were shutout twice. This might have been an even more thorough embarrassment than that loss, getting swept out of the playoffs in the first round by a team that had finished twenty-one points behind them. After this, the run to the Final of '92 felt like some mistake by the universe. Like someone had forgotten to lock the usual door and we escaped out before anyone realized what had happened. We had escaped into the light the previous spring, or at least as close as we'd ever got, and the powers that be were going to make sure that never happened again. Back under the bridges and caves we went while an extra lock and bars went on the door.

The Hawks would simply never "get it."

One Last Time
October 6, 1993
Panthers v. Hawks

We knew it was coming. The announcement of the "Joint Venture," the partnership between the Hawks and Bulls to build the United Center, had come years before. Ground had been broken the previous year. The construction rose right across the street from our beloved Stadium, and soon it was clear it would engulf the old girl. We didn't want to believe it I guess, but watching the construction grow and grow was like being kept on Death Row while they build the electric chair from scratch right in front of your cell. There was no stopping it.

I've come to somewhat appreciate the features of modern arenas. The escalators, the better food, the bigger and cleaner bathrooms, the wider concourses. But back then, knowing we were heading into the final season at Chicago Stadium, it was like having your heart cut out.

The Grand Lady of Madison certainly had her problems. It had no skyboxes. The concourses could barely fit three people across. The creatures living within it had morphed into something out of *The Princess Bride*. It only held eighteen-thousand people, and both the Bulls and Hawks were convinced they could draw more every night. It was faulty in some places. There was "water" on the bathroom floors. These were none of the things modern sports franchises wanted for their arenas.

But it was home. It was hallowed. It was envied across the league as the most intimidating place to play. And we made it that way.

That soulless monstrosity across the street? That was for people who didn't come to the Stadium (which I suppose was the point). It was for sweatered yuppies and lawyers from Highland Park. That wasn't for us, and we knew it. We knew we would be pushed higher and farther away from the ice, where we wouldn't have any impact. We knew we existed on the fringes of society, and we actually liked that. But now we could sense we were being pushed to the fringes of where we came to be together.

We didn't have to see the blueprints to know that the United Center would have no character. We'd already seen it with the new buildings that were popping up. We'd seen it in the new Comiskey Park that went up on the South Side. They would put the skyboxes in first for the corporate people and fill in the rest of the seats where they could. The floors would gleam, the walls would actually be white and painted. There would be no smoke in the building. There would be ads everywhere. We were getting brought out into the light, kicking and screaming.

As I descended more and more into punk sensibilities, with my teenage years rapidly approaching, this was a major crime in my eyes. Sometimes I would forlornly hope for some sort of construction accident that would delay the move for another year. Or maybe Wirtz would have a change of mind. Some natural disaster. Because I did not want to ever leave The Stadium. The United Center was for all my classmates and their parents. They didn't understand. They didn't know the roar, and we knew that wasn't going to transfer over no matter how many promises the Bulls and Hawks made about the place amplifying noise. They would get their wine and their better parking. What would we get? A bigger scoreboard?

That kind of malaise hung over the team and fans all season. There was something ending and would never be the same again. The Hawks would no longer play in a relic that had a feel to it, that other teams feared. They would just be another team in another glorified airport hangar.

The Old Lady's Last Stand
April 24, 1994
Maple Leafs vs. Hawks (Game Four)

Drawing Toronto in the first round didn't make a whole lot of people happy around these parts. It was the first playoff meeting between the two division rivals in forever, which held appeal for the crusty. But it was clear that the Leafs were far superior to the Hawks. They had gone to the Conference Final the previous season, and were basically screwed out of a Final matchup with Montreal which would have essentially ended the hockey world. They reloaded for this season, and boasted the likes of Gilmour, Andreychuk, Clark, picked up Mike Gartner at the deadline, and one or two others. And of course, Peter Fucking Zezel.

The Leafs flattened the Hawks in Game One of this series at Maple Leaf Gardens, in a game that featured ninety-one penalty minutes between the two. Because of course it did. It was ever thus. Gilmour and Andreychuk ran all over the ice doing whatever they wanted and had two points each.

Game Two was a much more tame and even affair, with Belfour at his best. He made thirty-seven saves, but he needed to make thirty-eight as Todd Gill beat him in overtime to send the series back to the Stadium with the Hawks up against it at 2-0 down.

The two next games at the Stadium were some of the more strange and wild of this Hawks era. Game Three saw Tony Amonte score four times, which didn't prevent the Hawks from blowing a 3-0 lead. They would eventually claw out a 5-3 win. There was life yet.

Game Four is one all Hawks fans remember if they're old enough. Apparently the strangeness hadn't had time to clear out. Gary Suter score the first three goals for the Hawks, and hat tricks from d-men was something you almost never saw. The Hawks blew another lead, this time a 2-0 lead that the Leafs turned into a 3-2 deficit. Suter's hat trick, power play goal halfway through the third tied the game, and they headed into overtime again. Clearly the Hawks had to have this one. None of us wanted to believe this was going to be the last game at the Stadium. Surely the Hawks had to make a stand.

It took less than a minute for a memory that is burned into all of us forever to develop. Amonte picked off an outlet pass from Todd Gill right at the Toronto line. Murphy picked up the turnover and hit Amonte skating behind the Leafs' net. Roenick streaked right to the slot at approximately 139 miles-per-hour and Amonte found him to bury one into an open net at which Felix Potvin never had a chance.

The noise and Pat Foley's call can probably be recited from memory by a huge swath of the fandom. Roenick streaked up the boards in celebration, sliding on his knees from one line to the other before being met by Belfour. Foley nearly fractured a larynx screaming, "HAWKS WIN! HAWKS WIN!" He came close to reaching a frequency only dogs can hear. The walls sounded like they were caving in from the euphoria of the crowd. Most people's favorite image is some fans climbing up over the glass where the Hawks were piled to touch or high-five Roenick, and Roenick seemingly being restrained by his teammates from climbing into the crowd himself to meet them.

Did we think the series had really turned? No, probably not. What we did know is that there was one last roar, whether we were there or listening to it on radio. One last moment where the sheer power of The Stadium could be felt. One last time when we were reminded—despite all the bullshit and ache of it—of why it still felt special and cool to be a Hawks fan. One last time that Roenick would bring us to our feet in our barn, before we all had to decamp across the street to a place that most certainly was not for us. One last time where it still felt like the most alive and dangerous place on Earth.

A lot of us can still close our eyes and see JR pumping his fist on his way back to the door that led to the stairs to their dressing room. We can still hear the crowd greeting each one with another roar. We can still hear Foley's appreciative, "The Old Grandlady of West Madison!" as he tried to describe the pandemonium still consuming the building. We knew the Hawks were overmatched by the Leafs. We knew that two more wins were unlikely. As it turned out, that was the last goal the Hawks scored in The Stadium. It was the last goal they scored in that series period, dropping two 1-0 decisions to send them home and the Stadium to a date with a wrecking ball.

But for at least one more night, it felt like the crowd lifted this undermanned Hawks team to heights to look one of the league's best teams in the eye and make them blink. It felt as if we were part of that win, and we were part of so many before. Teams would never fear the United Center, at least not the atmosphere, or so we thought. But they did the Stadium. For one last night, it felt like we were the difference.

The Night We Almost Made It
June 14, 1994
Canucks vs. Rangers (Game Seven)

  Against our wishes, the NHL playoffs continued without the Hawks. The Leafs overcame the Sharks, who had at least made us feel a little better about things by upsetting the Red Wings in the first round, in seven games before falling to the Canucks in the conference final for the second straight season.

  Out East, the Rangers had become not just the main story in hockey, but the biggest sports story going. For once, the NHL had caught a break in timing. Michael Jordan had "retired" (depending on your conspiracy theory) from the NBA that previous fall. Meanwhile, the Rangers had produced one of the best series in recent memory to get to the Final, winning in double-OT in Game Seven to get past the Devils. A goal of course scored by Stephane Matteau, which to this day I still have a hard time believing.

  This was hockey's chance to get onto the main stage and maybe stay there for once. Its most popular team in its biggest market trying to end the sport's longest championship drought. Having a classic series leading into the Final didn't hurt, and the Final itself being the best one since the Oilers and Flyers laid into each other only heightened the attention. Everywhere you looked or listened people were talking about the Rangers and the NHL, and not Patrick Ewing and the Knicks setting the NBA back about fifteen years. We were coming out into the light, whether the rest of the world liked it or not. Finally, everyone was going to see what we already knew.

  The day leading up to Game Seven was filled with talk about the game everywhere. In the papers, on TV, on the radio. It was almost like a Super Bowl. The tension was really turned up as the Rangers had blown two chances to win the Cup already, and were poised to give their fans the biggest kick in the balls imaginable. It was also the first Game Seven in the championship round since 1987. There's still something special about hearing the words, "Game Seven." Even more so when it's going to decide everything. It doesn't happen often.

  The game itself might not have been a classic, but the Rangers' celebration is one every hockey fan remembers. Madison Square Garden up for grabs as they spilled off the bench. Messier shaking with excitement while he had to wait for the pictures as he took the Cup from Bettman (Bettman didn't even get booed during this, giving you some indication of the euphoria). Messier had won five Cups before in Edmonton, and even one without Gretzky. But this is what he's probably best known for, and he knew it.

The Rangers were everywhere the next few days. They showed up on Letterman. Their parade drew throngs. They even showed up on *Seinfeld* during this run. They were far more visible than the Houston Rockets, that was for sure. Hockey was the story for the first time in my life.

My compatriot on our blog Matt McClure wrote a fascinating and brilliant piece years ago about the correlation between hockey fans and punk rock fans. Their provincial nature, their distrust of outsiders and mass media coverage, and many other factors, including how 1994 was the year they both almost took their place in the mainstream. Green Day, The Offspring, Nirvana, and a host of others were the biggest bands on Earth around then and The Rangers were all over television.

Of course, neither hockey or punk rock could stick. The NHL couldn't capitalize on the momentum from the Rangers' win due to their own stupidity and greed. They staged a lockout right after their shining moment, and by the time they took to the ice again Michael Jordan was returning to the court. They had missed their window. And they did it as only they could.

For the first time, and sadly not for the last, we would wait until January for an NHL season to start. It's a mistake the NHL still has never recovered from, made up of tiny mistakes that could have easily been solved had anyone with a brain been involved in proceedings.

Gary Bettman was hired away from the NBA a little less than three years before this, and he was basically hired to get the owners the salary cap they so craved. While there are myriad ways to go about making sure every team makes money in a professional sports league, a salary cap is the only one that doesn't see owners having to spend their own money to do so. Clearly, this had the most appeal.

If Bettman didn't have a warlord mentality, if the Players' Union didn't feel quite so threatened, if anyone with vision had a voice at the table, they would have seen the window the NHL had. No one had that voice. While Bettman didn't seek an exact model of the salary cap the NHL has now, the measures were just about the same. He isn't all at fault, though. The Players' Union should have seen the writing on the wall, should have seen the greater chance for marketing of their sport would lead to more endorsements and profiles for their players, which would have meant more money. They were only concerned with "winning," though. These two sides could have worked together quickly to not miss any time and capitalize on the momentum they had from the Rangers' win. They could have tried to avoid the anger that baseball fans were making quite clear, and which MLB still hasn't totally recovered from. But quite simply, the NHL and hockey is just too stupid to live.

If my fandom hadn't been ingrained so heavily at such a young age, they would have lost me. I was almost delighted, in some strange way, that baseball had decided to destroy itself. The Cubs sucked to high heaven, as they had for pretty much every season of my conscious fandom, and I was relieved to not have to watch them play out the string.

However, I was now at that age where sports were no longer all that mattered. I was thirteen, and this was the time when Nirvana, Soundgarden, Pearl Jam, Alice In Chains, and a host of others were changing the lives of kids my age rapidly and violently. Suddenly the conversations with my friends, the few I had at that time, weren't about sports but about music. Whereas the small sample of bands we listened to before sang about subject matters we would never understand like coke binges and groupies and demons, it seemed that these new bands were talking about things we were just getting into. "Hey, he's singing about having no friends and being an outcast. I have no friends and am an outcast! HE GETS ME!" Suddenly, they were the most important thing in the world.

Also, there were these things around called..."girls?" I'm not sure if that's how it's spelled. And I didn't know exactly what they were or what they wanted (and I didn't know at the time that would remain a mystery for the term of my natural life). What I did know then is they didn't want much to do with me but I knew I wanted something to do with them. Hockey most certainly didn't fit into that aim, at least not in my mind at that time.

The Hawks lost kids around my age group simply through their own irrelevance in this city. Loads more than just my age group as well. Hockey in general must've lost a great deal during this lockout, too. I still had a bond with it, a bond with my brother Adam that I could never desert, no matter how much the NHL and the Hawks tried to break it. But thousands if not millions around the nation didn't have nearly that strong of a bond. So when hockey went away, how many were quite content to fill the time with "Vitalogy" or "In Utero" and never come back?

I started a band with my best friend Mike. We named it after the digestive condition I still carry to this day. We practiced in his basement. This could have easily been my new path to fill whatever it was my Hawks fandom did. Had the winds blown another way, I might have never come back to hockey.

Thankfully, Bernie Nicholls made sure I did.

Nicholls had signed with the Hawks during the summer, when there was still hope the season would begin on time. No one had benefitted more from Wayne Gretzky's trade to Los Angeles, other than the Kings' owners, than "Pumper." Nicholls was a very effective scorer in his first six seasons of course, never totaling less than twenty-eight goals and topping forty twice. But then Gretzky showed up, and that number went to seventy.

The Hawks had better players than Nicholls, but no one who had put up a magical number like that. Savard and Roenick routinely racked up fifty goals or a hundred points. But back then those numbers merely made you an All-Star or among the higher echelon. Seventy goals was...well, it was out there. It was stratospheric. No Hawk had ever come close to that number.

The record for goals in a season by a Hawk remains Bobby Hull's fifty-eight. In my life Roenick's fifty-three in '91-'92 was the most I'd seen a player achieve. A player who scored seventy? Seventy? SEVENTY? That was like Olympus dropping off a resident on your doorstep. While Nicholls would never come close to that again, you kept saying to yourself when you saw him in the Hawks' red, "That dude once scored *seventy!*" He was like that dude in your class who first got to third base. So many questions, and you'd never understand the answers.

The addition of Nicholls actually led to the Hawks having a real, live power play. Sitting through shitty Hawks power plays was a badge of honor, something we all shared. This hurt our retinas. We couldn't figure out what it was. We wondered if it was legal. We kept waiting for the curtain to be pulled and revealed to the be the subject of a prank. But it never came, and they kept scoring.

Of course, they lost their first two games of the season and we all thought they should have just stayed locked out. What we didn't know at the time was that the scars of that lockout would eventually beget the massive 2004-2005 lockout. That the owners relenting only lead them to spend more money they didn't really have over the next decade. And that in turn leaving more and more small market teams either hopeless or breaking themselves to try and keep up. That Bettman would take losing so personally. That the players always thought they could get one over the owners, and the rancor between the two sides extending any dispute for much longer than it ever needed to go. It's like no one read twentieth century European history or anything.

Big things come from small beginnings.

The First Foray
January 22, 1995
Rockets vs. Bulls

Two days after the NHL season finally started, I made my first trip to the United Center. But it wasn't for a Hawks game. In some ways I think it's symbolic that it wasn't. As Kurt Cobain (even in death), Kim Thayil, and Scott Weiland only pushed me more into my punk ideology (up yours all you STP deniers), there was part of me that never wanted to see a Hawks game at the United Center. After all, this was a monument to everything I hated about sports fandom. It wasn't dangerous, it wasn't going to be loud, it wasn't dirty. This place didn't make me cool. This was pop music. I was not pop music.

However, that friend Mike I started a band with, his father had Bulls season tickets and he went regularly. He knew neither of us belonged among that crowd, with our flannels and ripped jeans (oh, we were in full uniform) but he also loved basketball. And he always wanted me to go, and every so often I'd relent. I guess I figured that I should go see what I was already so aggressively against. Not to see if I was right or wrong, of course, but to have my suspicions confirmed. There wasn't anything I was going to see that afternoon that would make me think this building would meet my standards. I knew how this worked, and at thirteen I already had the world figured out.

So on a snowy afternoon, I walked in. And the first thing I thought was, "This looks like a fucking airport." It wasn't just clean, it was sterile. It didn't smell. There was fresh paint still on the walls. It had shops and food concession stands that were actually in the walls, not sticking out into the concourse. It had clear signage. Big signage. All the employees were far better dressed than before. My shoes didn't stick to the floor. What gate was our flight? You could see all the concourses. There was actual art on the wall. What the fuck?

We took the escalator up, which only sickened me more. Oh sure, I hated the Stadium stairs. There were times I thought I might cry from the ache in my legs when it was over. Not that I would ever cry at the Stadium for fear of showing weakness in that place, because that would have gotten me killed or eaten. But dammit, that's what real fans did. It hurt, it sucked, but that was part of the experience. That's how you earned your joy at the game. And now any of those dumb fucks could just stand and make their way to the top with no effort? What kind of lesson was that?

As I'm sure it is in other arenas, when you're taking the escalator up from the 100 Level and you get on the same level as the 200, you can peer in through one or two of the entrances from the concourse to the seating bowl itself, or a small section of it. And from that very first glimpse, that preview, you can feel the sheer size of it. At first glance it kind of takes your breath away. You can't see the top of the 300 Level, but you know it's way up there. You can see how far away the other side of the arena is, though that's magnified by only getting a small window to look through. You can kind of sense the air being sucked into it. Even now, on the rare occasion, I look through those entrances and am still taken aback by the sheer mass of the building. Now it makes me feel like I'm about to see *an event,* but back then it was just the sheer mass of it.

We took the second escalator up, and I kept asking myself if this was taking longer than the stairs at the Stadium did. I just knew we were going up, and the windows to the outside proved that. That was another thing about the United Center that I wanted no part of. There were no windows to the outside world in the Stadium, and when I was there I didn't want to think about the outside world. And the outside world certainly didn't want to know about us. I wanted to be locked in a cage with my fellow psychos. These windows let in natural light, for fuck's sake!

We finally reached the top, and walked into the seating bowl. This wasn't Kansas anymore. The court was down there, but it wasn't as far away as I thought it would be from the top level. You could still see everything clearly. But this was obviously much, much higher. I didn't feel a part of anything that was going on down there (even if this was only the Bulls and basketball. BLECH). Whereas we were on top of the other seats in the old building, now we were merely observers, pushed as far back and as high up as they could manage without apologizing. This was the outer rim.

I didn't voice any of this, obviously. I didn't want to be rude to my hosts. But I spent most of the first half of that basketball game trying to figure out if I would be able to see a puck from the middle of the top level. I wasn't sure that I would be able to. Even sitting in the middle of the 300 Level I knew was higher than my usual standing room perch. And then I turned around to see if there was any standing room. There wasn't. And if there was, it was in a place I couldn't see. This wasn't surprising. They had told us the standing room would be greatly reduced in the new building, if not eliminated altogether. It looked gone to me at that point.

They had won. These...Bulls fans. To me at that age, even the hockey fans in this building were still just invading and unwanted Bulls fans. They had taken away the place where I had found a large part of my identity. The monsters roaming their quiet countryside had been eliminated so they could enjoy their picnic. And when we did arrive, we'd have to sit quietly, removed from everything we knew and were once a part of, so they could have their fucking mai tais in peace while looking all the way up to us with some kind of pity.

"Who sits up there where you can't see anything?" they asked in wonder, in my head.

"Those poor poors. That's all they can afford." I bet you can guess how I felt about their mythical pity that probably only took place in my mind.

This was a fraud. A sham. They killed what I loved.

At least Kurt understood (sidenote: he wouldn't have understood in any way).

A few weeks later, my brother and I headed to the United Center to see Tom Petty. We had seen the pictures on the news or in the paper, but this was the first time Adam and I got a look at the Stadium being torn down. On this night when we went, the entire west side of the building had been torn away. You could look right into the building and see three of the four sides still very much intact at that point. After the show at night, it was still lit up so you could see it. It was like getting to see an autopsy.

While it was cool to see the building in this way, the inside revealed to the outside, that doesn't mean our hearts didn't sink into our feet upon viewing. Sure, it was just a building. But it wasn't just "a building." And it was dying a slow, unceremonious death. And you could watch it, bit by bit, and its enormous replacement towering over it, intact, across the street, almost gloating. It looked even smaller when you could see inside of it, compared to the structure across the street that needed airplane lights.

I wanted to cry. You could almost see your memories and feelings pouring out of the now exposed seating bowl—exposed to the elements, the cold, the wind—that which had previously shielded us for a few hours from all the things we found outside the walls. I'm sure a lot of other people saw their memories, their relationships with loved ones and the team, pouring out of there as well whenever they walked by the opening torn into the structure. You get to keep those, but you have to hold on tighter when the place they were created goes away.

It was the last time I saw the Stadium standing in any fashion. By the time I made it back down to another game it was a parking lot. I hate that the last view I had of it was in mid-destruction. It should have been the last game I attended there. I hate that that view, despite how oddly beautiful it was, joins all the other images and sounds I keep within me. I should have waited until it was completely gone before heading to the United Center. Then again, when Tom Petty calls...

The Perfect Crime
March 16, 1995
Canucks vs. Hawks

This was a night of nine Hawks goals, and the strange thing was it wasn't the first time they'd done that during this season, nor the first time they did it to the Canucks. This began a five-game win-streak that would see the Hawks rise to the top of the Central for a brief moment. These new Sega-Hawks had my hockey buzz going full-throttle, to the point where it crossed into areas it most certainly shouldn't have.

Eighth grade was the second year where my grades had started to dip into the shitter. If you're connecting all the music I'd gotten into and this development, you're certainly not wrong. It was certainly a surprise to my parents, both great students themselves and accustomed to the brilliant report cards I had been bringing home through the age of eleven.

About this time, I had some big science paper due. And like all papers in science class, it required research to be done and for that research to be noted in a bibliography. I had no time for this. I wasn't going to research this kind of thing when I knew I could do a passable enough job on my own. I had drums to play and hockey to watch, damn it.

So on this night, with the Hawks pouring in goals on the radio in the background feeding my overzealous fever, I made up a bibliography. I made up the titles. And I made up the authors. And every author I made up was an NHL player.

In my mind, there was no way that my wool sock-wearing, middle-aged, female science teacher was going to be a hockey fan. And based on the fact that I never heard anything about it after, I guess she wasn't.

Plagiarism isn't the crime in eighth grade that it is in college. So even if she knew that "Physics In The Real World by Russ Courtnall" was total bullshit, it was probably more trouble to hassle me about it. I was a lost cause in her field anyway.

Sadly, I had that jaded view of hockey fans for far too long. Of course she could have been a hockey fan. There was no reason she couldn't have been. But that sort of view of what they should be and where they come from still pervades the game today. For the most part leagues and teams still can't quite fathom what it means to cater to female hockey fans, or even believe that they're there at all. It's either completely ignorant of their existence, or completely misunderstood with pink jerseys and "Ladies' Nights" talking down to them. It's basically the same point of view I had of my science teacher, which lets you know just how backwards it is. My thoughts on hockey fans at the age of thirteen shouldn't be a still very popular feeling amongst us adults in 2016.

I guess I should just be happy I didn't get thrown out of school.

Stop Caring About Jefferson
May 19, 1995
Maple Leafs vs. Hawks (Game Seven)

The Hawks closed out the regular season like Daffy Duck driving that car that Bugs had pulled the one key pin out of and it just fell apart around him, leaving him floating in the air holding a steering wheel.

That one pin was Jeremy Roenick, who had his knee shredded by Dallas defenseman Derian Hatcher on an April afternoon. We knew it was bad when it happened. We watched the Hawks' trainer give him a towel he could bite down on because of the pain. We searched our house for a similar object for a similar pain. Roenick never got hurt. This was finding out Santa wasn't real.

In response, the Hawks reacquired Denis Savard from Tampa. It seemed both desperate and yet a righting of a great wrong. Savard didn't belong in Tampa, but what was he going to do at thirty-four? We were happy he was coming home, but it seemed nothing more than a lark.

The Hawks would immediately embark on a thirteen-game winless streak. Apparently it wasn't just Roenick's knee-ligaments that were torn, but the entire fabric of the team. They pulled out of it just in time to finish fourth in the West and line themselves up with a second straight playoff series against Toronto.

The series did not get off to a good start. Then a funny thing happened. Denis Savard went supernova.

It's not that he piled up the points, though he eventually did end up with seven in seven games. But he was simply everywhere on the ice. It was as if being back in the playoffs and wearing the Hawks jersey had turned back the clock for him, at least for just a little while. He was the fastest player on the ice. He was weaving through guys as if it was 1984. It was like one of those commercials where everyone is playing with the hologram of some long retired or dead player or musician, except Savard was really out there. He was in 1984, and the rest were in 1995. The Hawks overcame going behind in Game Three with two Gary Suter goals and a shorty from Chelios to get back into the series. Savard once again led the way with an assist on the winning goal in a 3-1 win to even the series. Suddenly, the Hawks had life. There was something magical about Savard pulling out one more bag of tricks, and showing up all of us who thought he was done. You never doubt the master, after all.

Game Five saw the Hawks blow a 2-0 lead but Joe Murphy and Murray Craven made up for that with two goals in the third to put the Leafs on the brink. The teams returned to Toronto for Game Six, where the Leafs amassed a 4-1 lead a minute into the third. Again spurred by Savard, who at this point must have been drinking a Shakespearean witches' brew, this time with a power play goal, the Hawks stormed back with three goals in the third period to send it to overtime. Sadly, they couldn't complete it and something named Randy Wood got the winner halfway through overtime. Which meant a Game Seven to decide it at the United Center.

And this was something of a major problem for me, because the day between Game Six and Seven is when my entire eighth grade class decamped for Washington, DC for a class trip. On the one hand, I was giddy because we were staying in a hotel that had cable and of course it had ESPN, which just happened to be carrying Game Seven. I've got you now Wirtz, because you can't keep me from seeing home games on TV when I'm not in Chicago. I've outflanked you, sir.

On the other hand, the class was booked on a night bus tour for the night of Game Seven. I did the furious calculations in my head. The time difference was a boon, and an 8:00 pm puck drop meant a return to the hotel was possible to catch most of it, or at least so I thought. Had it dropped at 7:00 pm, I would have been fucked. God bless you, Eastern Standard Time. I wondered at the various stops, such as the Lincoln Memorial or Jefferson Memorial or the Pentagon or whatever else was on it (these were not my priorities), if I would be able to sneak into some restaurant or bar that had it on the TV. I'd have twenty minutes or so at each stop. Finally, in a desperate Hail Mary, I asked my teacher if I could just skip the tour. She was something of a hockey fan, because we had talked about the Hawks throughout the season and she could sense what this meant to me. But of course, they couldn't leave one student to his own devices in a hotel room so he could watch hockey. She said she understood, which was nice, but that I had to go, which wasn't.

Ok, not surprising or devastating. I didn't really think that tactic was going to work. So I just had to console myself that with the tour starting at

7:00 pm, and supposedly only running two hours, I'd probably be back in the room for the second half of the game. And getting to watch half of a home playoff game was certainly better than none of it, which is what I was accustomed to. This could be done. It was possible, I just needed the rest of the tour to cooperate.

I suppose if I look back on it, skimping out on the significance of all that we saw that night just so I could try and hurry everyone along was something of a waste. I couldn't tell you why I thought through sheer will and withering, icy looks would hurry this tour group along. I just thought I could. If I focused hard enough, it would happen. This was Game Seven, damn it! I had never gone through a Game Seven with the Hawks. Jefferson was a competitive man, he would understand. And that fucking statue wasn't going anywhere. I could come back to it one day if I felt the need, and so could the rest of these fuckwits. After all, on the trip's first night the entire class crowded around a payphone at Camden Yards so a classmate could relay the final minute of the Bulls losing to the Magic. You'll recall that was the year Jordan returned, and I delighted in their demise (the vengeance of seventy-two wins the next year was a tad over the top, I'd say). There was only one team in this town chasing a championship and it was my Hawks. I probably didn't win any favors with my class that night.

If looks could indeed kill, I probably would have slaughtered hundreds that night. Here were these people enjoying some of our country's most important shrines on what was a lovely night, blissfully unaware that my personal well-being was being contested elsewhere. And I had the rare chance to actually watch it. Not only was I missing a Game Seven, I didn't know when I'd get to see a Hawks home game again. You only got so many of these opportunities, so they couldn't be missed. Somehow, no one noticed my scowls and glares, taking them as a cue to get moving. Here I was dying and everyone just ambled and smiled their way around. Empathy is dead, people.

Finally, thankfully, we returned to the hotel in time for the third period. While my friends milled about our room doing whatever fourteen-year-olds in a hotel do (no, not that. At least I hope not), I locked in on the TV and didn't let anyone near it. This was my time. The UC was bouncing, and Joe Murphy tore it off the foundation with another unassisted goal halfway through the period. Patrick Poulin scored a mere twenty-six seconds later to effectively end it.

I was greatly relieved that my absence didn't cost them, that I had caught enough of it to feel like I was a part of it (and gotten one over on Wirtz), and that there would be more hockey whenever this godforsaken trip was over. Sure, I would miss the first one or two games of the next series, but I would be home for the end.

And on a night when I saw the Iwo Jima statue, seeing Joe Murphy score meant more to me. People like me aren't born. They're made.

The Hawks would go on to sweep the Canucks in the next round, but then face the Red Wings at the height of their powers. They barely generated any shots in Games One and Two, though only losing both by a goal thanks to Belfour's heroics. Eddie would give up a terrible goal in double overtime in Game Three, a Kozlov shot from center ice. I wonder sometimes if Hawks fans lost faith in him forever after that. Though they'd get a consolation win in Game Four. This was on the night of my eighth grade graduation, a ceremony I tried to sully with my speech decrying my school's insistence on suspending me, three times, for the length of my hair or metal shirts I wore. My parents and others loved it, and I'm sure the school's administration figured they were done with me anyway and didn't have to get too salty about it. The Hawks dropped out again in double OT in Game Five.

Probie
October 7, 1995
Hawks vs. Sharks
The summer after the exit to the Wings didn't bring about much change with the roster. Perhaps the Wings getting flattened in the Stanley Cup Final by the Devils convinced the Hawks that somehow they weren't all that far away. They essentially brought the same roster back, with Keith Carney taking Steve Smith's spot on the second pair with Eric Weinrich. Up front, rookie Eric Daze was brought up to bolster the scoring, which he did before his spine turned into graham crackers a couple of years later. But in reality, the Hawks were going to make another run with the core of Roenick, Nicholls, Murphy, Amonte, Chelios, Suter, Belfour, and the others.

Well, there was one other acquisition. That was of Bob Probert.

It's hard to know where to begin with Probert. He was actually signed the previous summer, but due to crashing his car drunk off his ass with traces of disco dust in his system, the league suspended him for the whole lockout-shortened season. The Hawks signed him before he even got to rehab, which lets you know just how much thought they put into this. This wasn't Probert's first run-in with the law or the league's discipline system, of course. He had spent six months in jail in 1989 for getting caught with booger-sugar in his underpants at the Windsor-Michigan border (though you probably needed something in your system to deal with being in Windsor, to be fair). Probert had to spend nearly the first half of the '92-'93 season not traveling to Canada with the Wings, because he wouldn't have been let back into the US due to his ongoing legal problems. If this sounds like something out of a cartoon or bad movie, it basically was. While everyone probably deserves a second chance, Probert was already on his third or fourth and it's not like Chicago is a barren wasteland for fun.

If that wasn't enough to make a team hesitate on Probert, there was the problem of what he actually was on the ice. Probert was probably the last true heavyweight goon who could actually play. He had broken the twenty-goal mark twice in Detroit, and he was far from helpless when it came to the actual game. The problem was all the times he wasn't playing the actual game.

Probert was a true menace on the ice, and while some of his fights live on as classics, there were far more dumbass penalties and retaliatory bullshit because he simply couldn't keep up. Even at just thirty, the miles were catching up, and his penchant for the nightlife probably wasn't helping.

But like what had come before, his signing signaled once again that the Hawks were trying to win a game that none of their competitors were playing anymore. Their main competitor had jettisoned him, though obviously for more reasons than just hockey. The Wings were now only worried about playing with the puck with speed and skill. They had left the barbarism behind. The Hawks would be joined in the West this season by the new Colorado Avalanche, after the Quebec Nordiques moved there. And this was a loaded Avalanche team Denver was receiving, with Sakic, Forsberg, Young, Ozolinsh, Deadmarsh. Sure, they had Claude Lemieux and Chris Simon, but they were built to play like the Wings as well. The Hawks kept spoiling for a fight after everyone had already left behind at the schoolyard.

There were other storm clouds gathering before the season even started. Jeremy Roenick was heading into the last season of his contract, and he didn't make much of a secret of the fact he wanted to be paid like the star that he was. And that the Hawks weren't exactly in a rush to do so. It was still a long way off and there was a whole season to be played, but every fan would be lying if they didn't have a sense of dread that got bigger with each passing day of Roenick not having signed a contract. We knew what happened to players that had earned a big contract from Bill Wirtz that went to actually go and claim it. Older fans had seen the cycle with Bobby Hull. There were others. Roenick going so public was not going to help matters much, either. Wirtz was cheap, and the only thing he hated more than spending money was being publicly called cheap.

The Hawks entered the season with a feeling of last-chance saloon. And they were doing it with Bob Probert.

Personally, I entered high school. And seeing as how I was attending the same school as my brother had and roaming the same halls where he had played Strat-O-Matic and talked hockey with his friends, I thought I would have the same sort of experience. But where his generation had grown up with Larmer and Savard and Secord, mine had Pippen and Jordan. I had a couple new hockey friends, which made for the first I'd ever really had. As if high school wasn't going to be hard enough, given that I weighed eighty pounds, at least I had a couple of allies.

A few months later it became public that Jeremy Roenick was

looking for a ten-year contract for fifty-million dollars total. This doesn't sound like much now but it was astronomical then, and it was an amount that you'd need the Hubbel to ever see Wirtz doling out. The Hawks claimed that they'd offered Roenick a five-year deal for slightly north of three-million per season.

Roenick and his agent were doing a lot of negotiating in the press, knowing his standing with the fans and the pressure it might bring to the Hawks. Of course, Hawks management couldn't have given less of a flying fornication what we thought, and their response to all this public posturing was cool, to put it lightly.

It seemed as if there was no actual negotiating going on, and Hawks fans knew deep down the terrible truth. Trade rumors had started to circulate, and generally where there's smoke, there's fire. Once the first rumor started to bubble, whether it was to Winnipeg or Philadelphia or the Islanders or wherever else would pop up, our hearts sank. It seemed like this was being discussed more than signing our best and most popular player was. The tea leaves were definitely conveying only one message.

What you know and what you feel can be two very different things, though. I knew it was likely over, but I didn't want to think about a Hawks team without JR. Surely everyone would come to their senses. Someone would get in Pulford's and Wirtz's ear about this being the one player they simply couldn't let walk away. Yeah, he did his share of bellyaching to everyone, but he was worth it. No matter how old you get, there's a part of you that's still that kid asking Shoeless Joe Jackson to say it ain't so (which no, never actually happened but let's stick with the fantasy here because it makes for a better story). There are times when you can't shake the fantasy or the idealism, even if you become more and more familiar with adult logic and cynicism.

The rest of the season was played with those clouds turning black. We lived in denial. We didn't think about him leaving. We thought if the Hawks could make a run, then there's no way he could leave. But we knew the Hawks couldn't make a run. We just never said it out loud. Every story in the paper or on TV rumoring Roenick's trade was greeted by me essentially sticking my fingers in my ears, just as I had about Adam Creighton years before.

As hope started to fade, it felt like this was the last time being a Hawks fan would feel like this. We knew the Hawks wouldn't go out and sign a player of similar ilk as Roenick. We couldn't see the cliff, but it was apparent on the map and the car didn't seem to be taking any alternate routes.

She's Gone
May 13, 1996

Avalanche vs. Hawks (Game Six)

The Hawks finished the year as the third best team in the conference, well ahead of everyone behind them. But they were also nowhere near Colorado and Detroit, existing on their own island. They swept the Flames in the first round easily, and drew Colorado in the second. I was filled with dread, and had to spend a good deal of time calculating all the things that would have to go right for the Hawks to get past a seriously superior Avalanche team. They did steal Game One in overtime, with Roenick pulling one of his last heroics in red to win it. The Hawks got clubbed in Game Two, 5-1.

Game Three was the game everyone remembers. Roenick then tied the game on a breakaway in the third, once again pulling the Hawks' ass out of a sling. If this was to be his last year he was certainly doing everything he could to make sure it went as long as possible. This goal started the famous war of words in the press between Roenick and Patrick Roy. Roenick should have had a penalty shot later in the third, and when told by the media that JR thought so, Roy said it wouldn't have mattered as he would have stopped him anyway. Roenick, when advised of this, impishly asked the assembled press where Roy was on the breakaway he scored on, and suggested he was in the stands picking up his jock. Roy check-mated this little verbal skirmish by claiming he couldn't hear what JR was saying because his two Stanley Cup rings were plugging his ears.

Game Three's overtime is one of the more famous in recent Hawks history. Less than a minute into the period, Craig Wolanin simply gave the puck away to Eric Daze at the Avalanche line. Daze laid the puck off for a streaking Sergei Krivokrassov to steam into the zone down the right wing. His shot deflected off Wolanin's stick and over Roy's shoulder into the net. You'll find many Hawks fans who can recite Foley's call word by word: "KRIVOKRASSOV'S FIRST EVER PLAYOFF POINT, NEVERMIND GOAL, IS AN OT WINNER!" It's like he couldn't believe the identity of the scorer that put the Hawks halfway to a big upset. And with good reason, because neither could any of us.

Something was a little off for us in the family though, listening to the game. Our mother had gone into the hospital the day before. Hospital stays were something of a regularity for my mother throughout my entire childhood. Years before I was born, she had contracted Hepatitis B from a bad blood transfusion after a rather serious asthma attack. Due to the steroids she was prescribed for her asthma, the disease was masked and was allowed to ravage her liver for a decade or more. It was simply shot.

But this was how it had been for basically my entire life. My mother had twenty percent of the strength and energy of a normal human being. But I didn't really know anything was wrong. I guess I just thought she was old. And about once a year, sometimes a little more, she'd have to spend a couple days in the hospital. I honestly didn't know how much simply getting through the day took out of her. I didn't know that having to run her own company full-time or more to keep the family afloat while my father's employment status faded in and out was far more than she should have ever been asked. I knew no other life.

The day between Game Three and Four, my father let me skip out on a day-long school field trip so I could make visiting hours at the hospital. Adam and I spent the early afternoon betting on horses, because that's what we did as a family together. Don't make that face. We then headed to the hospital.

When I got there, something immediately felt off. They had told us our mother was being moved to a different room, and when we found her she was just sitting in the hallway in a wheelchair. That didn't seem right. I walked up to her, and one of the blood vessels in her eye had popped or ruptured, leaving the area around pupil red. I was told it wasn't anything to worry about, but it made my mother look sicker than I had ever seen her. And my mother always looked sick. Things were not adding up in my head.

Finally they got her into her new room, and the three of us talked about horse racing and other things for a little while, just trying to have normal conversation under not normal circumstances. Visiting hours came to an end and we were told to go. But right before we did I walked up to Mom's bed, kissed her on the forehead, looked her right in the eyes (scary one and non-scary one) and said, "Mom, please come home. We need you. I love you. Get through this and come home."

It was the most sincere thing I had said to my mother in years. I don't know why I felt the urge. Perhaps for the first time I was scared. For the first time I knew that something wasn't right. I had spent the previous few years, as every teenage boy does, doing everything I could to anger her or push her away. My grades slipped. I just wanted to be with my friends or alone. I wouldn't talk to her about anything. I would get embarrassed or angry whenever she tried to talk to me about my life. None of this is abnormal behavior for a child I'm sure. But at that moment, seeing that my mother was actually very sick, I guess I saw just how stupid I was being. I could make it up to her when she got back home, because she always came back home after a few days. It would be dicey for a bit, she'd get some new medication, and then she'd come back home. I guess I just wanted to say something to her so she'd know when she did come back home, our relationship would change.

Those were the last words I ever said to her.

I went to school the next day, as normal. Somewhere around 10:00 am, as I headed to an English class, I felt my backpack being grabbed. I turned around and it was the principal's secretary. And then suddenly my father appeared behind her. What was he doing here? It felt very, very wrong from the first instant.

He walked up to me, hugged me, and whispered in my ear, "She's gone."

It's a cliché to say the world was spinning. But that's exactly what it felt like. There's no other way to put it. In just two words, the entire world has changed and you can't possibly find your feet. I kept looking around frantically, trying to orient myself, but nothing would stay still. I literally couldn't breathe. I kept trying to inhale but no air would come in. They pulled me into some office where I could finally ground myself just enough to start uncontrollably sobbing.

After a few minutes, while everyone was in class and I could exit the building without being seen, I went to collect my stuff and head home. On the short ride there and back in my room, all I could think about was the apologies I would never get to make. All the advice I would never receive that only your mother can give you. All the girlfriends (ha,"all") she would never meet. All the things she'd never see. Did she know that all my bluster and derisiveness to her didn't mean anything? Did she leave us thinking I didn't love her? Had I fucked up in a way I would never be able to fix? These are questions most adults can't answer, and at fifteen I was basically at sea without a sail or paddle.

That day felt like it went on for about two months. It ended with me lying in bed, listening to the Hawks and Avalanche slogging through two overtimes before Sakic ended it four minutes into the third overtime. The Hawks had managed only thirty-four shots in five-plus periods of hockey. The writing was on the wall for them and me.

Five days later, after our extended family had left and we'd had the services, my father asked me what I thought about going to Game Six. As I've said, the thought of going to a playoff game was still fantasy at this point due to cost and scarcity. What I didn't know is that Dad wasn't asking. He had already told Adam we were going. He knew that's where we needed to be, a good way for us to try to get back to our lives, as futile a task as that seemed at the moment. He had already purchased the tickets. This was my first trip to the United Center for hockey, and it was not just a playoff game but an elimination one after the Hawks got trucked in Game Five in Denver. What a way to make an introduction.

We arrived early to pick up our tickets and our *Blue Lines* of course. I was going to try to stick to the routine no matter how little it seemed to matter now. I got something of a laugh, which I badly needed, when the group in front of us in the will call line, which was completely comprised of the yuppies I had come to despise, were informed they had tickets to a different game. To me this was something of a victory. This wasn't for you, pal. You didn't belong here, not on this night. The stakes were too high, and only those of us this really mattered to should be in the seats. Take your Michigan State degree and your bleach-blonde self to Wrigleyville. This was serious business and you're not welcome At least karma was smiling at me in some way, I thought.

We sat behind one of the goals in the 300 Level, but only a few rows up. The ice looked bigger than I thought it would. It wasn't as bad as I thought. It was my first viewing of a video package and presentation to start a game, and I loved it. A big "10" remained on the board throughout it all, signifying how many more wins it would take to win the Cup. It made it seem epic. Though that "10" might as well have been "98" considering what the Hawks were up against.

I screamed my lungs out during the anthem, clearly working out more than just getting into a hockey fervor. I needed to scream. Here I could shroud it with others' screams.

The game started, and it would be another classic encounter between the two. The Avs scored first through Valeri Kamensky. I didn't realize how much more feeling the goals in playoff games contained than those in the regular season, especially when you're in attendance. The opponent scoring first in all the other games I'd seen didn't mean doom. But this being my first playoff game, the first goal against meant the world was coming down around me. There was real terror. And I had to throw myself into it all, if only for a few hours, because it was better than what I had been feeling the previous five days during which the world actually *was* falling down around me.

Halfway through the first, Denis Savard chased down a clearing attempt and corralled the puck at the line along the right boards. He had skated halfway across the ice to do so, his last desperate lunge to keep playing. He floated a puck toward the net that somehow eluded three or four bodies and Roy and into the net. The place erupted, I leapt out of my seat. Salvation. Savvy doing his best, for the last time, to try to make us believe that anything was possible.

The game remained tied late into the second, when the Hawks were attacking the net we were sitting behind. With twenty-four seconds left, Roenick picked the puck out of a jam just inside the line, and floated a puck toward the net with Nicholls screeching toward the net. It somehow found room between Roy's glove and the post, and from our vantage point I could clearly see the net just inside the post bulge and turn black. This coming after Roenick and Roy's war of words (say that out loud five times fast), the eruption was massive. JR had done it again, gotten the last word. After his teammates had congratulated him, Roenick made sure to give another full-body fist pump right at center ice where everyone could see it, making sure that Roy knew just how much he was enjoying this goal. The jumbotron showed Roenick sitting on the bench a few moments later, and he was still screaming, "YESSS!!!!" He was certainly milking it for all it was worth. How could anyone not have loved him?

(Ok, Nicholls actually tipped it in but we didn't know that at the time and I just prefer the alternate reality.)

The third period was not kind to the Hawks. This is where, after five games and two periods, Colorado's quality really began to show. No matter how hard the Hawks skated, they were second to every loose puck. They couldn't clear the zone, and when they did it was only to allow a line change. Belfour stopped several chances. But the Avs found two goals through Sakic and Kamensky (they never had an answer for Sakic). The minutes ticked down. We were going over the edge. This was it. We stared into the abyss.

It takes a while before you realize the season is going to end, at least when the last game is close. Up until the last minute or two you never even consider your team won't score a tying goal. They'll get a bounce, a deflection, a power play, one brilliant play. Of course they will. But when you get to one or two minutes left, you can't ignore it anymore. The impending doom actually weighs on you. Your desperation starts to feel like no match. It's just on the other side of the door.

With about a minute and twenty seconds left, the Hawks got the puck into the Avs' zone and Belfour headed to the bench. The puck kept relaying from behind the Avs' net to the blue line and back again as the Avs desperately tried to clear it and the Hawks desperately tried to keep it in. Finally Nicholls was able to get some sort of control of it and just flung it across the crease where it found Roenick on the other side of the net. Roenick was able to spit it back out to the crease, where Murphy had beaten his man to the net. He swept it into a yawning cage.

All of this was chaos to me on the other side. It happened too quickly and with too many bodies and with no organization to it at all. I just saw the puck get to Roenick, a slam of bodies, and then suddenly the goal light went on. I saw Murphy leap into Gary Suter's arms.

And then I was leaping into my brother's. It's the first time I remember losing control of my limbs and lungs after a goal. There was obviously more at work than just celebrating an extension of the series and season. I couldn't stop screaming, "YEEESSS!" just like Roenick had earlier. I couldn't stop jumping. After all we'd been through the past few days, all we'd been asked, we got this Hail Mary. Perhaps I was overjoyed knowing that there would still be joyous times even within this dark cave. The relief of not watching the season end only adds to the euphoria. You escaped the clutches. There would be life.

The first overtime only accentuated the third period. The Avs were so much quicker, creating clear openings that Eddie had to be at the top of his game to stop. Every time an Avalanche player wound up to shoot I would hold my breath. I wanted to turn away. And every time Eddie stopped it I felt my entire body exhale. It was all going to pivot on one moment. It was too much. Maybe I was lucky that my emotions had been scraped dry over the past week and that I couldn't fully stress out during this.

Belfour was able to get the Hawks to a second overtime. But five minutes in, he could hold them no longer. A mad goalmouth scramble, right in front of us, saw Eddie furiously looking for the puck. He couldn't find it. Sandis Ozolinsh, for some reason fleeing his defensive post to be in the crease, slammed the puck home from his back. Murray Craven slammed his stick on the ice.

That's the thing about overtime goals, especially ones that decide a series. They happen too quickly to process. I saw the puck slam into the back of the net. But I didn't know what that meant for a couple seconds. That much meaning can't be computed in an instant. And then you just sink.

We watched the handshake line. We watched the Hawks wave to the crowd before heading off. We watched JR linger after everyone else. He did his own goodbye. And then we knew. He wouldn't be coming back. This was farewell. I couldn't muster any more sadness. I was out of tears.

I knocked over a garbage can on my way out. I probably didn't get into trouble because of my age. Here I was, watching this era of Hawks hockey end, and heading back to a home that was forever altered and frightening. We were going to have to find our own way. It was clear I was going to have to take care of my father just as much as he was going to take care of me. My brother would have to go and find his life now that my mother wasn't around to be looked after.

A schism between me and the Hawks developed that night. One that wouldn't be fixed for many years. I had too much to do, and they were not going to be worth the effort to fit in as much as I had before. That much was clear. In a lot of ways, my childhood ended during that time, and Ozolinsh's goal was the final nail in it. Hockey and the Hawks would still be a part of my life, but walking out of the arena that night, I knew it was just going to be different.

...Has Left The Building
August 16, 1996

Like most of the moments of major events, or the ones surrounding them, I found myself at the OTB (off-track betting, for those who don't speak the lingo) with my brother. We didn't have anything else to do that day, neither one of us had a job to speak of, and betting on horses is just where we went.

Shortly after arriving, the news broke that Jeremy Roenick had been traded to Phoenix. The saga that had gone on far too long finally ended. This didn't come as a shock, but I still felt a sucking in my chest when the axe finally fell. It had dragged through the draft and the summer, and all the rumors were about possible destinations for JR instead of any contract signing. It had gone on so long there was a faint hope that maybe they'd just be stuck with each other. When Bob Murray appeared on the screen, we knew better.

This was not Bob Murray's fault, of course. He wasn't the GM. Bob Pulford was. And he was taking orders from Wirtz. But neither of the latter two were going to show up in front of the press to admit they were simply too cheap to sign Roenick. There was no winning with this organization, in any sense of the word, on or off the ice.

Murray's words rang hollow: "We just felt there was no way the agent was going to let us get a deal done." Yep, everyone's fault but the Hawks. They were as generous as could be. And Roenick meant well. It was the work of a demonic agent, one they couldn't possibly have bridged the gap with to make a deal. He was the unreasonable one, not the organization that wouldn't pay its star like the star that he was. This was standard practice, blaming everything on the evil creation of a sports agent.

I was in a rage. Everything I looked at turned red. Even though I had known this was coming for months, whether I admitted it or not, the final stab was still all-consuming. How could this team be so stupid? How could it come to this? Could they not see they'd have to pay someone this money to be competitive? So why not the player we all adored?

Trades like this feel so final. It's hard to imagine you'll never see your favorite player playing for your favorite team again. Did you get all you wanted out of it? Do you remember the goals and hits as vividly as you should now that there's a sum total to them? Do you feel short-changed?

The Hawks lost a lot of luster on that day. It didn't matter who came in return. They had just dislodged a major part of their identity. Our connection to the team was headed to the desert. He had come up through the system. We watched him grow as a player. He lived and died with everything as we did. No one else was going to be like that. It felt like JR understood us. He got it. It was another part of the old Stadium dislodged. The player who shook that old building now discarded from a team that made it more soulless to match the soulless building they now inhabited. No more would we see Roenick charging out on his first shift to turn someone into pellets on the end-boards, sending the crowd into a frenzy. No more timely goals that only he seemed to produce. It felt like being robbed. The finality is hard to come to grips with.

It's a good thing my Roenick jersey didn't fit anymore. I wouldn't have been able to bring myself to wear it again anyway. For once, I wouldn't be excited for hockey season to start. Why would I be? It was clear there wasn't going to be much to watch.

Strangers In Our Midst
December 6 & December 20, 1996
Canadiens vs. Hawks, Flyers vs. Hawks

These aren't remarkably special games in any way, other than they are the first games I ever attended with someone who didn't share my last name. Hockey was something between Adam and me, or my father standing in for my brother, but this was me attempting to open up my world a bit. This was me attempting to emulate the high school experience, or at least some part of it, that my brother had. Except the Hawks pretty much weren't worth it.

The first of these, against the Canadiens, I went to with my friend Graham and his father. While he was aware of *The Blue Line*, his dad was caught a little off-guard by it, let's say. I picked one up outside of the UC. This particular issue contained a "spotlight" section on then-coach of the Habs, Mario Tremblay. The image that accompanied it was not one of Tremblay, but a huge bullfrog. I went home that night and attached that to the cover of my binder for French class, because of course I did. My French teacher's reaction could be filed under "less than thrilled" when she saw it. I'm not sure Graham's father was impressed either, but he didn't say much. That was clearly the highlight of the game, as only Chris Chelios was able to get a puck past Pat Jablonski (yes, Pat Jablonski) as the Hawks meekly bit it 3-1.

A couple weeks later, Graham came with my brother and I to see our semi-annual trip to watch Eric Lindros. This was truly letting someone into the inner circle. It's one thing to accompany a friend on their family trip to the hockey game and be something of the "expert." It's another to let him into the whole tradition, that which helped define me. This was growing up, wasn't it? Soon my brother would have to go off to Miami for grad school (don't ask), and I was going to need a full-time replacement. Here was Graham's audition, I guess.

Tony Amonte blasted one home from the circle late in the second to give the Hawks a 2-0 lead. It was his twenty-second of the season in the team's thirty-sixth game, and it gave him the league lead at the time. There was still a thrill seeing a Hawk on top of any statistical category, especially when it was such a surprise. Amonte's high in a season before this was thirty-three and he was already at twenty-two. He was on such a binge, tuning in every night was like watching someone on a heater at the craps table. You enjoy the goals, but you also enjoy the shock that they just keep coming. He can't possibly keep scoring like this, you'd think. And then the next night he'd score again. There was something of an out-of-body experience about it.

Not that it mattered much that night or in the season. In the second period Lindros went into that mode where simply no one could handle him. He converted two close-in chances, one off a rebound and one on a drive from the boards, where he simply didn't notice there were Hawks d-men trying to force him off the puck. They might as well have just blown in his ear, for all the good they were doing. They were putting all their force into knocking him over or even just off-balance and he couldn't have been more unaware of their presence. He might as well have been out there by himself.

Lindros, at least early in his career before the injuries got the best of him, was one of the few players who could do whatever he wanted when he wanted. When he used the full breadth of that frame, there was little anyone could do about it. He was just a force of nature.

The game ended 2-2, and a few weeks later my brother headed off to Miami, and Graham had been fully indoctrinated. It was a new world. My psychosis ran so deep that it wasn't too long after this, perhaps in a bid to fill something the Hawks no longer could, that I started the intramural floor hockey league at our high school. It quickly became a wonderful, riotous mess where everyone tried to dress weirder (and also be less sober) than the next guy. The league would last well after I had graduated from high school. Sadly, it ended after some sophomore girls showed up to impress some senior guys, far too wasted. This once again proves that teenage girls, and really all girls, ruin everything.

Another One Bites The Dust
January 25, 1997
Hawks vs. Islanders

The Hawks continued to stumble and trip their way through the season, and the rumblings that Eddie Belfour was on his way out only grew louder. It became clear he could see where the club was heading, and there wasn't even a hint of a negotiation on a new contract. He was going, it was only a matter of when and what the Hawks could get in return. Only months after losing franchise linchpin Roenick, here was another one heading for the exit door.

Even before the trade, the near-certainty that he was going to be traded was pretty damn sobering. The Hawks were now a team that their long-serving stars wanted to flee. The Hawks were supposed to be a team that added through the season. They were one of the Original Six, for fuck's sake. And yet after years of mismanagement and miserliness, even those who had brought them closest couldn't see the point any more. Eddie wanted out, and we were all pretty sure that he wasn't going to be the last. The Hawks had become an outpost.

On January twenty-fifth, the Hawks pulled the trigger on one of the worst trades they ever came up with (at least until the next season). They sent Belfour to San Jose for Chris Terreri, Ulf Dahlen, and Michal Sykora. If you're wondering if those aren't the same guys who just changed your oil, I wouldn't blame you.

If the Hawks had gotten a handful of beans back for him, they would have done better than the haul the Sharks passed along, giggling all the way I'm sure. You know those interchangeable goalies you see in highlights from NHL games in the '80s or early '90s? They're wearing brown pads and usually falling over? That was Chris Terreri. He could have been any of them.

This is how the Hawks descended into hell. It wasn't just bad luck or age or an owner slowly driving off all the fans. It was management incompetence. And they traded him for nothing. At least Roenick had netted the Hawks someone who could dress regularly, at least before Zhamnov threw up all over said gear.

It was impossible to not see where this was heading. The Hawks were meandering along on the ice, and losing pieces that weren't being replaced either in the trade that sent them away or by any kid coming through the system. The Hawks didn't have a young goalie to take Belfour's place. They didn't have a center to replace Roenick. They had to chase whatever they could get, which wasn't much.

One Final Stab
December 12, 1997
Flyers vs. Hawks

The Hawks coughed and sputtered through the '96-'97 season. They barely scraped into the last playoff spot after the Belfour trade. They drew the Avalanche again. While the series went to six games because the Avs spent two games playing with their food, the final game was truly sobering. The Hawks gave up six consecutive goals after taking a 3-0 lead to end their season. We weren't even really surprised at how violently they coughed it up. This was the best they could do. And given how swiftly they were swatted aside, we knew that it was probably going to be a long time until they were in the playoffs again.

They headed into the following season with little hope. I still couldn't quite completely give up on them, at least not yet. By this point a group of friends had been convinced to go see a game together. I guess I figured that this would be the last chance to have the high school Hawks game experience that I had assumed would be a major part of my teenage years. The Flyers being in town seemed like the best bet to do it. This was the first game that we got ourselves to and from. We had driver's licenses (which seems terrifying now) and amongst a group one of us could find a car we could borrow. I guess this was our Dazed and Confused, though I would have much preferred Aerosmith tickets in '78.

I felt about as adult as I ever had to this point. We got the tickets on our own, because suddenly that wasn't hard to do anymore. We made our own plans, we got ourselves down there, we got ourselves home. This was something of growing up, I guess. If only this had been a trip worth doing more than once every few years back then.

It was also the last time I bought a *Blue Line*. It had ceased operations about a month earlier but was still selling its last ever issue for a few more games after that. The dwindling crowds at the United Center had made its tiny profit margins disappear, and the team certainly wasn't worth putting in the passion it takes to write in-depth about them regularly. This was just another death rattle in Hawks fans' experience. When the voice of the fans can't even be bothered anymore, that's scary. Whereas the writers of the *Blue Line* felt it was necessary to be the voice of protest and analysis before, even they though the fight wasn't worth it anymore. More to the point, they didn't see the fight in anyone else either. There just wasn't anyone there. It's not that Wirtz had "won," he had just simply negated any sort of fight at all. Which I suppose is a form of winning, though it's hard to claim victory when only friends and family are walking through the door.

Zhamnov scored twenty seconds in, which for a little while made it seem like the Hawks might actually hang in this one. The Hawks would toss seventeen more shots that period at Garth Snow, but the Hawks had punched themselves out, mustering just three shots in the second period before Chris Gratton, another player long rumored to become a Hawk but never did, scored the winner in the third. We camped back to the car having watched yet another Hawks loss.

I had hoped for some kind of exciting win that would convince this crew it was worth it to come back again. They didn't know quite how bad this Hawks team was, at least not all of them did. I wanted this to be a pillar of high school and college breaks and beyond, just like it had been for my brother. But the Hawks simply weren't up to it. It was a fun diversion, something to be tried once, and then move on. If I were to continue my fandom, it would basically be all alone again. This was just yet another betrayal, another letdown from them. I couldn't put up with much more.

Little did I know at the time, but it would be years before I would return to the United Center. I tried, I really tried, Hawks. But quite simply, you pushed me away.

The Hawks would eventually go winless in their last eight games of the season to miss the playoffs by a longshot and I was mostly glad about it, for a few reasons. One, in my anger toward what they'd become and what they'd destroyed, it felt like comeuppance. This is exactly what they deserved. For the first time in nearly thirty years, a Wirtz wouldn't have any playoff revenue. Maybe that was what would spur him to finally see what he had been doing wrong all those years. Fat chance, of course, but that was the hope. You sit and think about what you've done, Hawks.

On another level, it made my waning interest seem justified. Why bother following a hockey team that couldn't even manage the simple task of getting into the playoffs? That was still considered filling in your name correctly on the SAT. It was job #1, and the Hawks couldn't even do that. So why should I stick around? This was truly the mark of something that wasn't worth it, that was a drain on my time, my emotions, and now that I was of the proper age, my own money.

I didn't even watch or listen as the Hawks slipped away. When the curtain came down it was like finding out a faraway relative you'd lost touch with and knew was sick had finally passed. You knew it was sad, but you didn't feel sad. It was how this was going to go, and quite frankly, in your darker moments, you were somewhat relieved it wasn't something you had to think about anymore. You think of the times you had together, back when you were still a part of each other's existence, and grieve that those are gone forever. But you knew those were gone forever long before, and all the tears are gone now.

So Long, Captain
March 23, 1999
Hawks vs. Penguins

Looking back on it, the trade of Chris Chelios was pretty close to the actual definition of beating a dead horse. The Hawks as a team were non-factors, if we're being polite. The fanbase had already thrown up its hands and left. I guess in a way, this was the perfect time to trade your franchise's greatest defenseman. There wasn't going to be a furor over it, simply because no one cared anymore. After watching Roenick and Belfour go away and magic beans come back, there weren't any nerves left to rub raw.

Of course, sending him to the Red Wings was going to sting every Hawks fan, wherever their apathy levels were. It was bad enough that the Wings had now amassed two straight Cups and were the league's leading light. We could somehow stomach that they beat our skulls in every time and were going to do so for the foreseeable future. But for them to swoop in and take the Hawks' captain? This was Bart trying to make trades at the lunch table at the school for the gifted.

Chelios wasn't just the captain. He embodied what we all wanted the Hawks to be. He was from the city. He desperately wanted to stay even as terrible as the team was. He played every night like his game-check was going to pay the ransom for some family member held hostage. He was one of the league's best players even at thirty-seven. He talked openly about playing sixty minutes one night. He was hated by everyone else and loved by us. He had said previously he would never play for Detroit, because he felt the same way about the Wings that we did. He was a Hawks fan as well as player.

But the Hawks left him with no choice. They told the press before they told him that he was on his last contract with the team, which is really unconscionable. Sure, no one but him could predict he would play for nine more seasons after his thirty-seventh birthday, but there is no way you're supposed to announce that in the press. And Detroit was the only one making an offer, or so it seemed.

This was the final insult. After claiming to be equals for so long, the Hawks had to go hat in hand to Detroit to take whatever grift they were offering for a club legend. The Hawks once again got nothing for another star, setting the team back years. I'm sure this was the last straw for a lot of fans.

I had given up watching, but even I was hurt by the trade. It was such a clear demonstration of the differing hockey worlds the two teams were inhabiting. Chelios was going off to compete for the trophies he deserved and no longer would where he loved it most. We were left with flotsam and jetsam. It was revolting. And yes, I know what came back and his name was Anders Eriksson, but he might as well have been named, "Flotsam Jetsam."

And you could argue that wasn't even bottom.

College
December 4, 1999
Hawks vs. Bruins

I'm not exactly sure why I tried to buy back in the next year. If there was ever a time to make a clean break from the Hawks, it was now. I was off to college in Boston. I would never see their games, nor would I have the time to do so. I could even not be a hockey fan at all. It was all there in front of me. It was the first of a thousand lessons about how we can't run from who we are.

Perhaps I thought now in the bigger pond of college, that I would find more people who liked hockey than I had in my tiny high school. After all, this was Boston. This place was supposed to breathe hockey. And I did, and upon making a small circle of friends I had already planned to attend the Hawks visit to Boston in December. Sure, the Hawks sucked but the Bruins weren't much better. It was something to look forward to, or so I thought. I was really play-acting at it, trying to identify as Chicagoan more than Hawks fan, simply because it made me unique. But it was something.

The Hawks stumbled badly out of the gate that season, so badly that even a month or more in advance of their trip to Boston I knew I didn't want to scrape together what meager college money I had to go see them. There was a college experience to explore, after all.

In fact, the only time I felt any emotion about them that season was the night before they arrived in Boston. This was when they fired Lorne Molleken as coach, and also Bob Murray as GM—even though we knew he was never really the GM. And in a true showing of imagination, they installed Bob Pulford into both chairs.

Even though I hadn't seen a game in weeks, even though I knew they were going to hell, inserting Pulford as the coach felt...exceedingly backward. Here had been this guy who'd been incompetent as a GM for as many years as we could count. The guy who forced out Mike Keenan, the only guy to construct a team that came within touching distance of a Cup. Here was the guy behind the trades of Roenick, Belfour, and Chelios, and now he was getting more control? It was a giant, neon sign flashing "HOPELESS."

I remember firing whatever Hawks jersey I had those days out of my dorm room and leaving it in the hall for hours. I don't know how it remained there. That was the thing about being a Hawks fan those days. Every time you'd thought you'd hit bottom, or that they couldn't do any more, or that you finally couldn't feel anymore, they'd cattle prod you right in the ribs. I didn't think I could muster any sort of feeling about the Hawks anymore, and then Bob Pulford somehow stumbled (probably literally) his way behind the bench. It was almost like they had a bet to see how much they could enrage a fanbase that simply wanted to tap out. And to their "credit," they never failed.

The joke was on me of course. The Hawks strolled into the Fleetcenter, as it was known then, and won 9-3 in their first game under Pulford. It would have been a massively good time to enjoy with my Boston-resident friends. But I didn't want to feel anything good about the Hawks. I didn't want anything that made me pay more attention or give up more time. I wanted them to be "over there," where I could remain angry at them. Or I could not feel anything about them.

It All Goes Wrong
January 30, 2003
Hawks vs. Bruins

Quite simply, I missed the whole previous season. I spent a year in Leeds, UK for my junior year of college. My only hockey watching involved checking the score online the next morning. Of course, that was the one strange year the Hawks actually belched up a playoff appearance.

I returned home from Leeds, and a year without hockey and made it clear I couldn't go very far without it. In my exuberance to dive into hockey again after a year away, I had purchased tickets to see them play the Bruins in Boston as soon as Bruins tickets went on sale that fall. This was asserting my rediscovered desire to be amongst it again, or so I thought. But ten days before the Hawks arrived in Boston is when it all went wrong.

Sometime after a game in Columbus, Theo Fleury and a couple other Hawks started a brawl at a strip club. It was clear that his repeated trips to rehab and suspension hadn't really done anything to allay the demons within Fleury. Whatever steps the Hawks were taking weren't either, if there were such a thing. They'd ended up on the police blotter and in the paper, perhaps the only time the media actually paid attention to the Hawks in that period of time. This was the nightmare scenario we thought would await Bob Probert.

The Hawks remained mum on the whole thing by the time they came to Boston. And Fleury remained the centerpiece of the team. He scored the opening goal and clinching goal in a 3-1 win, one that saw Jocelyn Thibault make forty-four saves. My yells of "THEO!" were certainly accentuated to antagonize the Bruins fans around me who hadn't exactly been welcoming of an opposing fan in their midst. There was still hope that they could keep this together.

They couldn't. That win was just one of three they managed between January 17, right before the Columbus incident, and March 7. The team simply disintegrated after the incident in Columbus, highlighted by losing nine in a row to end any hope of a second-straight playoff participation. Brian Sutter only made things worse, unable to nurture any young talent or to keep the veterans interested.

As the losses piled up my attention to the Hawks simply couldn't keep up with getting through the last semester of school and my impending graduation. There were more important things (e.g. drinking) to be done. And the NHL was headed off another cliff anyway.

Bottom
December 11, 2003
Red Wings vs. Hawks

After graduating, the Hawks didn't spend a lot of time proving they needed to be a big part of my new, adult life. Actually, "adult" should have been in quotes there because adulthood is still a nebulous concept of which I'm still in search. But I was out of college now, had returned home to Chicago, and would have been perfectly happy to be somewhat of a regular at the United Center. Or I would have been if not burned out by Wirtz's ownership, or the constant zombie-rising of Bob Pulford, or the dysfunctional rosters they kept tossing out there and expecting us to accept.

Following the previous season's collapse after Theoren Fleury's what-have-ya in Columbus, the Hawks didn't make any effort to try to add to what was left. While I'm sure the cover story was to let Tyler Arnason, Mark Bell, and Kyle Calder ascend to the top of the team and carry it, that was hardly the reasoning.

It should be mentioned that there was a strange pall over all of the 2003-2004 season. It wasn't just here in Chicago. Every hockey fan knew that there was a lockout coming after the season. The owners and players had been talking about it all the previous year. And everyone knew it could very well cancel the whole next season. Gary Bettman was coming to get what he didn't get in the 1994 lockout, and he wasn't taking any less. The Canadian franchises were drowning, trying to keep up with what the American ones were spending in a currency far stronger than theirs. They had already lost Quebec and Winnipeg, and it wasn't clear that they could hold onto all the other ones they had. Bettman had lectured other owners about what they spent in relation to what they earned. But he couldn't stop them by simply lecturing. He knew a reset button needed to be hit. The union clearly became aware that was the aim. And the fans knew it, too. So why would the Hawks bother signing any free agents when it was clear that in the best case scenario, there would be a whole new system in place a season later?

The only significant addition to the roster, or what we hoped would be, was Tuomo Ruutu. Ruutu had been drafted two years before, and it was generally agreed the Hawks got something of a steal at the ninth pick. He was generally regarded as the best player plying his trade outside North America. Or he was during the next two seasons when he was still in Finland, because the Hawks refused to sign him to what he wanted as a draft pick. All we heard was that he was the most exciting prospect not on this side of the pond. He finally arrived for this season, but the lovechild of Gretzky and Zeus wasn't going to save this roster.

The Hawks started the season in middling fashion, to be polite, but whatever meager accomplishments they had were buried in the attention of Chicago sports fans by the exhilarating though ultimately doomed Cubs playoff run of 2003. I was working in a bar during this time, and I don't recall having the Hawks on the TV very much at this time. Turns out they were actually a game over .500. Had to look that up. Needless to say, not many people were paying much attention.

It was only a couple weeks after Mark Prior and Dusty Baker froze that the Hawks sank their season, and entire organization, to basically its lowest ebb. Starting on November 9, the Hawks embarked on a fourteen-game winless streak that left them eight games under .500 from which they couldn't possibly recover. They didn't score more than three goals in any of those games. They gave up forty-six goals in those fourteen games.

I was working alone in a bar on this Thursday night. It was the only thing on, so I had it on the TVs. It was actually a home game on TV, because ESPN was covering it thanks to the visit of the Detroit Red Wings, still the class of the league. There can't be much more of a helpless feeling than having not won a game in over a month and facing the team that had been rubbing our noses in it for now a decade. At the same time, it was almost a relief to play the Wings in such a state (and it would happen a few times over the years). Because really, how much worse could they make it? Could their fans' laughter be any more stinging than our own?

It happened other times, when the Hawks, as greatly overmatched as they were, would still play an inspired game against the Wings. As long as a hockey season is, the type of team the Hawks were wouldn't always grab the full attention of an opponent. And perhaps the Hawks played with more desperation out of fear of embarrassment. It was yet another insult, if we were capable of being insulted, that the Hawks were the mark of the hockey season's doldrums. A trip to the United Center for opponents was merely an appointment that had to be kept. Playing in an empty building against an incompetent opponent was just something that had to be done.

The bar wasn't much busier than the UC, so I caught most of the game. The Hawks took a 2-0 lead but blew that. They got the third goal but blew that lead too. Somehow, just fifteen seconds into overtime, Mark Bell streaked past everyone to score the winner. You could feel the relief pouring through the screen. Though the fans knew, and I suspect the players did too, that the season wasn't going anywhere, they were more than delighted to do that in the background. A winless streak that long grabs the attention of the hockey world at least, and it's the attention you want the least. You become the leading object of mockery from everywhere. That win meant at least the Hawks could remain anonymous for a while. At that time, that was the best we could hope for.

Of course, the win didn't signal any turnaround. They lost four of the next five. After that they lost five of the next six. The season was well and truly done by Christmas. They would go on to post the lowest points-total they had since 1958, and that's when they only played seventy games.

But the season didn't just peter out in obscurity, because that would have been too easy. The team's utter uselessness finally convinced the powers that be that a total rebuild was necessary. Or they knew the lockout would produce something of a do-over whenever hockey resumed after it. Either way, the Hawks jettisoned just about anything that wasn't nailed down.

Alex Zhamnov, who had simply picked up the captaincy off the floor after Tony Amonte left and no one was bothered enough to figure out if it belonged on anyone else, was traded to Philadelphia. Steve Sullivan, whom the Hawks never appreciated despite all his goals thanks to his size, was punted to Nashville for draft picks. He would only score fifty-five goals the next two seasons in Music City. Alexander Karpotsev was finally tossed overboard to put us out of our misery, leading to Pat Foley's famous rant on the radio about what a horrific experience it was to watch him as a Hawk. This rant probably helped get Foley fired a couple years later.

Oh, but that wasn't all the Hawks had in store for this complete Hindenberg of a season. Not content with settling for their antics the previous season, in March word came out of another bar fight while the team was on the road. This time it was Tootsie's in Nashville, and this time it was the coach, Brian Sutter, getting into it with one of his players, Tyler Arnason. Sutter didn't think Arnason was tough enough or cared enough, or some such drivel, and thought that challenging him to a bar fight would be the way to cure such an ill. Only the Hawks.

The impending lockout seemed almost medicinal at this point. We knew hockey was going away for a while, and the Hawks did their best to make sure we wouldn't miss it. While we knew we could never pull ourselves away totally, no matter how much we tried, perhaps if hockey pulled itself away we could learn what life would be like and how much happier we would be. This was taking away the drugs of an addict.

That June, at a friend's BBQ, I headed inside the house to watch Game Six of the Lightning-Flames series. I didn't really care, and no one there could believe I wanted to watch this ridiculous hockey. But I knew that the impending lockout would see hockey go away for a long time, everyone said so. I felt this duty to cram one more in, to be that weird, outsider watching hockey by himself at the party. I didn't know when I would again, and there was this little itch I couldn't ignore that said I might never.

The Lockout

As you see, there's no date to list. No game. Because there weren't any. There was no hockey.

At first, it's actually pretty easy to not notice that hockey was gone. The Cubs had their miserable ending to 2004 which ate up whatever anticipation of the season opening there might have been. Though the Bears were bad, they were under their first season under a new coach and were at least interesting. The fall is pretty well occupied. And the season, or what would have been, was already off to a rocky start. The previous June, despite how simply awful the Hawks were the preceding season, they couldn't capture the #1 pick in the draft lottery. Or even the second. That was the draft that Alex Ovechkin and Evgeni Malkin were so far ahead of every other eligible player that for months it had been described as a "two-player draft." I remember standing on the Western train platform talking to my brother at work, and telling him, "You know I didn't watch the Hawks much lately, but leave it to them to get the third pick in what everyone says is a two-player draft." They couldn't even suck right. It was so perfect. As any Hawks fan knows, this was the draft they ended up with Cam Barker. Didn't go quite as well as Ovechkin and Malkin. Again, the Hawks were Charlie Brown marveling that their trick-or-treat booty had yielded nothing but a rock.

And much like the Hawks, I wanted the NHL to act dumber and more selfish than any other league ever had. Sometimes a lesson can only be learned through injury, and this was clearly the league taking a blowtorch to its own face. We knew the league had been run horribly, we knew our team wasn't generating any love of the game for us, so I wanted to know if the NHL was capable of immolating itself. I was out of sympathy. Could they really be capable? As a parent would tell you (or maybe it was just mine?), sometimes you let the child hit itself in the head with something to learn a valuable lesson.

But as the leaves fall off the trees, and the air goes from crisp to biting, you notice that weekday nights feel off. Sure, we could always find something to do on weekend nights. But those nights at home, with the wind kind of whipping at the windows and snow on the ground, there was a gap that you couldn't miss. Life just didn't have the same rhythm.

I watched a lot of basketball with my father that winter. This was the year that the Bulls took a huge leap under the guidance under Scott Skiles. So they were actually winning and entertaining and it was a good way to spend lots of time with my dad. But every game I watched, I noticed I was trying to force emotion. I knew the moments that should be cheered, that were definitive, and yet my body didn't naturally react in the way it should. It just didn't raise my EKG.

Christmas came, and Adam and I didn't know what to do when he was home. There were no games to attend. We went to a show at one of our favorite rock clubs and they had the World Juniors on in late December. Usually, we wouldn't have paid much attention. But this was hockey on TV, so we locked in. This was also something of the first unveiling of Alex Ovechkin and Sidney Crosby. So it was worth a look.

I remember sitting in a Vegas casino in late January of what should have been that season, my first trip to Sin City. It was when they were in their last attempt to salvage the season with some sort of thirty-game impostor of a regular season. There were hockey writers I recognized on ESPN on the casino TVs, saying what was going on. Though I wasn't as attached, and though a thirty-game season would have been a sham, I have to say I hoped they could salvage something. Maybe I would watch, maybe I wouldn't, but there was security in having hockey there. It was foundational. And without it, no matter how little of a part it was, the structure felt unmoored.

Of course they didn't. A week or two later I watched *Miracle* on HBO, not because I was terribly interested in the film (the HBO documentary told the story much better), but because it was the closest thing to hockey that there was to watch. There were hockey sounds on my TV, and it felt comforting.

They canceled the season a couple weeks later. Even though we had been told for over a year that this would happen, it was still hard to grasp. Sure, we'd seen baseball destroy its playoffs and World Series before. But never had a league lost a whole season. Of course it had to be hockey to break that threshold. Who else would have?

While my fandom had wavered over the years, to be completely robbed of hockey was still deflating. I still identified as a hockey fan, and that still meant something to me. It still marked me out from the masses, which still mattered to me. It made me unique in some ways. And to have it stripped away, I was a tad lost. In a strange way, when they canceled the season it affirmed that I would be back more passionately whenever it returned. Which is totally backwards and not how a rational fan should act. But now I'd seen what life was like with absolutely no hockey or no Hawks around, even if only it was something at which to laugh and deride. To be around to be actively ignored. Now it wasn't even that. And honestly, I didn't like the view.

It's true what they say. Let go of something you love, and if it comes back you know it's true. We both had let go of each other, and afterwards, I knew that I was always in. I'm sick.

I Can't Quit You
October 5, 2005
Ducks at Hawks

Eventually, over the summer, the players and the owners came to an agreement. The owners got pretty much everything they wanted. There was now a salary cap, pegged at 54% of total revenues (they would learn later this wasn't exactly what they wanted). Because of how some teams had drastically outspent others, the NHL entered what was almost a fantasy-draft type setting. Teams were allowed to buy out contracts of players they didn't think would fit into this new, structured world, for two-thirds of the value of the contract. And none of that would count against the team's salary cap.

This was something of a reset-button for a lot of the league. Nearly a third of all players were now free agents. Teams could almost remake themselves entirely. It was hard to not get caught up in the wild movement of players all over the map in really a matter of days and weeks. Paul Kariya ended up in Nashville. Peter Forsberg went to Philadelphia. Chris Pronger went to Edmonton. There was the Marian Hossa-for-Dany Heatley trade. It was madness as teams had to do more than take a scalpel to their rosters to fit under the cap.

Considering how badly the Hawks had mangled their entire organization, they needed something of this cheat-code restart to try to make up a team that could make up the gap on the other teams. And with a cap, they kind of dove headfirst into the now bursting free agent pool. Of course, this being the Hawks they didn't do it correctly, but at the time we were so shocked at some new faces we didn't quite realize it.

They signed Adrian Aucoin, who had been a big, bruising defenseman in Vancouver and with the Islanders. They brought in Matthew Barnaby, who had been perhaps the most entertaining member of the really good Sabres teams of the late '90s. He seemed a perfect Hawk: a tough, physical winger who could actually score. And their big splash was bringing in goalie Nikolai Khabibulin, who the last time we had seen NHL hockey was backstopping the Lightning to a Stanley Cup. Back then, before we looked deeper to understand what really made a team win, a goalie who had won a Cup automatically was considered "elite," as annoying as that word had become. If you had one, then clearly you couldn't be bad because of that certification. All of the sudden, it seemed like the Hawks could be interesting again.

And I couldn't contain my excitement any longer. I bought tickets for the opening game. Anyone who was there will remember that every fan was given a mini-replica Stanley Cup as some sort of thank you for sticking it out through the lockout. My friend Craig couldn't wait either, and accompanied me. And of course, we got the student-discount tickets for eight dollars, even though neither of us had been in a classroom for a few years. The Hawks didn't care, they just needed you in the building. This ploy worked for a years.

After missing a whole season, and considering where the Hawks had been for the years previous, I don't know why I was even a little surprised at there being no buzz for the Hawks' opener. Even on the Madison bus to the United Center, we only saw a couple people in Hawks jerseys on the way there. I hadn't seen any downtown where I met my friend. It was almost as if we were just going to some show at the Metro or something, such was the pocketed feel of it.

And I guess in a way, I rejoiced in that. I was going back to being part of some secret cabal, and we all gathered in this place that no one else ever came. After some years trying new things and trying to figure out who or what I was (more "what" than "who"), I had come back to something of my true nature.

We settled into the 300 Level, and watched the introductions to this "new" Hawks team. It's amazing how quickly you can lose grasp of the league when your team sucks and you don't pay that much attention even for a couple seasons. Most of the names I recognized but couldn't have really told you about what they brought to the team (turns out it was mostly because they sucked and couldn't bring anything). I knew Curtis Brown had been in the league for a while, but not really as what. I knew Todd Simpson was a middling bottom pairing d-man but didn't really know where from. Ditto Jassen Cullimore, Jim Dowd, Jim Vandermeer, et al.

I knew Eric Daze was actually upright though, the only holdover from when the Hawks last really mattered to me. I knew Tuomo was the great hope, and I was excited to finally see him live. I knew that there were expectations for Arnason, Bell, and Calder. But I had never seen any of them. There was going to be a learning curve.

There were also a couple kids making their NHL debuts, or close to it. The names of Rene Bourque and Pavel Vorobiev make us laugh now. But there were two other NHL debutants that night. They were Brent Seabrook and Duncan Keith. Seabrook had the bigger buzz, being the first round pick that previous June and making the team at just eighteen. Keith had been a second-round pick three years before and had spent the previous two seasons in the Hawks system, back when their AHL team was in Norfolk, VA. But there was certainly less buzz about him than the higher-pedigreed Seabrook.

On that first night, what was obvious was just how much Keith could skate. What was also obvious is that it was in every direction except the correct one. He looked like that kid playing his first ever soccer or basketball game, and no matter how carefully you explained his position and responsibilities to him, he'd still go tearing into the other team's half at the first whistle. He was playing kindergarten recess football, while everyone else was attempting to play NHL hockey. But he did it so fast you couldn't help but notice.

What was also exceedingly obvious, even on that first night, is how ill-prepared these Hawks were for the "new" NHL. After the lockout, the league went under some pretty massive changes to the on-ice product as well as the off-ice structure. This is when shootouts were introduced. And the biggest change was a massive crackdown on all obstruction that had gone hog wild in the previous years. Players were no longer going to be allowed to hook, hold, grab, tackle, and assault the way they had for most of the previous decade. You go back and watch highlights from before the lockout now and you can't even believe how much was let go by the refs. Guys were basically water-skiing behind their opponents, or straight up tackling them to prevent scoring chances. Never was there a penalty. The NHL was determined that they were going to open up the ice and make the game fast again.

The Hawks were set up to play the game the old way, and it looked it. You could tell because someone was heading off the ice to the penalty box every two or three minutes. They were serious about this changing of the rules, and this is what hockey looked like for a while this season. Teams getting eight or ten power plays a night. When the teams did remain even with manpower, you could see that the Hawks were simply behind on everything. They had to grab and hold because they couldn't skate with the Ducks, who weren't even a remarkably fast team then.

It was also a discovery of what it was like to be at a Hawks game now. I hadn't been since the crowds really started dwindling. I had been when the building wasn't full, but seeing it half-full was still pretty jarring (and half-full is being kind). When Mark Bell opened the scoring that night there wasn't the roar that had become entrenched in my memories and down to the soul. It was so far from ear-splitting. We did the best we could but there weren't enough of us to fill that giant space with sound. That element of danger, even from just the noise, certainly was gone. It was just kind of a rise. Hockey didn't have the same soundtrack that had brought me back all those times over all those years.

The Ducks would score the next three goals, and the Hawks couldn't ever get even. But even though it was greatly different now, and even though I had this suspicion that despite the flashy signings the Hawks were going to be bad again, and even though the experience was different from all that I had grown up with, I felt content on the trip back to my apartment. I knew what I was now, at least in this sense, and life just made more sense with hockey in it.

This Is Not My Beautiful House
December 21, 2005
Predators vs. Hawks

The Hawks continued to blow, despite the addition of the handsome Sharp. But Christmas was approaching and that meant my brother was coming home from New York for a while, and that meant we had to go. He had also accepted hockey back into his life full bore, even if he hadn't let go to the point I had. He was a regular on the message boards as well, trying to fill in the void of being away. We went to the United Center the first chance we got, which was this night against the Predators. We hadn't been to the UC together in a few years, and our relationship didn't make any sense without seeing the occasional hockey game together. What were we going to do instead? Talk?

While I had seen the new "atmosphere" at the United Center, he had not. And I was not prepared for how it would affect him. I didn't give it any thought. I had assumed he knew what he was in for. I'm sure he knew what the attendance numbers had been but couldn't quite conceive of what that translated to in person.

The Predators certainly weren't a household name to anyone, even though they had constructed a pretty fast, entertaining team that could contend. They were still something of a hockey solecism to most fans. So this was one of the more sparse crowds I had ever been a part of, which is saying something, especially given those returning home for the holidays.

My brother couldn't stop laughing that we could still use the student tickets, delighted as the box office was to get anyone into the building. His laughter stopped upon entry, when he saw how empty the concourse was. That sank into outright depression when the anthem started. Those who were there in those days still tried to cheer their way through it, mostly on reflex. But it was like watching a cover band version of your favorite band in some dingy bar. It was sad. I could see my brother's shoulders sink throughout it. He just couldn't believe what it had become and how futile the effort was. This had been a part of him longer than it had me, and he still had more to come to grips with. I guess in some ways he was watching something he loved being on life support. The form was still there, but the life certainly was not. Whereas the anthem before had been raucous and intimidating, it was now something of a lame joke.

When the anthem ended and the five-thousand or whatever it was stopped cheering, he turned to me and said, "That was pathetic." There was nothing I could say to him. There was no answer. It was. I guess I just stared blankly, and hoped that expression would convey that this is what we had to get used to. I felt like I had let him down, even though none of this was my fault. Maybe I should have prepared him more. Maybe he feared we had lost something special forever. I guess we all did.

The game wouldn't help either of our moods. The Preds, who were light-years faster and more talented, pummeled the Hawks up and down the ice that night. It was 4-1 after two periods and it probably should have been 10-1. The Hawks really couldn't have been more inferior.

Halfway through the third period, with the score 5-1, Nashville's Jordin Tootoo, unquestionably their biggest asshole on the ice and hated by everyone outside of Tennessee, skated the puck over the Hawks' line. Todd Simpson dropped his stick and simply jumped him, punching him out of nowhere repeatedly.

It was embarrassing. That was the only word for it. The completely ill-equipped Hawks couldn't keep up, and this is what they had to resort to to save any face, at least in their minds. The Hawks couldn't play hockey with the Predators, so they played this. The Hawks were basically an abortion on the ice and an embarrassment off of it, with 5,000 people in attendance in the league's third-biggest market. This was beyond being the black sheep of the league. This was the dingy basement of the office where the weird guy worked that no one wanted to visit.

I think my brother was in shock. Seeing it first hand was more than he could handle at that point. He would get used to it, I guess. We all did. Maybe, like me, he was seriously scared that a major part of our sibling relationship was forever damaged. Maybe we were going to lose it. After all, how many games and nights were we really going to put ourselves through before it wasn't worth it anymore?

Of course we were back two nights later. Duh.

The "Rivalry"
December 23, 2005
Red Wings vs. Hawks

We had gotten the tickets before Adam had even come home for the holidays. Perhaps if we'd waited until he could see what was really going on, we might have opted out. The thinking at the time was that the trip the Wings made in around every Christmas was perhaps the only game that would have a full arena. Sure, it was at least half-full of Wings fans, which is a lot like choosing to spend time amongst infected raccoons, but it would be an atmosphere. We craved that.

Except the likelihood was that the Hawks would get even more paddled than they had two nights before. The Wings were once again the class of the league, having seamlessly transitioned from the old NHL to the new, without ever dropping from the top of the standings. They could even switch coaches, this time to Mike Babcock, and it didn't matter. Their fourth-liners would have been top-liners on the Hawks, and probably one or two of their minor leaguers would have been as well.

If I try to describe the sense of dread heading to the building, you'd be mystified as to why we bothered at all. And I wouldn't be able to tell you. It was just force of habit. This is what we were supposed to do. The one night the building would be full, we were supposed to be there. Even if it was akin to saying you were supposed to be in prison.

Strangely, the Hawks played one of their better games on this night. It's kind of amazing what a group of professionals can do when they are terrified of being embarrassed. That's all this was. It also helped that Detroit played like this was about as engaging as a driving test, which it was for them.

Arnason scored in the last minute of the first. Martin Lapointe added another a little over halfway through the second to give the Hawks a 2-0 lead. They got to the second intermission with that lead, and you allowed yourself to...well, I can't say "dream." Because one win in the middle of the season wasn't something you dreamed about. And if it was your life would be very sad indeed. Maybe hope? At least for one night there was now a possibility that our sad Hawks could get one over the mighty Wings and at least send all these invading fuckers out of our building grumbling. We could say, "Yeah, but you lost to us!" That's usually the very faint silver lining of being a fan of a team this bad. When you did get one over on a team you could have a good giggle.

The minutes ticked off and the Hawks kept leading 2-0. With fifteen minutes to go we were still relatively sure the Wings would come back. With ten minutes to go it was just kind of sure. With five minutes to go, we actually thought the Hawks would win.

Silly rabbit...

Kris Draper, Kris Motherfucking Draper, scored with forty seconds left and their goalie pulled. At least they did us the courtesy of pulling their goalie. Once that goal went in, there wasn't a Hawks fan in the building who thought they wouldn't tie it up soon after. It was predestined. Sure enough, the Wings won the ensuing draw, pulled their goalie again, and thirty seconds later Brendan Shanahan poked one home to tie the game.

I couldn't say I was surprised. I couldn't say I was upset. I wanted to laugh, but couldn't muster it. It was the absence of feeling. It was an emotional black hole. Worse yet, all the Wings fans were jumping up and down as if A) this was some sort of major accomplishment and B) they didn't think this was possible. And we knew that was a load of shit. Perhaps they were just lording it over us how easy it had been for their team. That no matter the gap between the two, they would always find a way to make it worse.

It somehow got worse. When things were reduced to four-on-four in overtime, there was no way I could conceive that it wouldn't end early. The Hawks couldn't keep up when they had five skaters. With the added space of 4-on-4, they were likely to end up with windburn.

The Hawks held on for three minutes, when Duncan Keith got hosed with a tripping call that Datsyuk performed a triple lutz on to get (a valuable lesson for Keith in his rookie season). A 4-on-3 power play to this team was certain death. I thought it wouldn't take more than twenty or thirty seconds. But the Hawks desperately clung on. They got to within touching distance of the end of overtime, and the lottery of a shootout felt like salvation enough.

Nope. Couldn't be that way. The knife had to twist. With one second left, Datsyuk banged one home from the right circle. We were sure in the stands it had come too late. They reviewed it. I didn't think it was possible, but when the ref got off the headset and pointed to center ice to signal a good goal and the Detroit bench erupted, my heart sank. I thought I was out of emotion. I thought I couldn't be disappointed or surprised. But this ending? They couldn't be serious with this.

In the span of three nights we had seen our team so badly outplayed it had to resort to barbarism and then watched its once-greatest rival have to actually try for all of four minutes to beat them. They had even teased us with good feelings and fun, only to wipe it away. Sisyphus...I get ya, brother.

Go West
February 11, 2006
Hawks vs. Kings

For the previous year or two, I had been leaking friends to Los Angeles. I suppose that's what happens when you hang out with mostly actors and comedians (I was the latter, at least so I claimed at the time). So it came to a point where I decided it was time to make my first ever trip to California. Yes, it took me until the age of twenty-four to get there. Of course, me being the way I was, the trip had to be centered around seeing the Hawks. Even though at home I really was struggling to find the motivation to see this tow-yard material team, I didn't hesitate on seeing them twenty-five thousand miles away. To play another tire fire in the Kings, no less.

You never quite know what to expect the first time you fly into L.A. You bounce between picturing the beach and palm trees to the smog-filled urban hell that most of my favorite bands sang about. You know about the freeways, but you really can't conceive of them until you see the whole system in action. In reality, Los Angeles is all of these things at once, covering a massive amount of ground. You can find anything you want there, but you're probably going to have to drive a while to find it. And also you quickly discover that everything written about Hollywood never bothered to tell you what a shithole it actually is.

I can't say I immediately liked it there. I found it to be pretty dirty and wildly different than what I had grown up with, which is obviously the point. All the bars were dark, and I mean really dark. They didn't even have signs out front. That haze that hangs over the city most of the year felt like it seeped into your head. And unless you have a lot of money, the beach and ocean are miles away. They're just a concept.

Still, when it was time to go see the Hawks play the Kings, perhaps the two worst teams in the league at this point, I was very curious. What were Kings fans like? Was it just a unique way to spend a day Los Angeles for them? Was it more a curiosity than a passion? And it was a matinee as well—because the arena has to be cleared for the much more serious business of a Clippers game that night, don't you know—so seeing a game with the sun gleaming in the concourse was going to be another trip.

The Staples Center's size and shape is the first thing you notice. Whereas the United Center is pretty formatted on the outside, the arena in downtown LA is central, not out in the middle of nothing like the UC. And it's perfectly circular, which is kind of weird. But it does feel right in the heart of everything, even if that was the heart of a very dingy downtown area at the time.

For some reason I was almost relieved that the inside was even more sterile than the United Center. It had actual stores and restaurants instead of just the normal concessions I was used to, making it feel more like a shopping mall surrounding a playing surface. There was a McDonalds and a Panda Express, with the prices jumped up about twenty-five percent of course. I guess I was happy to know it could be worse?

I came in with a pretty prejudiced view of what I would find amongst Kings fans. That was quickly cleared up. They were wearing just as many jerseys as you'd find in attendance at a Hawks game. And they were of all kinds of players, like Ziggy Palfy and Mattias Norstrom and a lot of Luc Robitailles and Deadmarshes. These people paid attention. They weren't all in the Gretzky silver and black.

When the puck dropped and we sat near the top of the arena, I quickly noticed that all these people grumbled about all the things we grumbled about. How their team couldn't win a faceoff or how this guy was too slow or how their power play would never score. I recognized this kind of hockey misery. It was my own; I was just watching it play out in purple and black instead of red and black. I knew these people, I had been surrounded by them for the past few months and really most of my life. They just had better tans than the ones I was used to. And maybe even more tattoos.

This was one of those really entertaining, bad games. Neither team had a goalie they wanted anyone to see them with, and neither team could really defend in front of them anyway. The Kings went up 3-1 and 4-2 at the end of the second, but the Hawks tied it with goals from Arnason and Lapointe three minutes apart halfway through the third. This was fun-bad.

The teams traded chances, not because they were so skilled and fast but because each team couldn't complete two consecutive passes or go more than a minute or two without handing the puck to each other. You got swept up in it, because that was a hell of a lot better than remembering you took time out from your life to watch these two teams.

Matthew Barnaby, in a brilliant exhibition of his usefulness during this season, put the puck over the glass with less than a minute to go. That meant his penalty would carry over into overtime, resulting in a more dangerous 4-on-3 power play. The last game I saw had ended on one, thanks to Pavel Datsyuk, and there was no reason to assume this one wouldn't either even if the Kings weren't in the same galaxy as Detroit. It only took Joe Corvo forty seconds to prove me right. Beaten by Datsyuk to Corvo, this was our lot.

It was a weird feeling walking out of the building. Kings fans were delighted to have actually seen their team win for once but a bit sheepish about blowing a two-goal lead and needing a power play in overtime to get past the Hawks. We traveling Hawks fans were somewhat glad they had put up a fight and been entertaining for the miles and money we'd put in getting there. You could feel a kinship between the two fanbases: "Yeah, we watch dreck too. But hey, it's still hockey, right?"

At the time I really had no idea it would be just over a year before I would move out there. Like I said, I wasn't impressed with Los Angeles on my first visit. My life at home was starting to spiral, but I thought I could save it. I had just been dumped, I was about to lose my job, and I didn't have a lot of answers. But I guess this was the first seed planted to let me know that I could find the things I loved and recognized here, too. There were people who lived the same way and felt the same way about things and loved the same things. Maybe without knowing it that was the first clue that I could give L.A. a try and not be totally miserable.

It's also funny to look back at this game after seeing some of the games the two teams have engaged in in recent years. It's hard to believe it's the same sport. When they did play those far more meaningful and higher-level games, I thought about those fans in the upper reaches in the Staples Center, bitching about Alex Frolov, and I know they feel the same way, too.

A year or so later, when I moved out there, I was out with a group of friends, or rather one or two friends, and a bunch of other people I just knew. I was introduced to a guy who was his boss, and he was in a Kings jersey. We immediately hit it off, talking about hockey. We were both so overjoyed to have that conversation, he starving for it amongst his fellow L.A. residents and my transplant yearning. You could always find a bond over how much you hated the Red Wings, and at least I knew that there was always a crowd, even out there, I would fit into.

The First Strike
July 10, 2006
Italy vs. France (World Cup Final)

     In the middle of the '05-'06 season, GM Dale Tallon realized he had gotten it all wrong. He had built a team for an NHL that no longer existed, and he quickly went about trying to tear everything down and rebuild in a way that would make sense in a league where speed and skill were now favored over size and snarl. We saw Patrick Sharp arrive, and after a few games my brother and I quickly concluded he could make a fine third center one day if he maxed out. Trained scout's eye, we had. A bunch of others were either called up or signed and given a look. But clearly the Hawks had some splashes to make.

     The soccer game referenced was the day before, actually. But I flew home the next day from a trip to Germany for the World Cup. After the long flight, landing at O'Hare somewhere around 3:00 pm, I turned my phone on to see one text message from my brother.

     "Marty Havlat."

     While I had been in the air, Dale Tallon had taken his first big swing in acquiring more speed and skill to the team (this was also a month after he drafted Jonathan Toews, so things were definitely changing). He had moved out Mark Bell in a three-way trade and got back Havlat and Brian Smolinski.

     I was over the moon. Havlat already had three twenty-plus goals seasons to his name. The previous season, though he only played eighteen regular season games due to injury (this should have been a warning), he had potted nine goals. He had made the real splash putting up up seven goals and thirteen points in just ten playoff games for a powerhouse Ottawa team. This was a bonafide first-line player who wasn't even in the prime of his career. The salary cap had made him impossible for the Senators to afford, and Tallon had taken advantage.

     It was a first real sign that Tallon and the rest of the front office knew what it was going to take. Marty could skate like the wind and really did have out of this world skill. We don't remember that now after all that went on in his three years here. But for Hawks fans at that time, here was something to watch. We hadn't had that since Amonte left, and maybe before. Even though the Hawks weren't going to be good, we knew that when we showed up to the building or turned on the television there was an excellent chance that Havlat would do something to bring us out of our seats. There was unpredictability again. That's what it felt like in July, when we desperately needed reason to believe that there was any reason to get excited about hockey when it arrived.

     Turns out it was the first step, it just wasn't a smooth one. But being on a plane in the middle of July and getting excited about a Hawks trade, instead of losing feeling in my extremities due to raging anger, was certainly unique and invigorating.

Sega-Hawks II
October 7, 2006
Blue Jackets vs. Hawks

The Hawks made other moves that summer that at least brought in NHL players. Michal Handzus, who wasn't a joke then as he sort of became later, was brought in to be the actual center that Havlat needed to get the puck. And he could still do that at that point. Other moves like Denis Arkhipov and Tony Salmelainen aren't as well remembered, at least in non-comedic fashion. Whatever all these players were, the idea was that they could skate (well, not Handzus). The Hawks may get beaten like a drum still, so went the thinking, but they're not going to get skated out of the building anymore.

The season opened in Nashville, a team harboring Stanley Cup thoughts and were clearly a team in Tallon's mind that had skated rings around and imprinted tire marks on the Hawks the previous season. However, even with the additions, something was definitely missing. For the first time in my life, the Hawks were on TV and Pat Foley was not announcing the game.

The previous May, the Hawks announced that he would not be returning as announcer. The reasons are still murky, but essentially they decided they didn't want the radio and TV broadcast to be the same, and they only offered Foley the radio job. I'm sure there was more to it. Foley had become just as tired of watching this dreck as we had and didn't hold back on a lot of broadcasts. The Hawks were certainly never in a mood to simply allow this kind of criticism from within to last for too long. Whatever it was, the Hawks had cut out another pillar of not just my childhood, but a lot of others' too.

It hurt. Whatever Foley said, we knew he was one of us. He had grown up here. He had the same edge about the Hawks we did. You could tell during some broadcasts he was always on the verge of swearing, which we were while listening to him. Almost all of my cherished Hawks memories to that point were narrated by him. The old Stadium was gone but he was still a connection to what brought us all here in the first place. He suffered the same way we did when it all went to shit. And now he was gone. It was another kick to the shins from the Hawks, robbing us of all that drew us to the team and game. It also didn't help that his replacement was Dan Kelly, who simply didn't have any idea what he was doing and just wanted to make everything sound epic. He was the dude in your dormitory who liked to do play-by-play just to show off his catch-phrases.

It's probably the most bonkers season-opening game the Hawks have ever or will ever play. They were down 2-0 before five minutes were off the clock. They were up 3-2 before eleven minutes had gone off the first period. The first goal was a breakaway from Havlat where he completely embarrassed Tomas Vokoun. There is something for every fan when the off-season's biggest pickup makes an immediate splash like this. It's, "here's what you've been missing" and "here's what you're in for" at the same time. It makes you feel instantly like you didn't waste all that excitement when you first heard about the trade/signing. You feel rewarded.

Havlat would add another goal and assist, and both teams would trade scores like it was speed-chess. The Hawks finally emerged from the looniness of it as 8-6 winners.

Who cared if it was bad hockey? Who cared if it didn't mean anything? The Hawks had scored eight goals in a game! That never happened! They hadn't done it since that magical power play year with Bernie Nicholls. They could keep up with a good team...at least when that good team played badly. They had a player who gobbled up that space. Four points in a game? That was allowed? By a Hawk? Those words didn't make any sense. That wasn't English.

After that game I had to charge out to the bar, because what else was I going to do? I needed to calm my nerves. I was frayed. And then I immediately got tickets to the home opener two nights later, because I had to be there.

It was another nutso affair, but this time the Hawks lost by a goal, 5-4. They had scored the first two goals through Handzus and Jeff Hamilton, but then gave up the next five. They stormed a comeback in the third, with Sharp scoring on the power play and then Havlat scoring from the goal line to bring hope. It was after that goal my brother texted me from New York, "Martin Havlat, Hart Trophy." It was funny to think about, but we were just reveling in this player putting up six points in two games and the Hawks pouring in the goals, even if only the shortest stretch imaginable.

I hadn't seen the Hawks with actual top-six forward talent in far too long. Watching Marty on the ice was something like seeing a football team with a devastating wide receiver but with a questionable quarterback. Sure, there were stretches where you didn't notice him, where he looked a wasted luxury, but every time he was on the field there was a chance he could streak down the field, singe whatever defensive back was covering him, have the limited QB just heave on up on hope, and change the game with a big catch and touchdown. It could happen at any moment. Whenever Havlat got room on the right wing to show off his world-class speed (and he did have that), or would make a one-on-one move in a tight space, this feeling ran through you *that something could happen.* Maybe it wouldn't, but it could. It could come from anywhere at anytime. We hadn't felt that anticipation in a very long time. Goals in hockey emerge out of chaos a lot of the times. There's a lot of battling on the boards or aimless skating, at least it looks that way, and then all of a sudden things open and there's time and space and a player gets a clean look before you can even realize what happened. It's like a traffic jam. You're not going anywhere very fast and you don't know why and just about the point you're going to snap traffic starts moving fast and you have no idea why you were stopped in the first place. Havlat could force his way through the chaos and make his own opening. It didn't just appear. You just had to watch him.

I was finally thrilled by a player, which I hadn't been in years. There was always a chance the Hawks could score with Marty out there. And I had finally heard the building roar when the Hawks were mounting that comeback. I hadn't heard that in so long, even though there probably weren't more than fifteen thousand people there. My pulse actually got into the danger zone (LANAAA!!!). After so long away, it was life-affirming to see once again what the sport could do to you. I knew I couldn't wait too much longer to get back.

The First Time, For Someone Else
December 10, 2006
Oilers vs. Hawks

When you've walked through the sludge long enough, and Hawks fans certainly had by this point, you sometimes forget what brought you to this in the first place. It's hard to remember what the game looked like, what the experience felt like, when you first became enamored. It's always a good idea to go with someone to their first game in that case.

I was definitely in search of a new hockey buddy. I had resorted to attending to a game or two alone, such was the state of things. I wondered if everyone else around me in attendance was looking at me as *that guy*, the weirdo who takes things far too seriously and whom no one can stand to be around. I was *that guy* pretty much in the rest of my life. I couldn't stand the idea that it had crept into this realm. This was not a situation I wanted to replicate too often.

A few days before this one, I ran into my friend Margaret at the gym. She asked what I was up to on the weekend, and I told her that on the Sunday my friend Dan and I were headed to the Hawks game. Her face got this kind of odd, curious light to it, as if I'd just mentioned an activity she'd never heard of (which was basically true). I might as well have told her I was going bungee jumping or calf-roping. It sounded so out of left field to her that she just had to know.

"Can I come? I've never been before."

Any request to join me was going to be granted with gusto. So we arranged to meet at the United Center, and instead of two student-discount tickets we would be getting three.

Of course, there's a paranoia when bringing someone to their first game, especially in this era of Hawks hockey where the building was half-full and the team might just throw a total clunker at you. In which case the chance at a long bond would be forever lost. So as the game started I would glance over to her every couple of minutes for any sign that boredom had crept in. Such fears thankfully proved unwarranted.

She was transfixed. She looked as if she was instantly learning a foreign language in the Matrix or something. She asked questions at a rate we could barely keep up with but happily did. She gobbled up the knowledge as if she'd found a water fountain in the desert. She almost seemed angry that this kind of thing had been kept from her until her early twenties. I don't know if it was the speed or the colors or what but I didn't care. It was just affirming to have not only gained another hockey companion, but created one. I felt like I had given someone close to me a gift. Or maybe I was just relieved that at least one less person would think I was completely nuts for devoting time and money to this.

One of my favorite moments of the night was after the Hawks had biffed an early power play, and we turned to our new recruit and said, "You've just sat through your first underwhelming Hawks power play. Congratulations. It's a rite of passage. If this becomes something you do regularly, you'd better get used to this." She probably only barely understood what we were talking about at the time, but she was delighted to feel part of the club.

It didn't hurt that the Hawks played one of their better games of the season on that night. Havlat was back from two months out injured (it was ever thus…). They scored two goals in the first to go up 2-0 and release any tension there might have been. During the second intermission, there was a promo on the jumbotron that featured Havlat on screen. While she had been fascinated by the game, being a red-blooded woman, she couldn't help but focus on Havlat on the screen as well. One of Marty's many features was being extremely easy on the eyes.

Of course, Havlat would top that by showing our new friend he could match his looks with his play. Early in the third, Havlat picked up the puck off the boards on the right wing, and streaked toward the goal we were sitting behind. He simply scorched past whatever defender was gasping for air trying to keep up with him on his backhand, made a small fake to his forehand to get Dwayne Roloson to move, and then roofed a backhand to the first strand of net behind the post and crossbar. It's one of the more impressive goals I've seen live to this day.

Well that was it. She was indoctrinated. There was no way she could escape now, and Havlat's brilliant display of skill was easily appreciated by hardened fan or neophyte alike. Where else would you see something like that? As we walked out she immediately wanted to know when we were going again (no, I didn't marry this girl).

It was also a good hockey rejuvenation exercise for me as well. While the last two trips I had finally seen Hawks wins and felt good about being in the building, there's something about seeing what it looks like for the first time to someone. You're reminded how special it feels to some to be part of the cult, to feel you know something that most don't. To know why hockey is so fun when you simply strip it down to watching the sport, not worrying about the standings or the owner or the direction of the team or what the building used to be like. Sometimes you just gotta get back to your Ramones records, y'know? Sometimes three chords is more than enough.

A Preview

January 3 2007
Canada vs. USA (World Juniors)

This game only gained context after the fact. It was Hawks fans first chance to get a real look at Jonathan Toews. He was the third pick overall the previous summer, and the organization didn't hesitate to pump him up as a franchise savior from the moment they made him so. The message boards were simply on fire with his work in high school and during his one and only year at North Dakota. But we couldn't watch their games on TV, at least not without great effort. The World Juniors were televised on the NHL Network, and he was a centerpiece of the Canadian team. In this semifinal, his Canada was facing a USA squad led by Patrick Kane.

Kane was already starting to generate buzz as the top available player in following draft, but with the Hawks still floating around .500 we didn't think there was much chance the Hawks would get the first pick or anything near it at the time. Even if they'd been awful, things didn't work like that for the Hawks ever. Things like bouncing balls never went the Hawks way, and even if they did we always suspected that the NHL powers that be would never allow a top pick, and an American one like Kane, to ply his trade somewhere where his home games wouldn't be on TV to the local populace. Put it this way: the NBA would have never allowed a star like this to be drafted by a lost organization like the Hawks. We can look back at this game now and remember it differently, but then we didn't know.

It was a pretty classic game, ending in a 1-1 tie. What was obvious then, even at seventeen and at that level, was how the game didn't just slow when Kane had the puck. It totally stopped. It was like everyone was waiting to see what he would do, terrified that they would be the one lit up by him. His hands, his skills with the puck were clearly so far above everyone else on the ice it almost seemed a joke. The game moved to his whim. He was the conductor.

Toews' game was a little harder to appreciate at first. He was on a more talented squad of course, so it was harder to stand out. But what was clear was how strong he was on the puck, and how he always seemed to end up with it. You might not have noticed much else but his name was always being spoken by the broadcasters because he was always in the right spot.

The game didn't slow in the way it did when Kane was in possession, it just sort of bent to him at the same speed. If he wasn't conducting it like Kane, he was first chair in every section.

Somehow the deadlock survived a frantic ten-minute overtime with four skaters apiece, with Kane just barely missing a chance to end proceedings. It moved to a shootout that has now gone on to be the stuff of legend. According to the rules of the tournament, after the first three shooters a team could send whoever they wanted back out however many times they wanted. Toews scored three times in the shootout, never missing, including the deciding goal. It was Toews's first heroic moment that we got to see, and though we had much bigger dreams than winning shootout goals we certainly could see the steel and verve in the biggest moments and wondered what he might bring here.

Now it looks like a sneak preview of what was to come. It wasn't then. All we knew was that Canada's most clutch player was coming to Chicago. They would go on to win the tournament and Toews would swear during his postgame interview, and everyone's lying if they tell you that didn't help endear him to fans. We had a fantasy that Kane would come with him, but at the time there was no inkling that would become reality. But looking back on it now, it definitely feels like the seed to what would grow.

The Downside Of Alone
January 19 2007
Wild vs. Hawks

Whatever hope had been generated after Denis Savard had been hired as coach quickly evaporated after the new year. The Hawks lost ten in a row starting on January fourth and would never come close to sniffing .500 again. They couldn't stop anyone from scoring, giving up forty-one goals in that stretch. We had a glimpse of good hockey, and it was quickly taken away and the light firmly stamped out as we returned to the doldrums.

Toward the end of the losing streak, I ended up back at the UC by myself to see the Hawks take on the Wild. I can't say I went because I was terribly excited to see the Wild. No one's ever terribly excited to see the Wild, and that includes the residents of the Twin Cities. I certainly didn't have enough money to consider it, having been out of work for a few months now. I guess the boredom got to me, sitting around the house with nowhere to go for days on end. At least the respite of a hockey game gave one day a center, a purpose. Or maybe it was just being out of the house. And hell, when you're miserable and directionless, perhaps there was solace in seeing a team that was in the exact same condition.

It's one thing to go to a game alone glowing in the buzz of the Hawks new star and the beginning of a new season, as I had done once in October. It's another to do it when the team is firmly in the muck, your life feels like it's spiraling, and it's fucking cold outside. Given the mood going in, you can probably guess how the game went.

I sat in a lifeless building watching the Hawks merely make up the numbers in a 3-0 loss to Minnesota. The rind of Chicago had gotten to Havlat as well. Late in the first period with the game still tied, he pulled up on a rush at the right circle and tried to find the point-man on the other side. Except there were three Wild players between him and that pass finding a safe home and he whipped it at about knee-height. I'm surprised Cam Barker didn't slip a disc trying to corral it. It led to Marian Gaborik having a breakaway from center ice the other way, and pre-injury Gaborik wasn't going to be caught by any Hawk if they had Marvin the Martian's rocket scooter. He easily beat Brian Boucher, filling in for Nikolai Khabibulin for the night. Just one goal, but the game was pretty much over then.

There is something pure, even on the wrong side of your feelings, about this night in my head. Here I was thrashing about in life, taking time out to then watch this hockey team thrash about with no one else to join me. That's probably best. I wouldn't have wanted to subject anyone I cared about to this fare. I belonged here, I deserved to watch this, but they certainly didn't. This was my burden. During this time, and games like this, you could feel a palpable sense from the few in the arena of, "We did this to ourselves." No one made us go to the games. We just did. We couldn't get angry anymore, we'd tapped that source until it was dry. We all sat there, watching it unfold as we almost certainly knew it would, and admitted to ourselves that this is what we get. We knew there was nowhere else for us to go. It had all the passion of a business conference. But sometimes you can't get out of the conference. And you sit there with everyone else, knowing it'll be over soon enough.

The highlight of the game was organist Frank Pelico's version of "Bear Down, Chicago Bears," saluting our local football team as they were about to embark on the NFC Championship Game. They would go on to lose the Super Bowl. That's the kind of time it was.

Maybe He's Looking For Answers
February 18, 2007
Hawks vs. Rangers

After the Bears lost the Super Bowl, there were no more distractions. I had to actually deal with being unemployed, single, nearly out of money, and approaching the end of a lease. This was the crossroads, and Eric Clapton wasn't coming to sing about my trip there. Which was fine, because Clapton is overrated by a factor of six. But I still had some shit to figure out. My brother invited me out to New York for the weekend to see our Hawks at Madison Square Garden. It also provided a chance to have a serious talk with him, as the idea of moving to Los Angeles started to really bounce around my head. Things had basically gone all wrong at home. The only thing I had was a very fledgling career as a comedian, and most of my friends had already decamped to southern California. Basically, this was the best bad idea I had.

We had that talk on the Friday, and he seemed pretty positive about it, which gave me a positive feeling about it. Which was enough to talk to my father about it when I got home, but that could wait a couple days. First, there was seeing the Hawks on Broadway.

I had been to Madison Square Garden once before, on my first visit to New York to see Adam. It was the center of that trip. Sure, it was a game pitting a middling-at-best Rangers team against a middling-at-best Penguins team. But it was still *Madison Square Garden.* It felt like a true center of...something. It was bustling. It was right in the middle of it all. You felt like you were at *an event.*

It was a true New York experience, that first trip. Because New York's enforcement of a drinking age in halfhearted at best, I had been out with my brother late the previous night. This caused the first of many instances where I visited him at his office at whatever ad agency he was working at and promptly passed out on the couch. It wasn't a terribly good look for him. It was a pretty apt one for me.

When I came to, we started talking about the game and hockey in general. And three or four times, someone my brother had never seen before would pop in with a similar greeting. "You guys talking about hockey? I'll talk some hockey!" In a city the size of New York, you can always find someone to join in about whatever it is you love no matter what pocket of the city you're in, even it's a couple palookas wanting to join the conversation of two hungover brothers about Petr Nedved.

Also adding to the experience was a uniquely New York sports conversation taking place in the rows behind us, where two truly New York sports guys, with the accents and arrogance and everything were sitting. They never shut up the entire game but they were so hilarious to listen to we didn't mind. When the game started, their conversation was all about the Rangers and what they needed to be good again. As the first period went on their thoughts turned to the Devils and Islanders. At the beginning of the second period, they had moved on to discussing the Knicks. Halfway through the second period, they were now on to the Mets' and Yankees' offseason. During the second intermission and into the start of the third, they had moved onto a Giants and Jets season review.

You would have thought there was nowhere to go after all of that, but you'd be wrong. Halfway through the final frame, having exhausted all New York sports discussion, and the game on the ice long decided, they moved on to wrestling. It contained this lovely sentiment, which I never will forget. And remember, this is said in a true, New York jabroni accent:

"Yo I don't like that Eart'quake. He's fat, he's bald, he smells, he got a big hairy crack in his ass I don't like him!"

You can't buy stuff like this for any vacation.

But this was the first time we got to see our team in Manhattan. Not that this team was in any way ready for Broadway. They had recovered a little from that ten-game losing-streak and had won four of five and five out of seven. But it was simply wins in the abyss. They were entrenched in last, and really the season had become about where they would draft in June and if they could develop any kids during the last portion of the season.

Seeing the Hawks on the road at this time was a weird experience. You obviously cared enough to go, but you spent the whole day praying your team didn't get brained, making the whole investment a bad one. It was one thing to see a bad Hawks team in Los Angeles the year before. The Kings sucked too. But the Rangers were actually good, with two generational star players in Jaromir Jagr and Henrik Lundqvist in goal. But still, it was a hockey game between Original Six teams at The Garden, and though I had already seen on game there it was more exciting to see your team there.

We hit a bar near MSG before, that was actually relatively crowded with Hawks fans. I wouldn't say there was a sense of community amongst us so much as relief that there were others just as deranged and you were with them. You almost wanted to ask them, "What're you in for?" At least we wouldn't be alone if it went totally sideways.

This was a game that featured Havlat skating with Tuomo Ruutu and Martin St. Pierre (and his comically long stick. No, not like that, perv). Ruti was supposed to be on Havlat's level but had only shown flashes. St. Pierre was simply the only center they had. And this was the one line the Hawks had that had any chance of scoring. It's a low place with not a lot of lighting. Months after all the excitement of acquiring Havlat, he now kind of felt like the Christmas present that ended up in the back of the closet. It was almost like we failed him. This was all we could find for him? An AHL center and a prospect still trying to find his way? Still, whenever they were on the ice we felt a semblance that they could miracle the Hawks' ass to something. Every other time we basically watched through our fingers, hoping it would become something less than humiliation.

The Rangers scored less than two minutes in on the power play. I loved the Rangers' goal song, but it's not exactly lovable when it's being sung after they've scored against your team. A goal that early sent terror through my brother and me, wondering if this was going to be a football score. We didn't even get time to hope. We were thrown from the boat shortly after climbing aboard. The Rangers scored again ten minutes later, and it's at this point that you start totaling up the cost of your tickets and time and wonder what else you might have done with it. It didn't really make me feel any better. And when there's that much time left on the clock, you either hope it runs quickly or it just gets fun-bad so at least you have a story.

The Hawks actually leveled out, and climbed back into it a bit when Havlat somehow found a way to pierce Lundqvist in the second period. That was the only hope, that he would have one of *those games* and we'd get a memory. It wasn't to be. The Rangers easily held off the Hawks for the last half of the game, cruising to a 2-1 win but not the humiliation we feared.

There is one play that sticks out, even now, though it didn't really mean anything to the overall result. The Rangers skated down toward the end we were sitting on a 2-on-1 with Duncan Keith being the only defender back. Keith slid down to his chest to try and block the pass, but whatever Ranger had the puck simply went around him to have a clean look for either a pass or shot. But at the last second, Keith wheeled around while on his stomach and whipped his stick behind him to break up the play. It was pure desperation, but it was a demonstration of how Keith could always live on the edges and find a way to not get burned. Well, sometimes not get burned, as in his second season he was still making tons of mistakes. But the kind of game he was trying to play had a steep learning curve, and this kind of thing was an excellent example of how he was learning, slowly, to pull himself out of trouble. He would get this kind of thing right more and more over the next few years.

With the decision to decamp to LA now made, I headed to the UC one last time with my friend Margaret, whom I had introduced to the game only months before. The Hawks beat the mighty Senators in a shootout after coming back from 3-1 down. It was about as good of a send-off as they could have provided then. I packed up the car a few days later, and sure I was making a huge mistake, headed off for my own manifest destiny.

A.B. I
October 4, 2007
Hawks vs. Wild

Most Hawks fans have a different date or time they would point to when things really began to turn around. It's actually a pretty personal mark, because everyone rediscovered their interest at their own time and pace. What I can say for pretty sure is that the summer of 2007 was a big part of it for everyone, and all the things that happened in it set the franchise in a new and far better direction.

Where to start? Let's try this. At the conclusion of the previous season, fortune smiled upon the Hawks as they actually won the draft lottery. We couldn't believe it, at least those of us who regularly manned the message boards. We were sure the NHL would never allow such a thing, and perhaps someone did miss an assignment. But they did, which gave them the chance to draft Patrick Kane.

That looks like a no-brainer now, but back then there was a fair amount of debate whether the Hawks should take him, or James van Riemsdyk, or Kyle Turris (seriously, there was). Kane's size gave a lot of people pause, and a lot of Hawks fans still thought of things in terms of size and snarl. But Dale Tallon never wavered, he knew exactly what he wanted with the top pick. And I was with him. Having seen Kane in the World Juniors, it was clear he could provide something the Hawks hadn't had since Savard. There was once-in-a-lifetime skill there. To be able to bend a game to one's will was something you didn't pass up.

That was combined with the news that Jonathan Toews would be leaving North Dakota after one season in the NCAA and coming to the Hawks. We had been sold on Toews for all of the previous season. Toews was being billed as the fulcrum on which everything would pivot, and we wouldn't have to wait any longer.

While it's a truly morose statement, nothing changed the Hawks' fortune and our feelings about them quite like the death of Bill Wirtz.

I woke up the morning of September 26 to a text from my brother that just said, "FINALLY." That seems so crass now, but that was how we felt. I didn't need to ask what he was talking about. I knew. I quickly opened the laptop and scoured the internet to read everything I could and all the reactions. I called my father, who was never one to be talkative on the phone, and asked him if he saw the news to which he responded "I can't believe I outlived that motherfucker. I was sure he would be perfectly preserved for a century or more." Hawks fans everywhere rejoiced.

Again, that sounds awful, and in hindsight it was in some ways. Bill Wirtz had a family and a lot of friends. But he had spent years destroying what we loved. He had unabashedly gutted this team and its fanbase. He certainly never cared what we thought. They had fallen behind all the other teams in the NHL by decades. Their home games were still not on TV. We couldn't even dream of playoff berths, much less Stanley Cups that only ten to fifteen years before were right outside our grasp. And I won't even get into how he borked all the liquor distribution laws in Illinois, making life harder for me and my fellow drunks. He was an obstacle to all that we wanted for the Hawks. We knew that getting him out of the way was the only way the Hawks could achieve anything. And we knew he wasn't getting out of the way until he died. He would never sell what had been in his family for decades. Wishing death on someone is clearly never acceptable. And we didn't wish death on Bill Wirtz. We just weren't upset when it came to him. It was a day we had all talked about but thought would never come. And suddenly the blockade was lifted.

The following days left us all dizzy. First off, Rocky Wirtz took control, when for years we had all been led to believe it was his brother Peter that would assume control of the Hawks. Rocky had been in control of the liquor business of the family, and was now moving to the other wing, which everyone had said he didn't have much interest in doing. Peter was then sent...somewhere? Nowhere near the hockey team, we know that. Bob Pulford, the undead executive who kept rising from his crypt to run some section of the Hawks for my entire fan life, was basically cast out to Siberia. Perhaps his picture was put up around the United Center with a warning to not let this man in the building. We didn't care. He was gone. Never again was he just going to wander into the GM's office and just be given the job because he couldn't find the door to leave.

Rocky also made it clear that he would do everything he could to get some home games for the following season on TV. While I lived in L.A. and had NHL Center Ice and could see every Hawks home game through the visiting broadcast anyway, this was beyond fantasy. We had never seen the Hawks regularly on TV when they were at home, and then within the span of days that was now a reality, or would be in a season's time.

For the first time in a decade, at least the better part of one, there was hope. We could see a path to a new age of Hawks hockey, which we hadn't been able to in so long. Obviously, looking back on it none of these were revolutionary decisions. Of course you'd want the games on TV, as there's no better advertisement for what you're selling. Of course you'd replace incompetent management and put people who knew what they were doing in the best possible position to succeed. Of course you give your customers what they want. It's a mark of just how backward and incompetent the Hawks had been that these seemed like decisions that should make up its own business course at Wharton or something.

Even being 2,500 miles away, I felt a connection again. Life in California hadn't exactly been smooth. I ended up working an overnight job in a casino, which is just about as glamorous as it sounds. The hours and the nature of Los Angeles didn't leave me a lot of time and freedom to create my own circle of friends or to be as committed to comedy as I would have wanted. I had friends, but they were mostly connected to my roommate. I spent a lot of time in the house in the afternoon by myself. And suddenly the Hawks gave me something to get excited about, which I needed. I was more involved on the message boards and whatever blogs there were than I had been, feeling that connection to home again. I had a community. At the time, it was enough.

So I definitely made a whole thing of Opening Night, in combination with a Cubs playoff game (that didn't go so well either). I ordered a pizza, which I almost never did, and told my roommate the living room was mine until I went to work at 10:00 pm. Thank you very much, Pacific time.

It wasn't quite the finished article. Toews had broken his finger in preseason and didn't play. The Hawks didn't score. But they actually looked...dangerous at times? They could play a little defense? That never happened. Keith wasn't just all over the ice for the sake of it. He was pushing the game. And Kane. It was just what I had envisioned, if only for one game. Yeah, he was small, Yeah, he was pushed off the puck easily at times. But there were several moments, with the puck on his stick, where once again the game slowed, waiting for him to do something. There was anticipation whenever he got time. And he seemed to have more time than anyone else who had the puck that night. The Hawks might have lost 1-0 to the permanently faceless Wild, but pretty much every Hawks fan couldn't wait to watch the next game.

It certainly made me feel a little better about Ted Lilly serving up that home run to Chris Young a couple hours later.

An Unwanted Service
October 6, 2007
Wings vs. Hawks

The Hawks returned to open the home portion of the schedule two days later, and they have not had a more awkward home opener, nor will they again. The building was full, and even though it was the Wings in town it was actually mostly Hawks fans eager to see their new toys in Kane and Toews (though Toews was still hurt). Of course, they didn't show up wanting to see a memorial service for Bill Wirtz. Which is what they got, and it made for something of a mess.

Looking back on it, or if you didn't know anything that went on, the concept of fans booing a memorial service seems downright evil. But the thing was, the fans didn't show up at his funeral to boo. We didn't impede upon anyone. This was our space. It was a perfect example, perhaps the last one of the old Wirtz regime, of just how out of touch the organization was with their fans. We were not Wirtz's friends. We were not his family. He had been taking our money for years and not putting it where it was supposed to go, back into the team. He had gutted our experience of being a fan. It was due to him and his policies that the players we came to love, who were our heroes when we were kids, were chased out of town. I spent way more time miserable about the exits of Roenick, Chelios, Belfour, Larmer, and whoever else than I ever did cheering Hawks wins. I wasn't alone. For a lot of us, being a Hawks fan was a big part of who we were and what made up our lives. He had turned that into something we dreaded, even mourned. Certainly it was understandable that no one was in the mood to hear what a great man he was.

I've never been one to simply ignore what a person was in life when they die. Richard Nixon didn't suddenly become a great man because he stopped taking in oxygen. Bill Wirtz was not Nixon, but that doesn't mean he didn't have a lot to answer for by his actions in life.

If it happened now, I'm sure things would be more civil. But Hawks fans never got a chance to air their grievances when Wirtz was alive. They had no following. He wasn't out anywhere where he could talk to fans. He didn't talk to the media or hold pressers. This was the one chance, I suppose, that Hawks fans had to let him know exactly how they felt. Maybe they thought he would finally hear this, or maybe they just needed to let it out. Hawks fans took it. I couldn't blame them, as ugly as it might have been.

I can't imagine what Rocky thought about it at the time. He must've been horrified. At the same time, Rocky is hardly stupid, and must have anticipated something like this. Maybe he thought Hawks fans would just stay silent. Maybe he just thought it would be awkward without being vicious. Whatever he thought, he clearly saw what the task ahead of him was going to be.

The True Power
October 19, 2007
Avalanche vs. Hawks

As I said earlier, the moment in time that each Hawks fan will identify as their marker of revolution varies from fan to fan. This night was would be the choice for a lot of folks, I'm sure. The Hawks had managed some exciting games already. They had Hail Mary'd their way to a win against the Stars a week before, scoring a tying goal with two seconds left before taking it in OT. They had beaten the Wings in Detroit. We were seeing things we hadn't seen in a very long time.

The home games were still not on TV, and being the afterthought of a sport that was an afterthought on the main stage meant you weren't exactly on Sportscenter a lot. Or at all. You existed in the shadows of the shadows. Jonathan Toews changed that.

Everyone remembers the goal. Toews picked up a pass from Kane streaking across the red line, and curled up the ice along the right boards. He split two Avs to get to the middle of their zone, and then undressed the retreating d-man before going around Jose Theodore to deposit in an open cage. It remains probably the best goal he's ever scored, and one of the best in Hawks' history on pure skill. And it was his fifth game.

I watched from L.A. on the Colorado broadcast, and even the Avs broadcasters stood up and cheered. They were simply blown away. Analyst Peter McNab said, "As we said in the pregame, this is the kind of skill that could bring a franchise back." That's exactly what I was feeling in my living room. Only Havlat in the previous ten years was even capable of thinking of what Toews had just pulled off. Suddenly, the Hawks had a player who would get them on Sportscenter, who would have people talking the next day at work, who would get outsiders wondering just what the hell was going on here.

It's kind of a minor note now, but it was that same night that Patrick Kane scored his first NHL goal to cap off a first period blitz that saw the Hawks go up 3-0. After receiving a pass between the circles on a rush he simply rifled one over Jose Theodore's glove. It was pinpoint placement. I can still see Toews leaping into his arms, more happy that Kane had scored his first goal than he was about his own masterpiece. The energy of these two children was infecting the whole organization. How could you not get swept up in it? Maybe it's silly to put too much meaning to it, but watching them celebrate, it felt like the first time you could tell they both thought they belonged in the NHL. That they were here to fuck shit up. I think I nearly cried back in California.

Of course, this being Savard's Hawks they had to blow that three-goal lead. Thankfully, Tuomo Ruutu tipped in a point-shot with a minute and a half to go.

Toews and Kane had both scored, and the Hawks won. It was how you would draw it up. I left a message for Craig in Chicago, telling him he should at least check the highlights to see what Toews had done. The response both elated me and kind of broke my heart.

"Oh, I was there."

He had gone with Margaret. Margaret that I had introduced to the game the year before, joking that he was "completing her training."

It was the first time since I had moved that I felt I wasn't where I belonged. Toews and Kane ushering in new era had begun at the United Center so spectacularly? I was supposed to be there, not getting ready to man blackjack tables at Hollywood Park before the sun came up. I guess you could say the seeds were being planted.

They're On TV!
November 11, 2007
Wings vs. Hawks

It may sound strange to say I was excited about a home games being on TV when I lived out of market and had been seeing all the home games anyway. But I was. We can all get caught up in symbolism.

This was the first of a slate of home games that Rocky Wirtz was able to get onto Comcast Sportsnet Chicago. It wasn't some national broadcast usurping the local blackout or any other shenanigans. It was the first home game that the Hawks meant to put on TV. It was another page turning, let's say. Even as far away as I was, it felt like an occasion worth noting.

I got all ready for the game, and headed to the bathroom to clear everything out before puck drop. And perhaps the universe wasn't quite ready to let me forget what being a Hawks fan was like. The toilet broke and overflooded. For a second I couldn't ignore the metaphor of once again standing in an inch of water in a bathroom while getting ready to watch the Hawks. So while the first televised Hawks home game was starting, I was trying to stem the tide in my own bathroom. Paradise clearly wasn't reachable, yet.

Once again, the Hawks toppled the Wings. Even though the story was that you could see the game elsewhere besides the arena, the energy in the building was palpable through the screen. Sure, the population of Wings fans helped the noise, but Hawks fans were once again sensing that things were changing, even if they could have stayed home to watch this one. Both Toews and Kane scored again, and Khabibulin was able to turn away a pretty furious Wings rally. The Hawks had now beaten Detroit three straight times. When we read that sentence then, it might as well have been in another language, such was the sense that it made. It was one of those things where you spent the hours after it just laughing out loud, and if you were in public you hoped they didn't come to take you away.

A week later, the Hawks would hire John McDonough away from the Cubs to be president of the Hawks. Some would tell you this is the most important move they made. At the time, it seemed immense. McDonough was revered in the Chicago sports scene, basically for turning Wrigley Field into the place to be even though the team was dogshit for most of his tenure. I barely remember and no one younger than me would, but there was a time when Wrigley would be half-filled for most of the season. McDonough changed that, mostly be selling the sun, the beer, the bleachers, and Harry Caray who was basically some combination of all three. It was billed as party central, and that's what it came to be.

The hardcore Hawks fans were certainly leery. While they rejoiced that the team was finally worth watching and that there was an owner who at least appeared to care about the team and fans, they certainly didn't want the United Center to become Wrigley West. We knew that McDonough didn't know anything about hockey, no matter what his pandering over the years would be. But he knew how to market a team, how to draw in more fans, we just didn't know what those kind of efforts were going to be. Was the wave coming to the UC? Would we be inundated with twenty-somethings not watching the game and screaming the whole time? Were we going to get priced out of the arena all together? No one views outsiders quite as suspiciously as hockey fans do, and McDonough was an outsider who might bring a whole host with him. We were guarded, to be polite.

But I was hopeful. I wanted the building to be full again, all the time. I wanted the Hawks to have a spot on the Chicago scene. I wanted people to know what I had known all these years. I was pretty tired of the shadows. And from what I could gather, McDonough was the man to do it. He would certainly institute the obvious measures the Hawks had ignored for so long that made the games and team a more accessible place for everyone. The Hawks had never really had a president. They never had someone simply in charge of the business side. If nothing else, McDonough's hiring felt like another move to become a real, live, functioning sports organization.

Really, all he had to do was get out of the way. I should have been more suspicious when he talked about running into the Stadium to catch the anthem in the '60s, when pretty much everyone agrees that the Stadium crowd didn't start cheering the anthem until the '80s. We didn't know it at the time, but this was going to be the easiest job in the world. The changes were simple but they seemed revolutionary, given how much in the mud the Hawks had been. The easiest way to get people into the building and turn them into fans is to win, and the pieces were already in place for that.

Have to admit, he did that. Except when it came time to take credit, of course.

Rebirth
December 23, 2007
Oilers at Hawks

This is the night I mark as the Hawks' rebirth. This is the night that probably set out a path that would lead all of us to here. It still sticks with me as a time when I and many others could physically feel a switch be flipped.

The beginning of December hadn't been kind to the Hawks. They lost six of seven to lose whatever momentum they had generated to start the season. Denis Savard was not exactly astute at turning things around when they started to go bad. When things started to go sideways, either Savard never changed anything or he tried to change everything, nothing in between. It wasn't exactly the mark of a steady hand.

They were able to arrest the slide right before Christmas with a win at home over the Predators. Three nights later was a coming-out party of sorts for them, as they beat the still formidable Senators in Ottawa on Hockey Night in Canada. Toews scored in overtime to win it. There is something in the NHL about being on Hockey Night in Canada, where it doesn't feel official until you do it there. The Hawks hadn't been featured on there in a very long time, but now with Toews and Kane there was definite interest. That kind of performance made people take notice. They were a curiosity, if nothing else.

They returned home to face the Oilers the next night, a Sunday night. My brother and I had returned home from Christmas. His excitement over the team had boiled over and not only had he gotten tickets to this one weeks before, he even splurged for seats in the 100 Level. I hadn't sat that close since I was a kid at the Old Stadium.

I remember more about that day than I should. First of all, it was so cold it was personal. That's how we always described it. It was like the air was getting back at you for something you did to it. It wasn't just cold, but there was a biting wind that felt like it was ripping your skin off to deposit the cold air directly into your organs. There is no jacket for this. You feel like your eyes could sink all the way back into the middle of your head just to avoid it. Maybe if I'd remembered this feeling walking to the arena, I wouldn't have signed up for a job that would have me standing outside on nights like this.

My brother was housesitting for a friend in the Gold Coast, as my father's apartment couldn't house all three of us. We watched the Bears play the Packers there, and while the Bears season was well lost before this (weren't they all?) they did manage to hump it up to win a game the Packers really had no interest in playing. They just wanted to get back to their jackets and heaters (hmm, this should have been a clue they would biff that game at home in the bitter cold to the Giants a month later). Right after the Bears game ended, we headed to the United Center. The building was full due to the proximity of Christmas and the excitement about the team. This is what I had been looking for.

Almost everything worked out perfectly. My two hockey friends, Margaret and Craig, were in the building as well. And the two seats next to us were unoccupied through the first, so we were able to sneak them in to sit with us. The plebes had infiltrated the aristocracy.

You forget what the sport looks like that up close. Just how fast everything happens and how big some of these guys are. You wonder how the human mind can be trained to make decisions at such speed when you're right up in it.

Seabrook scored on a blast from the point for a power play goal in the first. The Oilers notched two before the period was over, including one from Dustin Penner on one of the odd nights he could be bothered and hadn't overeaten at the pregame spread. Sharp scored his eighteenth of the season, as Kane danced around a couple defenders along the boards right in front of us to center for him to deposit home from basically a foot and a half. Seabrook scored a minute into the third on an odd-man rush at the other end of the ice from us.

Khabibulin had to withstand a furious Oilers rally to keep the Hawks ahead. The Hawks couldn't get out of their own zone. No icing or timeout could save them for the final two minutes. It was all happening right in front of us. Each save or blocked shot out of desperation just brought the crowd into more and more of a frenzy. It was feeding on itself. By the time he made his last save the building was separating from its foundation. The Hawks saw it out, and you could feel the catharsis.

There wasn't much of an organization to it, but after they had congratulated each other the Hawks players kind of lingered to salute the crowd which was still jet-engine loud. Their retreat into the dressing room didn't stop the crowd. They kept standing, stomping, and cheering. It just kept going. A couple minutes later, the player emerged from the tunnel to come back out for another salute. It was basically an encore.

I had never seen that before. Not just at the United Center or the Stadium but anywhere. The players drawn back out to the playing area simply because the crowd begged them to. There was a lot more going on here than simply celebrating a win.

When McDonough was hired, the first thing he said was, "Hawks fans, it's time to come back." What he meant, at least I think, was that it was time for all of us to let go everything we'd been carrying for years. Our frustration, our anger, our depression, our apathy. It was time to let it go. This night felt like the physical manifestation of that release. Here we were screaming over a win over a nothing Oilers team, and there had to be a reason. This was the entire fandom finally letting it all go. This was us telling the team we were ready to love them again, to be a part of it again. And the players coming back out showed them what this city could be for them, and how ready they were for it, too.

We had our team back. Not only back, but something more than we'd ever seen. Sure, they had good teams before. But never had the organization as a whole cared about us in this way. This was new. We were ready to have them be a part of us again, and the added bonus was that they were more than ready to play that role.

I couldn't shake the feeling of that night. I would return to L.A. soon enough, and though I wouldn't say it out loud, inside I knew I couldn't live somewhere for too long without this, what this had become. It's amazing what a game between two non-playoff teams can be, if all the circumstances break just right.

Bloodlust
December 26, 2007
Predators vs. Hawks

Needless to say, one game wasn't going to slake our hockey thirst. So three days after that landmark night Adam and I headed back, and to our familiar haunt of the 300 Level. You can only interlope among the glitterati for so long before you need to head to the familiar.

It's a shame that the NHL no longer does Boxing Day games. Moving them to December 27 doesn't remove all the heat from them of course, but all arenas had an extra edge as people escaped being cooped up with their families for two straight days. Everyone is so happy to be somewhere else and to yell at people that don't share their last name. Now, by the time the twenty-seventh rolls around everyone is pretty much exhausted.

Halfway through the first, Martin Lapointe took a penalty, and I leaned over to my brother and said, "Shorty. Right here." It's just one of those things you say to be funny, no matter if you believe it or not. That sunshine-y optimism just for the sake of it. Scoring shorthanded goals had become something of a specialty for the Hawks that season though, given that Sharp and Toews were both used to kill penalties. They racked up seventeen of them that year, with Sharp himself collecting seven. So it wasn't totally out of left field, but I'd be lying if I said I really believed it was coming.

It only took a minute. Toews stole the puck, drifted into the Preds' zone, got around two Predators to center for Sharp camped out in front of the Nashville net. Just like he had done the previous game, Sharp didn't miss. My brother kept punching me in the arm. "Sammy, you called it!" I didn't really. I said it more out of hope or a slice of comedy than expectation. But I was happy to take the credit. Toews scored five minutes later, with Sharp returning the favor of an assist. This was when the line of Sharp-Toews-Kane was basically doing whatever it wanted. Somehow the league took forever to catch on to Kane being able to hit a cross-ice pass to an open Sharp to one-time one home.

The Hawks never let the Preds all that close, running out 5-2 winners in front of another bonkers building. But the night's events were not over. Far from it.

There was a meaningless draw with four seconds left or somewhere around there. Right after the puck left the linesman's hand. James Wisniewski and Jordin Tootoo had their gloves leave theirs. We didn't know it at the time but Wisniewski had already blown out his knee. He still had a score to settle. He proceeded to pummel the ever loving shit out of Tootoo.

I left my senses. I stood there screaming, "FUCK HIM UP, WIZ!" I yelled it so loud I think I nearly pulled an oblique. I could watch myself absolutely baying for blood but couldn't stop. I hated Tootoo with every fiber of my being. He was the leading punk in the division, with his big dumb face and his big dumb game. I didn't know it at the time, but we were coming full circle. Two years earlier, almost sitting in the exact same spot, we had seen Todd Simpson jump Tootoo after the Preds had simply skinned the Hawks alive in front of an empty and lifeless building. Now the Hawks had returned the favor, and a pummeling of Tootoo was capping off the complete opposite result in a building that must've sounded like a prison riot. This was some kind of closure I couldn't recognize then. I know why some people still cling to fighting in hockey. There can be a truly satisfying bloodlust, as dangerous as that probably is.

Wisniewski came to represent a lot of things I came to resent later. The idea of Wisniewski was a hell of a lot better than the reality. The idea was a head-banging nut job who could flatten opponents before heading up ice to unleash what was a hellish shot. He was an basement punk show on ice. The reality was he was constantly out of position chasing those hits, and he took so long to get that shot off the he rarely could get it by anyone. His positional sense would have crashed any GPS. But for one night, one moment, he turned me into an animal. I was at my most base, and I wouldn't have traded that for anything.

Man is an animal, after all.

Into Hell
January 4, 2008
Hawks vs. Ducks

In some ways, the season peaked with the win over Nashville. The Hawks lost the next three. Two of them were to the Kings, the second being on New Year's Day by a score of 9-2 in Los Angeles where Toews got hurt and would miss the next six weeks. They were helpless without Toews, and we all knew it. I returned to L.A. the next day, and looked at the tickets I had to see them play the Ducks in Anaheim two days later with a feeling of dread. After all, the Ducks were the defending champs and the Hawks were showing up without their main weapon. I could sense what I was in for, but there was no turning back now.

The first sign this was going to be one of those nights was that it was one of the six days per year in southern California where it never stopped raining. There is no part of going to a game in Anaheim that isn't utterly miserable, and that starts with the commute to Orange County. A downpour wasn't going to make it any more enjoyable. Thankfully, because I had found one hockey friend in the entire fucking place, I could at least use the carpool lane. That still made for a forty-five minute drive into the urban hellscape that is Orange County.

You arrive at the Honda Center, and unless you got there at 10:00 am, you're going to park three-quarters of a mile from the fucking place. And you're going to wait to do it. And this being Anaheim, as soon as you exit your car in your Hawks gear you're going to be taunted by some dickbag in a Ducks jersey that hasn't even had the tags removed yet. What the fuck did these people know? They had never trudged through a foot of snow with a blistering wind that made death seem like sweet relief to watch Alexander Karpotsev.

You enter the building, and it has so little color it made the United Center seem like CBGBs. At least the lack of any nearby escalator to the top level gave me flashbacks to the old Stadium. The game started, and I didn't even have time to get comfortable before Corey Perry scored sixteen seconds in. Corey Perry. Perhaps the biggest ass-rash in the entire league, with his dumbass, hang dog face and his habit of punching anyone who wasn't looking. The dude probably elbows his own kids in the ribs from behind during breakfast. That feeling I had a year earlier in the Garden, where I didn't know how badly this could get away from an outgunned Hawks team, returned. I had driven all the way down to suburbia-gone-wrong in the rain for this?

Sharp somehow bundled one in off a scramble in the second, giving me some hope. During the third period, with the Hawks attacking the end I was sitting at, a puck squirted out to Rene Bourque between the circles on the power play. He was all alone, and the one thing he could do was shoot. I rose out of my seat, just in time to see him ring one off the crossbar and out of play. The guys behind me politely put hands on my shoulders to console me. I just stood there with my hands on my head. I had seen salvation, and then it was snatched away. And now I was getting patronized by fucking Anaheim residents. Do not fear death, dear friends. Because there is Anaheim.

As the minutes ticked off and the Hawks didn't really threaten an equalizer after Bourque's miss, a chant began in the rows behind me. I know it was started by high schoolers, I was sure, because I could hear the crack in their voices.

"Blackhawks su-uck!"

Yes, they had turned "suck" into a two-syllable word. These dumb shits couldn't even get that right. And I had to sit there and take it. Here I was, having recently quit the casino, having blown pretty much every last dollar to drive to Anaheim in the rain to watch this and have to listen to this. Hello darkness, my old friend.

Opposing View
February 2, 2008
Hawks vs. Sharks

Unemployment continued after returning to Los Angeles. This may come as a surprise, but as it turns out the area is flooded with youngish, moderately talented fuckwits pining for simple ass jobs that allow them to chase whatever far-fetched dreams they have and most certainly won't catch. Interviews came and went, including with one woman so much dumber than me that I basically had to interview myself so she could get the right information. Los Angeles was turning into a very cold place while the sun always shined.

So I didn't have much to do, and the Hawks became pretty much my closest friend. Days on which they played at least gave me a purpose, something to center the day around. They weren't always rewarding but they were usually pretty damn entertaining. Combine that with whatever feeling of community I could get from the message boards before and after games, and at least I felt somewhat moored to something.

By this time, the Hawks had become something of a story around the league. Not that they were good, but lots of press and fans were excited to see the collection of young talent that the Hawks had. They were being tipped to be the next big thing in the NHL, if things broke right.

It was funny, at the start of the season when I would turn on opposing broadcasts, and the Hawks were treated as the sad sack organization that they'd been. This was an easy two points for whoever the

Hawks were playing, and if the game was taking place in Chicago there was always a commentary about how empty the building was and what it used to be like in Chicago. No broadcaster could refrain from talking about how far the Hawks had fallen. Fast forward a few months, and suddenly opposing broadcasters and media were at least curious, if not excited to see what the Hawks had to offer.

This game probably only sticks out to me. It was on a Saturday afternoon and I had nowhere to go. Toews was still hurt, and the Sharks were one of the league's powerhouses. It set up to be pretty ugly. But the Hawks, and in particular Nikolai Khabibulin, put in a heroic, defiant performance to lose 3-2 in a shootout.

What stood out is this was one of the first truly dominant games from Duncan Keith. The Sharks broadcast team couldn't stop gushing about his skating. He had one particular rush that started behind his own net, streaked past two forwards, entered the Sharks zone, and then did a half spin-o-rama right inside the line to get himself to the outside and back to his point. It was Keith in a nutshell, complete frantic, loosely organized, exciting, and ultimately effective. Keith was just starting to figure out how to apply his skating and other skills to really be noticeable in good ways instead of bad. He was bubbling underneath the surface, behind Kane and Toews. But it was becoming clear that he might just be the most important cog in the machine.

Hearing opposing broadcasters gush about other players than Kane and Toews always felt like our excitement was justified. We thought there was more to the Hawks than two players, and it was becoming clear to everyone else that was true. Part of the appeal of turning on the Hawks in a far-away market was to see just what the opposing views were of the Hawks. It was a nice perspective.

And I had nowhere else to go.

The Dumbest Game Ever
February 23, 2008
Hawks vs. Kings

Due to the weirdness of the NHL schedule, the Hawks were back on the West coast not even a month later. This time they were armed with a healthy Toews. Their stop in southern California also coincided not just with my friend Dan's visit from Chicago, but a business trip for my brother from New York. It was the perfect storm. So clearly, we were headed to the Staples Center.

Adam was able to somehow con the agency into paying for tickets that were about ten rows behind one of the goals. The game started innocently enough, with Peter Harrold opening the scoring before Patrick Sharp tipped in a Keith point shot on the powerplay to tie it. We were right behind that goal, and I still remember Keith pointing to Sharp right after to signal he saw he got it. It was so nonchalant. So easy. It felt like these two could do that whenever they wanted.

The second period was one of the more enjoyable my brother and I had shared in a while. The Hawks scored four times in the frame's opening ten minutes, with Havlat, Toews, Andrei Zyuzin (that's right), and Jason Williams all notching to give the Hawks a 5-1 lead.

We had never seen the Hawks win on the road together, and I had only done it once (in Boston, in college). Seeing them surge past a team like this in an opposing building was more gratifying than I could have imagined. There is always a bit of a fear when you see your team on the road. You know that if it goes sideways, the people around you aren't going to be sharing in your feelings. You don't know that someone around you isn't going to get a little too obnoxious. You wonder if your effort is going to be all worth it.

Four goals in ten minutes was going to spare us all of that, surely. It's relief and excitement in one. I didn't feel the need to taunt the Kings fans around us; they had it just as rough as we did, but at least I was sure they would leave us alone. Or so I thought.

This was Savard's Hawks, after all. Nothing was ever finished either way. Mike Cammalleri scored halfway through the third period. The three of us did some quick calculations. Three goals to go with ten minutes left still seemed a more than manageable ratio. This was the Kings after all, and they sucked harder than the Hawks. It was uneasy, but hardly panic.

Tom Preissing scored three minutes later. Now it was moving beyond uneasy. All it would take is one bad bounce or one bad call and the Kings would be within one shot. It was tangible now, and the building being excited wasn't helping our cause.

Patrick O'Sullivan scored with a minute left, and we knew exactly what was coming. Toews had a chance a shift later to ice it with an empty net goal, but his shot barely ticked the stick of a diving Jack Johnson to send it off course. The Kings came back down after collecting the puck, and there was only ever going to be one ending.

Being at the opposite of the end ice, we couldn't see exactly what happened. We just saw a scramble in front of the net, the fans behind the net leap to their feet with their arms in the air as the red light went on, and Anze Kopitar wheeling away in delight. The Hawks had blown a four-goal lead in ten minutes, sending the Staples Center into rapture and leaving the three of us feeling like the loneliest people on Earth. Everyone around you is standing and jumping in a furor, and you're sitting there just watching it. You're at the party you were never invited to.

The game went into overtime, and there was some salvation two minutes later. The Hawks gave up a couple prime chances that by some miracle didn't go in. James Wisniewski got the puck to Seabrook who came down on an odd-man rush. His blast was stopped but Sharp was right there to bang the rebound home. We could clearly hear him scream "YEAAAHHHH!!!" as the rest of the building fell silent. I can still see the look on his face as he skated off to the corner. We cheered more for the fact that we could get out of there without being totally embarrassed. I shook hands with a couple of Kings fans on the way out of the row. There was shared camaraderie, as they'd watched their Kings come up with enough stupid results that they could appreciate someone on the other side of it. We'd all been there before, after all.

For an hour or two after the game, all three of us would every so often look at the other two and say, "What the hell was that?" We were just confused. It was a perfect illustration of the Hawks that year. Capable of brilliance and utter idiocy simultaneously. Whatever it was, you always had to catch your breath afterwards.

The next night, the three of us decamped down I-5 for Anaheim, hoping a Hawks team armed with Toews would make for a far better experience than without him. How did that go? Let's put it this way: The argument between Dan and Adam over the best cover of "Whiskey In The Jar" on the ride down was the highlight.

There are many ways I try and describe the Medieval torture chamber that the "Ponda" Center is. But there is only anecdote that I need to make my case airtight. Next to the seats we had for the night, a season ticket holder had the two between us and the aisle. These were two of the four season tickets he had. The other two tickets were located on the other side of the rink, so that he could always sit in the end the Ducks were attacking. The ensemble was complete with his Ducks leather jacket that I'm sure he wore to bed.

Certainly, the money he spent on four season tickets on each end would have cost the same if not more than just two seats at center ice. This was also the time that the Ducks were sporting Chris Pronger and Scott Niedermayer on their defense, two of the greatest blue-liners of all time. I don't know, maybe you'd want to watch them play defense up-close once in awhile? As for the leather jacket, that probably answers itself.

Let me ice this one off by telling you that the two periods he sat by us, he complained to the various fans around him that certain Ducks weren't fighting a lot these days, because Ducks fans were sure that their league-leading fight total was the reason they were defending champions. I couldn't write this character in a fictional setting any better. And of course, when he did bother to talk to us he wanted it to be clear how little he had ever thought of the Hawks and how much more powerful the Ducks were. I'd like to find that guy now, but never will.

The First Heritage Night

March 7, 2008
Sharks vs. Kings

Pretty much from the moment that John McDonough was installed and Rocky Wirtz was fully entrenched as running the Hawks, they tried to illustrate how different things would be. They got a slate of home games on TV, and then added a few more as the Hawks actually became an interesting story. They had new, clever ads featuring the players for the games on TV and for Hawks tickets. The players were popping up on local morning shows, doing more and more interviews than ever before.

The big stroke, with emphasis on "stroke," was this first "Heritage" night they planned, which is when Bobby Hull and Stan Mikita were going to be honored. Honored for what exactly, no one was terribly sure. Both of their numbers had long been retired by the team.

Certainly, their relationship with the Hawks under Bill Wirtz after their playing days were over was at best non-existent, at worst toxic. Wirtz never really forgave Hull for bolting for Winnipeg in the WHL for more money, and he had no relationship with the team afterwards. Some claimed it also had to do with the team's inability to secure his son's services. Mikita also had little to do with the Hawks after he was done playing. It was said that he and Bob Pulford couldn't be in a room together, the scars of many battles in the faceoff circle representing the Hawks (Mikita) and the Leafs (Pulford) not even close to healing.

So this was McDonough and Rocky's grand gesture to show that the way things had been done in the past were over. That there would be a connection to the players of the past who had been frozen out before. It was to show that everyone was welcome back, be they players or fans who had cut the team adrift long ago.

Of course back then we didn't much consider the moral conundrum that this indeed was, and would later entangle the Hawks in some hypocrisy that they naturally didn't give a flying fuck about. Did I know about Hull's past of wife-beating and Nazi-sympathizing remarks? Yeah, I mean, I knew. I didn't give them much thought, but I knew they were out there. Most fans did, too. Did I or the rest of us think about it when he and Mikita came out onto the ice that night on the back of a '60s Corvette? No, we didn't. And we should have. While 2008 doesn't sound that long ago, it is very long ago in how we think about these things now, or at least how I and hope others do. Certainly no mainstream outlet mentioned this part of his past in the lead-up to this ceremony. And the alternative outlets didn't have much of a voice yet, at least not in Chicago.

I and the arena didn't care, though. All I could see was a full building screaming out its collective lungs for two playing legends who hadn't been in the building in years. All I could see was a real organization coming together, a real fandom ready to explode in growth, a real happening. That's the package the Hawks wanted to present. Not enough of us, including me, ever took a moment to say, "Y'know they're honoring a wife-beater, right?"

It really wouldn't have to cost the Hawks anything not to do this. The Hawks could have rebuilt their following without these kinds of heritage nights. Their play on the ice and their marketing was enough. But this was the first time the Hawks only had to concern themselves with the show, the gleam. They could put on the grand spectacle and no one would feel the need to look behind the curtain. And it's something they've gotten away with ever since.

Epiphany
April 13, 2008
San Jose v. Calgary (Game Three)
Oh right, we did this already.

A New Era
October 13, 2008
Predators vs. Hawks
To say the summer of 2008 was a whirlwind for Hawks fans would be quite the understatement. There were too many changes both on and off the ice. My own personal life being tied to that whirlwind only added to a summer I still can't quite wrap my arms around. It felt like it took about seven minutes.

After having that epiphany while watching the Sharks and Flames, I spent the next couple months chasing down and talking with the original editor of *The Blue Line,* Mark Weinberg. Finding him was certainly a chore in itself. He wasn't known to a lot of people, keeping to himself and his projects after giving up the publication. Eventually, after some digging, I was able to wrangle an email address from someone on a messageboard. It was just about the biggest shot in the dark I could find, but it's all I had.

So I emailed him, saying who I was and explaining that I thought it might be time to bring *The Blue Line* back, considering the season the Hawks just had, the seasons they were poised to have, and the interest in them actually climbing. The building was going to be full again, and it was going to be filled with new fans. The older ones might still want a connection to when they first started attending games, something to make them feel like they were on a different level. And the newer fans would want to feel cool, too, or something.

When I think back on it, what I expected was that I made a credible argument and that I would be able to contribute to it from Los Angeles. I certainly was not going to compete with Mark and the publication I revered by starting my own alongside it. While it certainly wouldn't be a full-time job, at least it would be something. He responded pretty quickly, which was exhilarating because I had spent months sending inquiries about jobs without hearing anything. This, if nothing else, was a viable lead.

I sent him some stuff I came up with, both written work and photoshops, and he loved them. This was also found gold, because I had basically spent a year and a half watching my comedy career get kicked in the skull in the giant sea of Los Angeles. The nadir was about this time, doing an open mic at The Laugh Factory on Sunset at like 4:00 pm on a Tuesday in front of three people, all the while the host never turned his microphone off and it was picking up his pen writing on a pad on his lap throughout my set. I think I knew it was over then.

I returned home for a weekend, mostly to meet with Mark. It was there that he told me he only wanted to do one issue of *The Blue Line*, and that he then wanted to see me create my own program that he would help me launch. A new program for a new era of Hawks hockey.

This meeting took place at Kuma's Korner, and if you've been there you know that thanks to the combination of their other-worldly burgers, the constant metal on the stereo, and maybe a touch of their beautifully tattooed staff, you walk out of there in a daze. To have my entire future altered left me in a state where I definitely should not have been driving afterwards.

I spent the last couple days at home asking various friends and my father and brother what they thought. All of their responses were extremely positive, some even saying they'd never heard something that made so much sense before. My father George and Adam were a little more guarded, as you'd expect, as both were still positive on the whole L.A. thing (probably just to have a host when they visited). But I knew when I got back on the plane to L.A. that I was only going to be there a short amount of time. I broke the news to my roommate, and basically packed up my stuff at the end of June and hit the road home.

I spent the next few weeks and months just coming up with comedic things for future issues or just trying things out, or teaching myself InDesign. Of course, I nearly scrapped the whole thing the first and only time I posted anything on one of the messageboards. I had made it known that *The Blue Line* was coming back, and finally somewhere in August I had worked up the gumption to present a fake-election comparison of Cristobal Huet and Nikolai Khabibulin, this being 2008, to gauge where I was at.

And it got ravaged. Back then I had no idea what the natural state of internet commentary and messageboards were when you submitted something you had created. It was pilloried from pillar to post. The comments calling it "lame" or "stupid" or "fucking awful" piled up. I felt ill. Had I made a huge mistake? Weren't these the people I had to make laugh if this was going to work? I had done hundreds of comedy sets where I couldn't get anyone to belch, much less laugh, and shrugged most of them off. But this I couldn't take.

Mark assured me I had what it took, that I had showed him stuff that was far funnier than anything he and his crew had ever done for *The Blue Line* (a blatant lie but I was happy to hear it). I pressed on, sleeping on my father's couch, but terror was only the beginning of what I felt. I found a print-house in Elk Grove that would be able to produce the program, even on weekends, and suddenly the table was looking set.

Things were no less boring for the Hawks. They had splashed on Brian Campbell in free agency, a true marker to what they wanted to become. Campbell was the most sought-after free agent defenseman that summer, and the Hawks not only wanted his puck-moving skills but to show the whole league and every player in it that they were now going to be a destination instead of a wasteland. Their previous ways were dead and buried forever. They weren't afraid to spend money, which caused every Hawks fan to fan themselves vigorously.

They also, strangely, signed Cristobal Huet, the most sought-after goalie on the market. Huet had just backstopped a miracle Capitals run to the playoffs. The thing was, the Hawks already had a goalie in Khabibulin that they were paying all the money. Even if this salary cap world was still new to us, paying two goalies a quarter of your cap or whatever it was then was obviously folly.

Khabibulin had been a disappointment for the three years he'd been in town, there was no debating that. He couldn't stay healthy, only making more than fifty appearances once. His best SV% in those three seasons was .909. It was fair to not count on him, but you would have thought you would have moved him along before giving another goalie a big duffel bag with a "$" on it. But again, the Hawks were showing the NHL that they were going to compete in every way.

There were other moves off the ice as well. The Hawks re-hired Pat Foley, which we had pretty much guessed was coming but was still exciting to hear. This was something of a bone to the holdover, lifelong fans. We never wanted to see Foley go, and it was basically an insult to our sensibilities to hear him doing AHL games in Rosemont. He belonged on our stage, and now that our stage was actually something worth being on, he should be back.

The Hawks were also the recipient of the Winter Classic, which was going to be held on New Year's Day at Wrigley Field. The NHL had launched the tradition the previous season in Buffalo, and now the Hawks were going to be the center of the hockey universe for the first time since probably the 1992 Final. Even the NHL could see where the Hawks were headed and were going to latch their star as early as they could. It's still astonishing what can happen in the timespan of one year. In 2007, the idea of the Hawks being involved in the signature event of the regular season was so abstract as to confuse Picasso (though maybe confusing Picasso wasn't all that hard). One owner death, a few young, exciting players, some marketing, and look what can happen.

Beneath the radar, the Hawks hired Scotty Bowman as a consultant. We didn't hear much about it at the time, and if we did, we might have wondered what the father of the assistant GM would cause to the actual GM down the road. But McDonough and Rocky knew they needed someone to look at the hockey aspect of the organization with fresh eyes and tell them what needed to change and what didn't. They certainly didn't know (though they might claim now that they did), and you couldn't find a better resume than the elder Bowman's.

The Hawks had commercials and billboards everywhere, and for the first time had a "Training Camp Festival" for the opening of camp at the United Center. Usually, training camp for the Hawks opened in the dark, buried behind Bears football and if there was a competent baseball team in town. Clearly, McDonough and Rocky were not going to simply accept a backseat. So they created this event with a 5K charity run and other games and things for kids and whatever else before you could go in for free to see practice.

And this was my debut as well. I created an eight-page, mini version of *The Committed Indian* previewing training camp. I was going to hand it out for free at the festival promotionally. Also, though I didn't realize at the time, it would get me accustomed to wandering around the United Center with no general direction as I would spend the next eight years doing. I ambled around the parking lot, handing out copies to whoever I could find. Some looked excited, most looked bewildered (and that didn't really change over the years), but hey, this thing was launched, whatever it was going to be.

The season did not get off to the start anyone had envisioned. The Hawks lost their first two games on the road, in New York and Washington, and didn't look particularly good doing it. They returned home for a very anticipated home opener against Nashville. And I helped produce the last *Blue Line* and took up residence on Damen Avenue on the south side of the arena to help peddle it. They had allowed me a half-page ad within this opus (the thing was like thirty-two pages or something). Most everyone who knew what it was was delighted to have it back, if only temporarily, and I made sure to tell everyone what was coming after a few home games. Mighty oaks from little acorns, and all that.

It was also the first game I attended as a season-ticket holder, a lifelong dream of mine (which tells you something about my life goals). Though my brother presented me with a whole pro-con list when I told him about the idea of returning home to do the program, I think he already knew what my answer was going to be. About two weeks before the season, I called him at work to ask if season tickets were an investment I was going to have to make, and his answer was simply, "Oh I took care of that. You should be getting them any day." I couldn't miss the message. This was his belief in me (as well as guaranteeing himself a ticket whenever he came home for a visit). As brothers, you don't ever come right out and say shit like that. You have to read between the lines a bit.

As a kid, you dream of season tickets because going to every home game sounds like pure fantasy. It was going to be part of your life routine. Work/school, family, Hawks games. You'd become friends with everyone around you, developing something of a new family. They'd know you by your first name at whatever bar you chose for pre and post-game revelry. You'd know all the vendors and ushers. You'd be something of a small celebrity within this tiny world. I remember seeing people interact as a child at games who were clearly season-ticket holders. It was like they came from another planet. I didn't have any idea what season tickets cost, but to me, holders must've made all the money in the world. Parents of my friends who had season tickets to the Cubs or Bears seemed god-like characters. To me, that's what being an adult meant back then. It meant you could go to the Hawks whenever you wanted. That you'd earned that right. Now that I had them, I felt...well, not like an adult. That still hasn't happened. But I did feel I'd passed onto a new level, let's say.

So Craig and I made our way to our seats, MY SEATS, for the first time in section 320. This is where I would be watching every anthem (well, actually, I wouldn't because I would be selling the program and just heading in, but I didn't know this at the time). This would be the angle I would have on every big Hawks goal. These would be the people I would high-five or complain to. This was my station. My section would become something of a part of my identity.

The Hawks lost this one in a shootout, their third-straight loss to open the season. Behind the curtain, it sealed Denis Savard's fate as coach, with the organization wanting to streamline and get a professional coach to mould this young lineup. They already had a GM in Tallon they didn't hire, so now they wanted a coach that they did hire. We could have read the tea-leaves. The Hawks had hired Joel Quenneville in the summer as a "scout," though his right-hand in Marc Bergevin put his house up for sale in Quebec immediately after that signing. Some say if Q hadn't gotten a DUI that summer they would have started the season with him, but that we'll never know. But clearly, Quenneville was never going to be just a scout for anyone, and you have to think he was promised something when taking on the role. It was obvious that senior advisor Scotty Bowman had told them they needed a real coach, Savard was always the elder Wirtz's loyal pet, and the Hawks acted on it. And lo and behold, Quenneville was already in the organization. Funny, no?

Whatever was going on, the entire ship for the Hawks and for myself was into the water.

The Debut

October 31, 2008
Stars vs. Hawks

 "Welcome to The Committed Indian. Inside you'll find all the sections you loved long ago in The Blue Line, and hope you will love again, such as The Fight Card, Hawks Record When..., Top 10 List, and more, and we've also tried out a few new things. And to celebrate, tonight only, we're giving it away"

 That's how it started. A brief note to the readers that we were trying to carry the torch over from *The Blue Line*. It's funny, I always said "we," because I liked the image that there was a team of goofs, trapped in some dark room with a bare light bulb and only cheap whiskey around, producing this barely coherent hockey newsletter before laying waste to each other. Like it looked like the basement of that house where the Stones recorded "Exile" (geez, self-aggrandize much?). But in reality, it was just me, though I had a ton of help with the blog. Anyway, it was time to take the stage, and I didn't really know if the crowd would go crazy.

 I decided to give the first one away for free just to get our name out there. This was also the first time I met my blog companion in person, Matthew Killion. He and I had only conversed via email before that, as he was kind enough to let me use his nascent blog *HereComeTheHawks.com*, as my online wing. He was coming to help peddle the program, and I suppose if we told him then from that night on he wouldn't be rid of me, he would have questioned all of his decisions.

 It's framed on my wall now. It was only twelve pages then. It was filled with fake ads because I hadn't found any true sponsors yet. It had the same stat pages and fight card *The Blue Line* had, trying to hold onto some traditions. It spotlighted Mike Modano, but used a picture of his pop-star wife instead. It had the same "Hawks record when..." page the old program did. I was doing my best to parrot what I knew.

 Even though I was giving it out for free, I was terrified no one would want it. You'd be surprised how many people turn away from something that's being handed to them when you're on the other side of it. Though I guess if someone looking like me tried to hand me something, I'd be highly suspicious as well. Looking back on that issue now, the margins were beyond fucked up. It was unedited and looked it. It was a giant mess. But it was a funny mess, and it meant well, and that at least got through to some people. You can do a lot in life if you're funny and you mean well, I suppose. But that first night, I couldn't eliminate the possibility that I would be scoffed at, or worse, ignored. Just because you're paranoid doesn't mean they're not out to get you.

 After we handed them all out I headed into the arena. I can't really tell you what it's like to walk around the concourse or look around the seating bowl and see people reading this thing. That feeling never really went away, but on that first night I wanted to walk up to everyone whom I saw with it and hug them (which probably would have ruined future sales). For all I knew, they were throwing it away as soon as they read the first page, but I didn't care at that point. We were on the scene, for better or for worse. People were carrying around something I created. I almost flew to my seat, such was the lifted feeling.

It was time to start swimming, just as Dory would have wanted.

If You Want Blood, You Got It
November 14, 2008
Blues vs. Hawks

My first, "only in my life" occurrence.

This was the first game where the air had turned cold and crisp. I used to wear what I called, "smoker's gloves" when selling the program, because it was easier to handle cash with my fingertips exposed (and easier to smoke). It kept most of my hands warmed, but from the top knuckle up would have some issues. I kept the programs in a gym bag slung over my shoulder and would have to reach in pretty often during the night.

With about half an hour to go, I noticed that every program I handed out had something of a red blotch or streak on the front or backpage. I just assumed it was a printing problem, as our title bar was in color and red. But it was every program. I was curious at least and made a note to contact the print house about it the next day.

About ten minutes before I was going to wrap up and head inside, I found out what the real culprit was. Due to the cold, my fingertips had gone numb. The skin had also dried out, and with reaching into the bag of programs and having them rub against the edges of every program, I had opened up a pretty severe paper cut. But due to the cold I couldn't feel it. And because the skin had dried out, it wasn't healing or clotting in any way, so for a paper cut it was somewhat gushing blood. And I was bleeding on every program I handed over to a customer.

I didn't know whether to be terrified or to burst into laughter. Could I get sued for this? Would everyone be horrified? Would they even notice? I came inside for the game and my companion for the night could tell by the expression on my face that something was off. When I told him what had happened outside, he remarked, "Well, you can't get more 'hockey' program than by handing out one that has your own blood on it."

I suppose that's true. So don't ever doubt what my dedication was to the process.

Fully Operational Death Star
December 26, 2008

Flyers vs. Hawks

　　December of 2008 was a time that most Hawks fans were walking around like zombies, like they'd simply taken too much soma and could never come down. The Hawks were on a seven-game winning-streak, and only two of them were by a single goal. They hadn't won that many games in a row in over twenty years, and the hockey they were playing hadn't been seen around these parts in far longer than that. This was the first iteration of the Matrix, the one that didn't work, because we honestly did keep trying to wake up from the dream we thought we were having.

　　The Hawks had completed a Western Canada swing right before Christmas, starting with that 9-2 win over the Oilers and wrapping up with an overtime win in Calgary thanks to Duncan Keith and then a really impressive win over the Canucks the very next night.

　　The Boxing Day game had an extra charge for all sorts of reasons. One, as always, it was the Boxing Day game and a lot of people had a family-related rage to get out. Two, the Winter Classic was now imminent and the excitement was growing, a feeling of being legitimized right near our fingertips. Third, it was the Flyers visiting, and the Flyers were growing into something of a power on the other side of the league. They too were loaded with young, fast, forwards. They were about a year ahead of the Hawks, as they had made the conference finals the previous season before bowing out to the Penguins. These were two of the more exciting teams in the league. Also, it was the fucking Flyers. Who didn't get in a frenzy to scream and cheer against them? That's their purpose, after all.

　　Adam returned home from New York for the holidays, and he could barely contain his glee at getting his first look at our seats and this Hawks team. He also couldn't wait to see what my job looked like, watching me peddle the thing outside Gate 3 and people reading it inside. I guess this was the return on his investment.

　　He joined me at my spot for a little while, and couldn't stop giggling that already so many people knew my name as they bought their program. I tried to introduce him but he would rarely let me. When he would people were thrilled to meet him, as I'd already mentioned him several times in the program and he also contributed a column here and there. I guess it was the first time he saw me as something of an adult, even if it wasn't all that close to being one. But here I was with a full-time job that I created and loved, and for the first time he could actually see it growing toward success. I didn't realize it at the time, of course. I never did. All I saw was him laughing at me. After all, that's what little brothers are for.

　　I met him inside right before puck drop. The anthem was particularly raucous. The din never really died down because Andrew Ladd scored barely a minute in. Sharp scored a minute later in a first period blitz that had the entire building pulsating. This was rolling on E. The onslaught never stopped. The Hawks outshot the Flyers 14-1 in the second period without scoring somehow, unable to break down the wall that was Martin Biron. He finally relented in the third where the Hawks scored three times, including goals from Versteeg and Bolland that came a minute apart to once again threaten the stability of the structure. The Hawks ended up outshooting the Flyers for the game 38-18. There was only one team in it.

This was the heavy metal hockey we had missed for so long. This felt as close to the Old Stadium as we ever had at the United Center. The noise never stopped. The Hawks were running a visitor out of the building. We walked out with our ears ringing and our chests pounding. It was a stern test for all the senses.

It felt like one of the few things that had been amiss in my brother's and my relationship finally fixed itself. The head-banging, ears-ringing chaos of good hockey. Finally, the puzzle had all the pieces again. We had circled back to when I was a kid and he was in high school. This is where we had started, and after years in the wilderness we finally had returned.

The Great Outdoors
January 1, 2009
Red Wings vs. Hawks

The Hawks won the next one in Minnesota, to give them a nine-game win-streak. It's a funny thing being a fan of a team on a winning-streak, especially when you're eyeing some landmark on the schedule ahead. While we were utterly delighted by the Hawks' streak, streaks do end. And you couldn't help but see this home-and-home with the Wings, the second being the Winter Classic, and feel trepidation. Even though it makes no sense, having won nine in a row only made us feel that losing to the Wings was more certain. That's just how our minds work. It would just be a thing Detroit would do, shit all over the best stretch of Hawks hockey that we'd ever seen, or at least in a long time.

The Hawks headed into Detroit for the first half of the double only trailing the Wings by four points in the standings. Because of the delirium from their performances over the month, a lot of us thought the Hawks could catch them by winning these two games. We had taken two losses early in the year to them, stinging losses, but now the Hawks were rearmed and retrained. This was the real team we wanted to show them.

Yeah, that didn't work either.

The Wings completely outclassed the Hawks in the first game. It was capped off by Dan Cleary railroading Patrick Kane into the boards in the first period, and it didn't really get any better than that. The first period saw Pavel Datsyuk simply pass the puck into the net on Khabibulin's short-side, as Khabby was completely screened by Tomas Holmstrom. It looked like a drill in practice to them. Franzen added another power play goal in the second, a period where the Wings piled up twenty shots. They added another two in the third. They probably could have scored ten. They were the pillow applied to smother our face.

"Ah, but wait until the Winter Classic. We got caught looking ahead to the big event." That's what we told ourselves. Maybe somewhere deep down we knew better but denial is such a comforting friend.

The whole Winter Classic experience was surreal. In some ways, Hawks fans going outside in the daylight was a cool metaphor. This was something of an unveiling for the whole city of what we had been experiencing for the past season and a half. We had been confined to the shadows, locked in a building on the west side for basically our entire fan lives. It was still something of the basement to Chicago. Now our party would be visible to all. The Hawks had the stage all to themselves. And they were going to show those who hadn't been indoctrinated yet what all the noise was about.

However, the noon start time made work somewhat tricky. I can't recall where I woke up on New Year's Day, I just know it wasn't at home. So I had to get back home and then back to Wrigley before 9:00 am. Ever try that after a New Year's Eve? The usual group of vendors I had finally assembled were all at their homes for the holidays, so I had to ask a bunch of close friends to help. Luckily, they were all going to the game anyway so it wasn't too much to ask.

Covering Wrigley though was much harder than the United Center. At the UC the gates are essentially on either side of the building, and most everyone is just coming from the east or west. Wrigley, of course, has four gates and everyone comes from everywhere. Secondly, while security and the cops had become used to my presence outside the UC, if begrudgingly, the ones at Wrigley had no idea who I was or what I was doing and had no problem punting me and other vendors all over the place. And the last thing I wanted to do was get to know the inside of a paddy wagon, not on what was supposed to be my biggest day.

I sent two cute girl friends into the bars along Clark to try to get pre-gaming fans to buy. Of course they were usually kicked out, and one of them was even refused by Billy Corgan. As if I didn't hate post-1998 Smashing Pumpkins enough (remember this, it comes back).

I headed in after a couple hours on Addison. Even a half-hour before the game started the place was already full, as everyone wanted to see what a hockey rink looked like on Wrigley's playing surface. This was an event, to be sure. I couldn't contain my feelings. I was starting chants and taunts like I was a college frat boy. First thing I saw was Jonathan Toews streaking around during warm-ups, acting like the child he still very much was. You could see that he wasn't alone in trying to take it all in.

NBC had set up some sort of card collage for the seats during the pregame ceremonies. However, on my side of Wrigley, the first-base side, once every Hawks fan realized they were holding up part of the Wings logo, they immediately tore them up and threw them away. We could only be asked so much. We all sang the Canadian national anthem at the top of our lungs, which for some reason was performed as well as the American one. We did our best to carry our anthem tradition outside, but obviously the open air makes it harder.

Finally, the game started. If you haven't been to an outdoor game, it's weird. The strangest part is the sound, or lack thereof. Inside, because it's enclosed and the PA generally mics the ice, you can hear the skates and the sticks. At Wrigley, you couldn't. It was like watching hockey on silent film, unless someone cracked a shot off the glass in front of us. Also, because of the positioning of our seats in the 200 level at Wrigley, once the play came to our half of the ice basically every player had their legs cut off from view. We could only tell what was going on by the positioning of the players. In the opening minutes of the game, Brent Seabrook pulverized Dan Cleary into the Hawks bench, some retribution for his hit on Kane in the previous game. If this had taken place in the United Center, we would have heard the crunch against the boards and maybe even a bit of his crashing into the bench. Outside, it all happened on mute. Without the sound, it took a second to compute what happened. We saw Seabrook skate into him, and then it was just Cleary's skates cartoonishly sticking up from the bench and a delayed roar of approval from the crowd.

I eagerly anticipated the roar of a Hawks goal. I wanted to know what Wrigley would sound like, what 40,000 instead of 20,000 sounded like, after a goal. We didn't have to wait too long. While on the power play, the Hawks created a scrum right in front of the Wings goal. Versteeg found the puck and simply rolled it into an open cage and past a lost Ty Conklin. At least that's what I found out later when I saw the replay. We didn't see it, it was cut off from view by the boards. We saw the scrum, and we saw Versteeg wheel away in celebration, and we heard the portion of the crowd that could see what was going on roar their approval. We joined in later. It wasn't quite like the eruption I had dreamed of. More a wave.

The Hawks were hanging in much better than they ever came close to the previous game, though some of that had to be attributed to the adrenaline of the occasion, the pretty dodgy surface and wind making smooth play a near impossibility. It looked more like rugby than hockey.

The Wings tied in six minutes later, also on the power play. Three minutes after that, the Hawks got another power play. The puck was jammed up along the boards in front of us, and then suddenly we saw Havlat approach the crease, and suddenly the puck was popping right up under the crossbar. Versteeg had somehow made a blind pass to Havlat in front, but we only got the end result. Again, a delayed reaction. With less than a minute to go, Ben Eager skated around the outside and behind the net and attempted a wrap-around. We heard him yell, and we saw him lower to one knee and pump his fist, so we just assumed he scored. He had.

The first intermission was filled with me and other Hawks fans scrambling around the concourse trying to find where to smoke. And then watching fans' disgust when the employees told us we couldn't leave the building like we could at the United Center. A group of hockey fans nic-fitting isn't exactly the most pleasant bunch. The 3-1 lead kept it pretty civil, at least. Clearly the Wrigley staff weren't used to as many grizzled fans looking for a fix all at once, as baseball didn't really train them for that.

And that's where the wave peaked and broke back. Whereas the Hawks could out-energy the Wings for a period, maybe even two, they couldn't do it for sixty minutes. The Wings also had the wind advantage in the second. What was stunning was just how hard the Wings worked, especially along the boards. They were never close to the biggest team but thanks to their legs that never stopped that never came close to mattering. As what we could see best was the work along the wall, we could see how the Wings won every race and battle. We knew about their skill and smarts, but this was what made it all so powerful. Hudler scored twice in the opening half of the period. Their legs kept churning. The Hawks' legs started to flag a bit. With three minutes to go, Datsyuk skated down on Cam Barker. He did more than turn him inside out. He turned him right-side-out after that and back again. What he did to Huet in net is best left unsaid, in case your children get a hold of this. I don't want to give them nightmares. Even though it was 4-3, it felt as if it was 10-3. While the Hawks had spent the previous month outclassing opponents, they were on the receiving end now. It was painful to see that there was another level to go, and just how hard it would be.

Maybe what made it worse is that two rows in front of me, a Wings fan who had to be in his fifties would turn around after every Wings goal and hold up four fingers, representing the number of their recent Cups. Did I feel some leg muscles tense in anticipation of leaping over the intervening row to maul him? Yeah, I did, but thankfully they didn't find too many allies in the rest of my body. Wasn't he too old for that crap? His Wings Starter jacket should have been a clue, and his Wings winter gloves another. I was in my late twenties, I could still act like a child. But this windbag? And there was nothing I could do or say. They were the standard still, and he was reveling in it. I still see him in my sleep sometimes, the image forever burned into my memory bank. Every Hawks fan has their own similar image, I'm sure.

The third brought no reprieve. The Wings scored two goals seventeen seconds apart (remember this number) early on and it was over. Huet was pulled. Mockingly, the sun began to emerge from out behind what had been a normal, grey, winter day in Chicago. Your timing sucks, Ra.

I instructed everyone who had helped sell to meet me in front of a bar at an intersection down Clark street from Wrigley. As usual I wasn't very organized, didn't have any rubber bands or anything, so they just dumped the cash they had collected into the gym bag carrying the leftover programs. To this day, one of my friends still jokes that I get paid in bags of cash. It had been worth being there, for sure. It's a day we won't forget. The day the Hawks were the center of the sporting universe. Too bad they got a foot in the ass in the spotlight.

Hoth
January 14, 2009
Sabres vs. Hawks

Ninety percent of the time, my job was and is a total blast. But Chicago winter is always around to give you perspective in violent fashion.

There's always a stretch in a Chicago winter that gets advertised ahead of time. Be it a blizzard or a cold snap (or often, both), about a week before it hits the news is rife with warnings about what is coming. So I can't say I was surprised when this night hit. Actually, yes I can. There are some points in a Chicago winter that you can't be prepared for. So let's say I kind of knew what was coming, or that I knew something I couldn't handle was coming.

The high that day was -2. Not with windchill. That was the actual temp. The windchill was somewhere in the negative twenties. I had warned the vendors for a week that if they didn't think they were up for it they didn't have to come. But I had made a promise to the readers that we would be out there every game. I thought there was some street cred to be earned, I guess. Ah, youth. My father spent the whole afternoon trying to convince me that I didn't have to go through with it. I told him he was wrong. He couldn't get angry at me for being hard-headed. I had learned that from somewhere after all, and he knew exactly where.

As the hour to leave for the arena came closer, I almost got excited. It was something of a challenge. It was like hiking up a mountain or something. Let's see if we could do this. If we could get through this night, there was no night we couldn't handle. I was going to beat the weather!

When you're gearing up for a night this cold, when you first step out into it you tell yourself it isn't that bad, no matter how bad it actually might be. You're basically expecting to turn into a popsicle the minute you get out of your car, so when you don't it feels like something of a victory. The wind hasn't made its presence known yet, so your skin still feels like it's attached to your body. The first five minutes, you're fairly sure you're the toughest human being around.

My vendors were waiting for me, and I greeted them with a huge smile. It's like we were getting ready to go play a football game we knew we were going to get slaughtered in. But hey, let's have some fun with it. It'll be a story, right? Dying is a day worth living for, and all that.

After about ten minutes, the enormity of it sank in. Or rather, drilled in right to your soul. There's being cold, and then there's this, where any exposed skin hurts immediately. You're fairly sure you could get to a point where you could snap off your fingers like twigs. Your feet feel like blocks, that is while you can still feel them. Most everyone who bought a copy expressed utter shock we were even attempting this. Some bought out of pity. Some just handed over ten dollars and told us to keep it for the fees we would need for our forthcoming stays at the hospital. One of my vendors gave up after half an hour. I couldn't stop him. My friend Adam who was helping out just kept roaming around the arena, fearing that if he stood still he would die. But it eventually ended, and I didn't die. Neither did he. I assume.

　　　　This was also the first night I experienced one of the more gross phenomena of my job. On nights this cold or close, I would usually wrap my Liverpool scarf around my face. Ever since I could grow one, I've worn a goatee or beard to conceal that fact that thanks to my father, I don't have a chin. Just a straight line from my bottom lip to my Adam's apple without any hint of a distinction or corner. So for the hour and a half I was out there and having my breath blocked by my scarf, that air had to go somewhere. I didn't know where, but I would find out.

　　　　I joined my friend Jake in my seats, and throughout the first period I couldn't help but notice liquid dripping off my face. At first I just thought I had spilled a portion of my beer, but it continued even after I'd finished that Bud. What I came to realize is that my breath had condensed on my facial hair while outside and frozen, and now that it had melted in the warmth of the inside of the arena it was dripping off of my face. It wouldn't stop. I was disgusted, and hoped no one else would notice.

　　　　At least the Hawks won.

　　　　I came home and emailed Sean Gallagher in St. Louis to see if he had any similar experiences running a similar outfit there. Of course he did. In his first year as editor of *St. Louis Gametime*, on a similar night he had fallen into a puddle and watched as his jeans basically freeze. He had two other vendors that night. He sold one program. One vendor sold another. The third quit.

　　　　So see? It's always worse in St. Louis.

Hard Hat Night
February 27, 2009
Penguins v. Hawks

　　　　The Hawks continued to rumble on through January and February, though not quite at the heights of December. The Penguins rolled in for what was a very anticipated game.

　　　　Some of the luster came off of it when Sidney Crosby got hurt a couple weeks before and wouldn't play. The Penguins didn't come to the

United Center the year before, so we were deprived of seeing our first Toews v. Crosby matchup. More luster came off when the Pens turned out to be a total mess for the first half of the season. They had tuned out their coach, Crosby was hurt, and nothing was working. Shortly before this game they had fired said coach, Michel Therrien, and hired Dan Byslma. When they arrived on Madison, they weren't even in a playoff spot.

Now, I'm not saying that I would have had the foresight to see what could go wrong with a hard hat giveaway, where 10,000 fans were given Blackhawks plastic hard hats. But it's not my job either, and I'd like to think that whoever is in that position would at least have considered the possibility of what was to follow. Then again, they had "Bat Day" at Yankee Stadium for years, so maybe I'm just naive in trying to believe the best in people.

The Penguins jumped out to a 2-0 lead in the first period, but Toews answered with one before the frame was up on the power play. He added a second, also on the power play, early in the second period to tie the game. Later in the second period, Toews appeared to tip in a point-shot for his hat trick goal.

Again, I don't want to be too harsh. But someone, you'd like to think, in the organization could have done the math of adding thousands holding plastic hard hats, and the bevy of scoring talent the Hawks boasted and concluded that it could get a little silly. But no one did. So after the puck hit twine, hard hats rained down on the ice. I can still see the look on the faces of The Ice Crew, using the shovels they would normally dig up snow as protection from the raining hard hats while they tried to pick up the ones that had already hit the ice. I would love to tell you that no one was aiming for them, but I know that's a lie. Their expressions all said something to the effect of, "They said this job was supposed to be fun!"

The thing was, the goal didn't count. Thousands of hard hats hit the ice for nothing. Toews' stick was above the crossbar when he tipped the shot, and the look on his face after he scored somewhat told the tale that he knew. The Penguins would score two late goals to take a 4-2 lead into the intermission.

There was little doubt though that Toews was going to go looking for his hat trick goal. It came on another power play with two minutes gone in the third. Cam Barker found him with a cross-ice pass, and everyone could see that Penguins goalie Marc-Andre Fleury hadn't gotten over and Toews had a whole net. Hard-hats were in the air before the puck was even off Toews's stick. And there were more than the first time? Where were they coming from? Did people run down to get theirs back after throwing it on the false alarm just to throw it a second time? Did they hand them back?

Strangely, I don't recall the Hawks ever doing a hard hat giveaway again. I wonder why.

The Marty Renaissance
March 3, 2009
Ducks vs. Hawks

An OT win, and an OT goal that saw Martin Havlat completely scorch Ryan Getzlaf to score. How does it get any better?

This marked just about the most brilliant stretch Havlat put together as a Hawk. It was even better than the first bank of games he had in his first season, because it meant something. Toews and Kane were hitting something of a wall, and Havlat was picking up all the slack. This was the exclamation point to a nine-game point-streak that saw him net fifteen points. He was the Hawks best player by a mile during this time, and really the rest of the season.

It was validation for those of us who never stopped having affection for him. After all, he was the only light in a very dark ocean merely a couple seasons before this. Because he was the team's best player, he bore something of the wrath of fans when it all went sideways. He was called soft because he was often injured in his first two years. He was accused of not caring. Some thought he was playing in a strop because Toews, Kane, and Sharp had become bigger stars and he was no longer the focus. Others thought he was just playing for his next contract, heading into free agency as he was.

That was all bullshit of course. He was finally healthy and he was finally playing with players who could hang with him offensively. He was still just about the fastest skater the Hawks had, and one of the few who could create his own shot out of nothing. He could still bring you to your feet like few others, just like he did on that night to end the game. He had started the season slowly, until Q put him on a line with Ladd and Bolland. Things just took off from there.

Sadly, this was probably as good as it ever got for Marty. His career never hit these heights again. There were flashes, but his body always let him down. But we'll always have his first few games as a Hawk, and we'll have this brilliant stretch when he was one of the best players in the NHL. If nothing else, he was a great transition from the dark days into the light and watching him flourish in both.

The Doldrums And Fuckwit 319
March 15, 2009
Islanders vs. Hawks

What Hawks fans hadn't dealt with in a long time was a losing streak that actually felt like it was costing the team something. We'd seen losing streaks of course, more of them than perhaps any other fandom. But they didn't *matter*. Those seasons had no stakes. It just meant they were more adrift than they already were. When the pile of losses reaches the sky, you don't really care if it gets there in spurts or in a consistent drip. Thus we dubbed them the "March doldrums." It cratered with this afternoon tilt against the afterthought Islanders.

The Hawks surrendered three first-period goals to the Isles. They were eventually down 4-1 after a Mark Streit goal nearly halfway through the third. Kane would manage a goal with two minutes left but the Hawks were never really close. They threw twenty-eight shots in the final two periods at Peter Mannino, but couldn't break him down.

Wait, who? That's what you're asking, right? Yes, Peter Mannino. It was one of two starts he ever made in the NHL. He made forty saves against the most up-and-coming team in the NHL. In any other setting, it would have been a story I would have loved. But not when it happened here, not when I was coughing up a Sunday afternoon for this. It really couldn't be more perfect. If you were writing a story about a man who gets one NHL win in a miraculous performance, you might name that character Peter Mannino. That's central casting right there. You know things aren't going your way when a goalie that sounds either A) made up, B) was probably working security outside on Madison the previous night, or C) both, is stonewalling your team.

If nothing else, it was a callback to the bad old days that still weren't all that far in the rearview. How many times did we sit in the United Center and watch some jamoke get his first career shutout or first multi-goal game? How many sad-ass teams like the Islanders came in to get a win they couldn't get much of anywhere else over the past decade? How many times were the Hawks one of the few sparks of light for a team also spending most its time in the woods and in darkness?

Of course, not everyone I saw it that way. When I dreamed of being a season ticket holder, I only thought of the friendships and camaraderie I would feel with those I sat near every game. I didn't consider that someone close by would be the opposite of that, and represent pretty much everything I abhor about Hawks and hockey fans in general.

I didn't really notice him for the first few games. But then I couldn't help but hear all the dumb shit he would yell during games from the section one over from mine. It was usually something to do with hitting someone or fighting. Let me put it this way, the jerseys I've seen this guy wear (and keep in mind he's at least in his fifties): Grimson, Carcillo, Bollig, Scott, Magnuson (and probably not because Maggy was a really good guy). That's just a sampling. You can imagine my heartbreak when he showed up in a Cubs jacket after an Opening Day game at Wrigley. I didn't want him in any associated group of mine. It was as if he thought he constantly had to remind everyone around him that there was a time when he was really tough or something. You can't miss him now. It only took my brother a couple games in our seats to dub him, "Fuckwit 319." That moniker has stuck ever since, and he's been a fixture as well. I've frequently told him to shut up whenever he shouts one of his nonsensical hockey hypotheses. I'm hardly alone. On the few occasions he's decided to respond to the ever-growing ocean of voices that would prefer his larynx fall out, it's the usual claim that the money he pays earns him the right to yell whatever he wants however loudly he wants. Our enjoyment never comes into consideration, of course. That's what happens when you think you're a poet laureate. At least I had the decency to keep my raving lunacy to written form where it only bothers the reader.

I didn't really know that a fourth loss in five games was call for major changes. Silly me. Anyway, as time ran out he yelled out, "FIRE TALLON!!" I couldn't tell you why. Perhaps the pickup of Sami Pahlsson and the deadline didn't satiate his bloodlust (though I guess blood being a liquid you would "slake" bloodlust). Maybe the removal of James Wisniewski from the roster made him feel like less of a man. I don't really want to think about it too much. But there's always one, and we have ours.

So long, JR
March 25, 2009
Sharks vs. Hawks

The Hawks ended up losing seven of eight games in this stretch, sending most fans into an utter panic. Again, it had been so long since things mattered that it felt like it might be slipping away. Our fantasies were starting to darken. And for the newer fans who weren't accustomed to the length and rhythms of an NHL season, they were even worse. They didn't know that it could be easily salvaged.

They pulled out of it with a win over the Kings, just in time for a visit from the still conference-leading Sharks. The clamor over the Hawks' streak kind of overshadowed that it was likely to be Jeremy Roenick's last regular season game in Chicago. As it turned out, it was his last game in Chicago at all.

The Hawks and Sharks played yet another classic, as they always did during those years. The Hawks blew 4-1 and 5-3 leads, with Joe Thornton finishing off the comeback with two minutes to go. It was played at an incredible pace. There were chances galore, and it moved to a shootout.

Kane and Toews both scored, and Roenick was the second shooter for the Sharks and had to score to extend it. He was only in that position because of some injuries the Sharks had. I can't remember a more confused reaction from a Hawks crowd then when Roenick came out to take it.

Again, there wasn't much build-up to this being Roenick's last game here. The Hawks had bigger issues at work. He had already retired once, though immediately took the Sharks offer to extend his career. It had been over ten years since he had been a Hawk. How many in the building remembered? It wasn't official, but when he hopped over the boards there was a sense from those of us who did remember that this would be the last act of his we would see live. We were caught off-guard as it was sort of rushed upon us. We didn't know we'd get a singular moment like this.

There is a natural tendency to boo former players, but Roenick never warranted that. Some did out of reflex, but most of it was half-hearted. They were drowned out by those just cheering. Did we want him to score? Some of us did. We didn't want to see JR's last act on Madison St. be one of failure. But the Hawks needed the win, too. They were trying to climb out of the small hole they had dug during their doldrums.

There hadn't been a pregame ceremony or anything, because Roenick hadn't officially announced this was his last season. But we knew. His contract was up, he was thirty-nine, and he was basically playing on the fourth line in San Jose. This wasn't how we would have wanted to say goodbye. But here it was.

He didn't score, and while the fans cheered a win, it was a bit sheepish. This wasn't the sendoff that Roenick deserved. This was his last performance. I walked out somewhat deflated. I hoped the Hawks and Sharks would see each other in the playoffs. Maybe just one more time, so we could get Roenick's final goodbye right. He was still one of the biggest reasons I became the fan that I was. I almost wanted to run down and thank him. I even thought because McDonough was always interested in giving the people what they wanted, the Hawks might even sign him to a one-year deal. Or maybe I hoped. But I knew the truth.

It was symbolic, that he was in some ways an afterthought for a good portion of the crowd as we focused on this era of Hawks hockey. He harkened back to a different time. And with all that had gone on, that era was now buried. I guess he didn't apply in the same way anymore. But to a lot of us, we recognized the significance when he hopped over the boards that one last time. If this season was about turning pages and filing things to the past, this one was just one more. But it was one of the more painful.

A Rivalry Born
March 29, 2009
Canucks vs. Hawks

Thanks to the blip the Hawks suffered through in the first half of March, the stranglehold they had on the fourth seed in the West suddenly became tenuous. The Vancouver Canucks, who had floundered through most of the season, were suddenly charging. They'd won ten of fourteen and came into this one just two points behind the Hawks. Suddenly hosting Game One of the playoffs, which we had been dreaming of and has just assumed was the Hawks' destiny, was looking very much in jeopardy.

It was the first game I had gone to that felt like it had actual stakes.

Sure, the Hawks had played some other "big" games that season and the one before. Any game with the Sharks or Wings were "big" because they were the other contenders in the West. That game with the Flyers felt "big," but that had to do with the time of year and opponent and not really what they were playing for. There was obviously the Winter Classic, but that was more event than stakes. This one had a direct impact on the standings of both teams. The air was certainly charged.

And the Hawks got stomped.

The Canucks played just about the best defensive game the Hawks had seen that year, smothering their forwards and leaving the d-men no space. Luongo barely had to do anything in net. The Canucks only led 2-0 heading into the third, but it felt like much more. It was impressive.

Of course, that's not what anyone remembers from this game. Shortly after Shooty Twin (Daniel Sedin) made the score 3-0 and essentially ended the debate, Dustin Byfuglien crashed into Luongo. He may or may not have punched him, I've never been sure. The Canucks were, and it torched a full-out brawl. We hadn't seen anything like it in years, with all ten skaters participating. It also included Alex Burrows, gentleman that he always is, pulling Duncan Keith's hair when Keith started to pummel him. With unhinged jackasses like Kevin Bieksa and Shane O'Brien on the ice at the same time, the kindling was always there.

Suddenly, the Hawks had a new rival, and their most bitter. All it took was one ass-kicking in a game the Hawks really wanted, and one big brawl and suddenly Canucks-Hawks games weren't the same for years. This is what the NHL has always misunderstood about trying to create "rivalries." They happen organically. Sure, there are traditional ones due to history and geography, like Montreal-Boston or Chicago-Detroit. But there aren't those for every team. Los Angeles-Anaheim will take decades to have that heat. Florida-Tampa Bay will probably never. Some of these things take circumstances on the ice. The most heated rivalry in the league before this one was probably Colorado-Detroit. They weren't geographically close. They had only been in the same conference for less than a season when they played a classic conference final that set them trying to one-up each other for nearly a decade. Hawks-Canucks was now on that path.

Before this night, Hawks fans didn't think much about the Canucks. They played on the coast late at night. They were in the other division. They hadn't been a playoff opponent in fourteen years. But after seeing Burrows trying to turn Keith into a hair donor and Bieksa chasing anyone that was much smaller than him, Hawks fans had a public enemy #1. We paid attention to every one of their results. We geared ourselves for a playoff series against them. Things weren't the same.

Suddenly, when the playoff matchups were set a couple weeks later, it wasn't just Hawks and Canucks fans eyeing the possible matchup. It was hockey fans everywhere. It doesn't take much to start a raging fire. That's what Smokey has been trying to tell us all for years.

Back Where We Belong
April 16, 2009
Flames vs. Hawks (Game One)
 The Hawks closed out the season winning six of seven games, including the last two of the season over Detroit. In the end, that loss to the Canucks didn't end up mattering, as they caught Calgary in their division and the Flames fell behind the Hawks, so the Hawks would host Game One of the first round after all.

 The three days before the first playoff game, I could barely sit still. I must've written the program for that game in about twelve minutes. It was the program I had dreamed of writing when I had the idea to do it in the first place. I was going to get to do this for Hawks playoff games! What an honor. *The Blue Line* had wrapped up operations before the last Hawks' playoff appearance. It almost felt like stealing. I went back to that program, to see what I wrote in my editorial, and it was a quote borrowed from *St. Louis Gametime:*

> *"This game, this date with destiny for the Hawks, is for you and me. It's for the season-ticket holders who kept the faith through the lockout, the dismantling of the team, and the non-playoff years. It's for people who showed up on Tuesday nights vs. Columbus for three years. It's for people who braved the ice storms on game nights since the lockout. You diehards, you knew who was here when we were finishing last. You know who you are. This game, this night, the Hawks make a triumphant return to the playoffs, it's for us. Bill Wirtz can't take it away. It can't get traded to Phoenix. It can't blow out its knee. When the team takes the ice, roar. Scream. Yell your bloody head off. You've earned it."*

 That's what it felt like. We were finally out of dungeon, never to return. We had sat through so many lost nights, so many shitty power plays, so many blowouts, so many bad goals, and then slogged back into Chicago winter nights for this. A night the arena would rock on Madison like it had across the street.

 And yet, I guess I wasn't the people I wrote about. I didn't have season tickets through the long march into nothingness, and probably wouldn't have either if I wasn't the normal, broke, just-out-of-college pisshead. I turned off on the team. I didn't sit through those Tuesday nights against Columbus that were exercises in Nihilism, at least not a ton of them. I was an ex-pat who then repatriated. There was only so much I could take.

Everything about it is still something of a blur. First off, my usual route to the arena was altered, because they cut off Madison to traffic. So I was late to my spot as I had to wrap around to where I normally parked. Second, I almost got arrested.

To be clear, what I was doing was completely legal. Because the program was a written newsletter or publication, you don't actually need a license to sell it outside the arena as long as you're not on their property. Within six feet of the curb is considered the public way. That doesn't mean certain security guards or cops were aware of that, and there's nothing a cop loves more than someone who knows the law better than they do. Remember when you were younger, or possibly later, and you dealt with a real hard-on of a cop and he reacted to everything you said to him like it's the dumbest thing he ever heard, even if you were right? Yeah, I saw that a lot that season, but never really had any trouble.

About five minutes after getting to my normal spot and dispersing my other vendors, I was approached by a guy who was actually running operations in the parking lot across the street. He told me I had to move or I would be arrested. I explained to him I had been selling the program from this very spot every game the entire season with no issues. He said this was the playoffs so rules were different. I told him I was fairly sure that "playoff hockey" didn't alter the laws of the city. He gave me one last warning that he was going to have me arrested if I didn't move. I tried to assure him that I wasn't doing anything wrong and everyone in the building was aware of me.

He called for a police car to come take me away. I was somewhat terrified. Though some conversations or arguments with security and police took a little while to be resolved, I hadn't ever had a cop car called for. Not even close. This was my biggest night to date, and I was going to spend it with a new pair of bracelets?

Thankfully, he didn't really get an answer over the radio and went to look for one. I'm fairly sure whoever he talked to told him to get a fucking life and leave me alone, because he walked to a point across the street from me and motioned that all I had to do was move about ten feet to my left. I guess he had to save some face.

We sold every copy with about half an hour to go until puck drop. For the first time I had underestimated demand. Eh, can't win 'em all. The atmosphere outside was incredible. Everyone was smiling, which as you know amongst a group of hockey fans is a true rarity. People were starting chants outside. It was almost as if I wasn't the only one who couldn't believe it. It was a hockey amusement park.

The anthem was electric. You'll recall that a couple weeks before this, the Bears had acquired Jay Cutler, and at the time we all thought he was a savior. Well, the Hawks had him drop the ceremonial puck and the fans in the 300 Level were so charged up they were belting out the lyrics to "Bear Down Chicago Bears" along with Frank Pelico's organ, and for a good few minutes afterwards. Before the actual opening faceoff was as loud a roar as I'd heard for some goals. We had finally arrived.

The last time I saw a playoff game, I was a child. Now I was...well, a bigger child. But I was more invested this time, obviously. So I didn't remember the tension that comes with playoff hockey. Everything's volume gets turned up. The hits are a little harder, the saves a little bigger, and everything is met with greater reaction from the crowd. And your heart-rate...well, it's probably not healthy to watch your team in the playoffs, at least when you're inexperienced. Everything is sharper.

While we were practically frothing at the mouth, the Hawks definitely came out nervous. They were hesitant, and far from crisp. They were outshot 10-5 in that first period. Halfway through the period, David Moss scored off a scramble in front of Khabibulin's net. I'd have to say the reaction of the crowd was mostly confusion. This wasn't in the script. We had waited so long, we were so juiced before the game that we just assumed it would carry over to the Hawks themselves and they would simply roll over the Flames. This didn't follow.

As the second period developed, the Hawks found their feet more and more. They were creating far more chances and showing how much faster they were. Little more than halfway through the period, Cam Barker caught Mikka Kiprusoff leaning the wrong way and snuck a wrister from the boards by him. The building exhaled more than roared. Now we were back on script.

Not so fast. Early in the third the Hawks got caught on a bad pinch and Mike Cammalleri and Daymond Langkow were released on a two-on-one. Cammalleri made no mistake with a one-timer off Langkow's pass, and suddenly the Hawks were trailing in the third. Again, didn't anyone show the Flames the script we had all written in our heads?

The Hawks pushed and pushed, and with about five minutes left Havlat, just about the most experienced player the Hawks had when it came to the playoffs, picked up a turnover in the corner and curled toward the net. His first shot was saved, but the rebound was not. The Hawks swarmed after that. Shortly after came a TV timeout to give the Flames something of a reprieve, but the United Center crowd didn't notice. We stood and screamed all the way through it, responding to the surge the Hawks had just put forth. I wonder if that will happen ever again. There were no "GET LOUD" graphics on the video screens. There was no exhortation from anyone. It was raucous. There could only be one result after this, surely.

The Flames survived into overtime, but only barely. I was something of wreck before overtime. My first playoff game that I'd even seen in twelve years and I was going right in the deep end? This wasn't fair.

Thankfully, the Hawks didn't put me through much of it. Because as the puck dropped, I really wondered if I had what it took to get through it. The last time I saw a playoff overtime live, the Hawks organization died. Right off the opening draw, Bolland picked off an Eric Nystrom pass. He entered the Flames zone with Andrew Ladd steaming toward the net. Havlat trailed Bolland and demanded the puck. Bolland obliged, and Havlat had the easy task of shooting through a Ladd screen past Kiprusoff. Easy for him, at least.

I lost control of my limbs. I simply mauled the guy sitting to my right, who wasn't anyone I knew. The place was chaos. It took all of twelve seconds. I ran through the concourse just screaming "MARTY!!!!" For what would be far from the first time, I leapt on my brother's back in excitement (he had come back from New York for Games One And Two. He wasn't going to miss this). I was six years old again.

The funny addendum to this story is that I and my two blog cohorts, Matthew Killion and Matt McClure, were asked to do a radio show on a talk radio station in the burbs after the game. Playoff hockey tension drinking does not lend itself easily to driving to the suburbs from the United Center, but we managed (though I had to drive McClure's car). While waiting in the production studio, the show's producer didn't exactly have to decode a puzzle to see we'd had a couple at the game. She went down the line, first asking Killion how many he'd at the game. "Three." Then to me. "Four." Then to McClure. His answer didn't come immediately, which already gave it away. He was adding it up in his head. Finally, not before Killion and I could bury our faces in our hands to conceal our laughter and embarrassment, came his unsure response. "Eleven?" We might as well have told her we were aliens, such was the shocked expression on her face. She declared there was no way Matt was going on air. He somehow did, and I don't think we made a fool of ourselves either.

At least that's how I choose to remember it.

The Hawks would take Game Two, but fail on their first two tries to win a playoff game on the road. Game Five would be the first unveiling of "You're Not Fucking Winning This Game, You're Not Fucking Winning This Series" mode, as the Hawks blew out the Flames, and carried that over to the next, the clincher. There was just a gear they would hit in the playoffs where you knew they couldn't be beat. We just didn't know how many times we would see it then.

The Crazy Train
May 11, 2009
Canucks vs. Hawks (Game Six)

I'd be lying if I told you I expected anything out of this series when it started. Was I settling? Maybe. But considering where the Hawks had come from, a 104-point season with a first playoff series win in thirteen years certainly felt like a hell of a stepping stone. The problem was it was the Canucks lying in wait, so settling for a defeat to them wasn't going to lie peacefully. While they had missed the playoffs the year before as well, they had been in the playoffs the year before that and it at least felt like they had more pedigree than the Hawks. On paper, maybe it just felt like it wasn't quite the Hawks' time yet. It had all come too fast.

The series swung from one pole of emotion to the other, sometimes by period. The Hawks came back from multiple goal deficits in both Games One and Two. They lost the first in the last minute, but won the second, taking us from happy to be there to thinking they could actually win the series. That lasted one game, as Luongo was brilliant in a Game Three win. And just about the time it was feeling like it was slipping away, Havlat came up with a late equalizer in Game Four and Ladd won it in OT, causing me to nearly throw my friend Ashely into the press box above me.

Game Five set up as the biggest game for the Hawks organization in over a decade. This was their sternest test, a best-of-three series now with two games on the road if required. Game Five showed just how much testicular fortitude the Hawks had. Byfuglien opened the scoring, only to be pegged back by Ryan Kesler two minutes later. The second period once again saw the Hawks impose themselves on the Canucks, but they once again sucker-punched their way to a lead through grinning doofus Mats Sundin. However, Byfuglien found the net again on the power play with less than two minutes to go in the period.

Playoff hockey can be such torture. Though the Hawks had been the better team, though they were creating more chances, though they had kept the Canucks shots and chances to a minimum, heading into a third period tied you know that it only takes one moment, one slip, one bounce. You can do everything right, but it can all be undone by a strange confluence of events that sees some hopeless shot hit something on its path to nowhere important and into the net. A bad call from a ref can undo all your work. A rough piece of ice causing the puck to bounce over a stick and onto someone else's. You know all this, and you have to watch anyway. You are not promised justice.

The Hawks were all over the Canucks again, but couldn't find a breakthrough. The minutes ticked off, and with each one that disappeared into the ether the margin of error disappointed. Now you knew that any slip would leave not nearly enough time to make up for it. Every moment got more and more decisive.

With less than seven minutes to go, bullhorn and embodiment of a beer fart Kevin Bieksa took a needless high-sticking penalty. This was the chance. At the very end of the power play, Kane somehow kept a clearance in at the line. He had no business doing so. He shoveled the puck over to Keith whose shot was saved and Kane collected the puck at the right circle. He waited and waited, slowly closing in on the net. Unbeknownst to the

Canucks, Bolland had circled behind the net and to the other circle. We could see it on TV, but they couldn't. When Kane slid the puck over to him, we could see he had the whole net open, Kane having sucked Luongo out to deal with the shot he was sure was coming. All of us at the bar leaned forward on top of each other. It went into slow-motion. If I could have reached through the screen and shifted the puck to the net, I would have. It felt like five minutes. Just collect it and deposit it, Dave. Why isn't it there yet? Was it this easy? Bolland made sure that it was, and I nearly hit my head on the ceiling fan at the bar celebrating. Havlat would go on to add an empty-netter.

In the span of a few days, I had gone from merely being happy that the Hawks were still playing to now expecting a Western Conference Final berth. The Hawks had leaned and leaned on the Canucks for the past two games, and it felt like they had taken their will. They were returning home for what felt assuredly like an easy clincher. How could the Canucks get off the mat? It all lined up. The Canucks were merely a prop at this point.

Silly rabbit.

I took my seat, sure I was going to see the guillotine come down on a Canucks team I had come to detest. That's what happens in a long playoff series. Seeing the same guys for five or six games breeds contempt. You just want to see different people. The Canucks came out with the desperation you'd expect of a team facing the end. They took the lead halfway through, confusing the United Center. Didn't you know your role, Vancouver? We were assured two minutes later when Kane streaked down the right wing on a two-on-one and easily beat Luongo to the blocker.

Everything was going to plan in the second. Versteeg and Toews gave the Hawks a 3-1 lead halfway through, and we felt the train was back on the tracks. Only thirty minutes from handshakes, as the Canucks would assuredly just fold from here. They had to be out of ideas. Routine as it gets, I thought.

Not so much. Shooty Twin and Shane "Here, Drink This" O'Brien scored three minutes apart to send us to the intermission tied. Again, I felt cheated as the script in my head was not being paid proper attention. I just wanted to keep pointing to it until everything followed correctly.

It got worse before it got better. Mats Sundin scored for the second straight game, after being a myth for the entire playoffs before. I can still see that dumbass grin on his face as he had his arms outstretched. Were they going to take it all away from us? No, because less than two minutes later Adam Burish, of all people, found a rebound in the slot and slammed it home, and then made sure he celebrated right in front of the Canucks bench.

We still weren't close to done. Brouwer got called for goalie-interference, and it only took Shooty Twin mere seconds to dance through two Hawks to rifle one home from the slot. We had gone from terror to relief to terror again in the span of about seven minutes. The ride was far from over. Somehow, Sami Salo and Willie Mitchell completely whiffed on a ring around, and the puck found Kane behind the net. Luongo, still under the impression that Mitchell and Salo were competent, was unprepared for the puck to come out the other side and Kane easily beat him to the other post. We were tied again, and I was about ready to pass out.

Forty-nine seconds later, with O'Brien in the box, Toews attempted to center for Sharp but the puck bounced off Alex Edler and behind Luongo. Three goals in less than two minutes, swinging us from the panic of having missed a series-clincher to in the lead. Three minutes later, it was over and Kane had his first signature moment.

He picked up the puck at center ice, and moved into the Canucks zone, cutting across from left to right just inside the line. He let loose a backhand that probably had no business going in from there. But it did.

For those entire playoffs, I had been wearing a Hawks hat that had been a giveaway at a previous game. I wore it waiting for this moment. I tore it off my head, made sure to get a good flick of the wrist upon release so that it would hold its line, and watched it sail over the ledge of the 300 Level. It was the first and only time I had thrown a hat. I then hugged anyone within distance, including people two rows in front of me. I watched Kane streak back into his own zone to leap into Campbell's arms.

I could barely catch my breath. The Hawks had broken Luongo, for years after. They had gone further than we ever thought they could. Every time they looked like they had blown it, they simply laughed and came up with a tying goal merely minutes later. Just like in Game Five against Calgary, they had found the "You're not fucking winning this game, you're not fucking winning this series" mode. The Canucks were helpless. And they were done.

I drove back to my local bar, where it's still something of legend the way I jumped into compatriot McClure's arms. Suddenly, it wasn't ridiculous to think the Hawks were a Cup contender. They were in the final four. Only really good teams got there, right? It was the stuff of fantasy.

Of course, all that was in the way was Scum.

A Bridge Too Far
May 22, 2009
Red Wings vs. Hawks (Game Three)

Even though the series with Vancouver had only gone one game less than the minimum, there was still a huge break before the Conference Final began as the Wings went the distance with Anaheim. That time frame had allowed our euphoria to dissipate. The reality of playing the defending champs, the benchmark team of the league, and the team that had been supplying our nightmares landed with the force of champagne hangover while living next to a construction site. It seemed like it was too big of an ask. We talked big, we tried to convince ourselves, but deep down in places we didn't talk about at parties, we knew the truth.

Game One revealed this. Though the Hawks were able to tie the game early in the third period, they were a step behind the Wings all game. They gave up forty-three shots. It's sobering to see the finished article right in front of you, and having it do just about everything you do better.

Game One's aftermath saw perhaps my lowest moment as a writer. In a postgame wrap on the blog I referred to Jiri Hudler as "Faggy McFagFag." I was still at an age where I thought it was ok to use that word as long as it wasn't directed at a gay person. That it was something you could use amongst your friends. Obviously, I couldn't have been more wrong. I'm still embarrassed by it. I was rightly called out for it by our readers and my co-writers. We can't run from our mistakes and who we used to be, and we shouldn't be afraid to as long as we keep striving to be better. But needless to say it didn't help ratchet down the enmity between fans of our blog and the visitors from Wings blogs. I'm lucky I wasn't fired from the network we were on, and had I done it a few years later I almost certainly would have been. Timing is everything, even when you're being a homophobic puke.

Game Two was worse in some ways, only because the Hawks played much more evenly with Detroit. They came out flying, Toews opened the scoring and though the Wings took the lead again, Toews tied the game in the third. The captain wasn't afraid, wasn't shying from the stage. But early in overtime Brian Campbell turned the puck over at the Detroit blue line, leading to a 3-on-1 rush the other way that Hjalmarsson wasn't going to be able to do anything about. Mikael Samuelsson slammed it home like it was Sonics-era Shawn Kemp on an alley-oop. The bar we watched from had a fair few Wings fans in there, still the bandwagon team and always eager to exhibit the superiority they glommed onto because of it. A brawl probably wasn't all that far away. But we were too deflated. The Hawks had definitely thrown their best punch, and it wasn't enough.

We headed to Game Three on the West side, and all I really wanted was for the Hawks to make one last stand. I knew they weren't going to win the series. But I wanted one last game that I'd remember fondly. And I got it.

The Hawks stormed out of the gate, leaving nothing in the tank. They went up 2-0 on two power play goals a minute apart from Sharp and Ladd. Late in the period they had a chance to end the game in reality. It's just a shame that Havlat nearly had to be decapitated to get it.

He got Kronwall'd. A puck rang around the boards in the Hawks zone to the right boards. Havlat was looking down to pick it off the boards, which is the only invitation Kronwall ever needed. He completely trucked him, laying Havlat out with his eyes rolling in the back of his head. Margaret, who had become Marty-smitten and hockey-smitten only two seasons before, clutched my arm like a scared child. Was he dead? We couldn't be sure.

The Hawks got a five-minute power play out of it. They didn't score. We knew what was coming.

Didn't take long. The Hawks had punched themselves out in the first. Even though Sami Pahlsson gave them a 3-0 lead less than a minute into the second, there was great trepidation in the building. It only took the Wings five minutes to find three goals. Like the classy and done-it-all team they were, the Wings had simply ridden out the storm and asserted themselves. Even worse, Khabibulin had gotten hurt and Huet had to finish out the game. He hadn't played in a couple months. He had lost the job to Khabby. I watched the third basically through my fingers. At some points I just wanted the Wings to score, the axe to fall, to put me out of my misery. Belief was only pain. Take me, darkness.

Somehow, the Hawks survived the third. It was a reprieve. Early in overtime, Pahlsson had the puck in a scramble in front but saw Sharp streaking in from the left point across the slot. He backhanded a pass to him, and Sharp didn't miss. The place was up for grabs.

Did I think the series had changed? No, I didn't. But we had one moment. One game where we showed them what we could do.

Of course, the Hawks went on to embarrass themselves in Game Four. They lost 6-1, and the third was filled with petulant and selfish penalties. Even Joel Quenneville lost his mind, berating the refs from the bench for the whole third. He blamed them after the game, even though the Hawks had lost by five. He called one penalty "the worst call in the history of sports." Meanwhile Detroit chuckled to themselves, acted professionally, and just took the win that was on offer. The difference could not have been more clear.

They embarrassed themselves in other ways. Somehow. Havlat started the game. Two days after being completely knocked cold. The tradition of how the Hawks handled head injuries feels like it started here. There was no way Havlat should have played, and he wandered around in a daze. It turned out to be his last game as a Hawk, and it was a deplorable way to be one. I don't doubt his competitive spirit, but someone is supposed to protect the players from themselves. This wouldn't be the last time the Hawks would mistreat brain injuries. Quenneville later, half-heartedly, tried to claim that it was a different injury that kept him out of Game Five and had him questionable for Game Four. Maybe he was trying to make it seem like he and the training staff weren't completely, tone-deaf monsters. I wasn't buying it.

Making Game Four worse was that I didn't have a program to sell. Whatever equipment the print-house I went through was using had a malfunction, and the game being on a Sunday there was no one to call. My last issue of my first season, and the only people who saw it were me and my imaginary friends.

The Hawks fought valiantly in Game Five. They went down in the third but tied the game late. I watched at home, alone, for the first playoff game in a while. I couldn't be out in public to watch it all end. I wanted to go through it on my own. The Hawks had chances in overtime, though they shouldn't have even gotten there. Franzen had a chance to end it with less than ten seconds left in the third, staring at a completely open net. Somehow, Huet flicked up a skate to divert his shot. But after four minutes of ridiculously furious action, those fucking Joe Louis Arena boards spit out a shot right to Darren Helm on the opposite side of the net from Huet, and he couldn't get there fast enough. It was over in a second.

McClure tells a story that later, out front of the bar I would have been watching from had I felt I could be trusted to be amongst people, a girl took a header off her bike. The ambulance that came was marked #43, the same as Helm. He couldn't not remark on the indignity of that, whatever condition the girl may have been in.

Every Hawks fan wanted the next training camp to start the next day. The season had been such a joyride, it was hard to take it ending in such a way. We knew what was coming. After the initial pain, there was only anticipation. Training camp was three and a half months away. It felt like years. I couldn't really fathom going that long without watching or writing about the Hawks. It was just too exciting.

The First
August 9, 2009

We laughed it off at the time. It seemed too silly. We probably should have taken it more seriously.

Hockey summers hit their nadir in August. The draft is well over. Free agency has died down, with only scraps left. Training camp is still too far away to worry about. Basically, this is when everything goes dark, turns off, and we all worry about something else for a time.

So because of how dim the news stream is, Patrick Kane getting arrested for beating up a cab driver late one night doesn't really register the way it would in January. It's something of a footnote, a comedic outlier. Baseball season is entering its pennant chase phase, football preseason has begun, hockey couldn't be more in the background.

It seemed too stupid to be real. He beat up a cab driver over twenty cents? Everyone was in a hurry to dismiss it as a drunken mistake by a kid. I did too. But there was a little nag inside of me as we did, tiny enough to ignore. Because I had been twenty or twenty-one before. I drank a lot then, and it wasn't even that long ago. Did I ever come close to this? Of course not. Did anyone I know? Maybe one or two and because they had that potential I didn't hang out with them regularly. What kind of madmen, even on The Creature, does this?

There were other questions we should have been asking. The stories of Kane's nights out in Chicago were already starting to bleed into the gossip back channels. They weren't the legendary myths they would become, but there were whispers and secrets. If anyone had taken the time to really put it together, we could have seen it was all going to be a problem.

But no one wanted to. He was the floppy-haired kid who was obscenely talented. We just wanted it to go away so we could get back to dreaming of the season to come, one which would not have the ending we wanted without him. Maybe we could have headed more off at the pass.

The Hawks made him do the press conference thing. He looked apologetic and embarrassed, even if he was just playing a role set out before him. That was enough. It shouldn't have been.

We should have been asking what if it had been Derrick Rose who was gotten doing that? Or really any black athlete? Would Chicago fans have been so quick to forgive? Even at that young age, wasn't this the mark of someone out of control? Who wouldn't listen? With no punishment, why would he?

Less than a year later, Kane went on to reference the incident during the parade. It was all a joke to him. Something he was laughing about in the same way we did when it happened. It didn't matter to him. It didn't matter to us. He knew he had gotten away scot-free. No one would ever reference it again. Not anyone who mattered, anyway. And we let it slide. It was cute. It was funny. We had won the Cup. That's all that mattered, right?

Sometimes I wonder what we helped set the stage for.

Summertime Rolls, And A Marker
October 12, 2009
Flames vs. Hawks

The summer of 2009 was about the most anticipated in Hawks history. And it didn't disappoint. After the steps taken in the previous season, the Hawks were installed as favorites to win it all almost immediately. I couldn't remember a time when the Hawks were preseason favorites, or when all eyes of the hockey world were on them before a season ever started. To say this raised the tension and stakes would be undercutting it by some margin.

It didn't get off to the best start. Before free agency, the GM Dale Tallon somehow didn't extend contract offers to all of the Hawks restricted free agents by the deadline to keep them restricted, causing all of them to be unrestricted free agents. Without going into a bunch of legalese, the collective-bargaining agreement stated that all free agents must receive a qualifying offer by a certain date. They can either accept, which they almost never do, or reject it but then the team has the right to match any offer they get from another team. It helps keep the price down on younger players, essentially, because teams in the NHL simply don't extend offer sheets to restricted free agents. Now Troy Brouwer, Kris Versteeg, Ben Eager, Cam Barker, Colin Fraser and Aaron Johnson were free to get offers from anywhere without any restriction. How much money this ended up costing the Hawks against the cap is hard to tell, but we can safely say it didn't help. Because of the added money, a greater urgency descended upon the upcoming season because it was obvious that the Hawks were not going to be able to keep this team together, as Jonathan Toews, Patrick Kane, and Duncan Keith were getting massive raises.

It stank from the start. While Tallon was the GM and took responsibility, there is simply no way that he was personally faxing or putting the offers into envelopes to send to the respective agents of the players. Much like Savard, the new regime had inherited Tallon as GM and it wasn't a huge leap to think they wanted their own guy to streamline everything. And it just so happened that their trusty advisor, Scotty Bowman, was the father of the assistant GM, Stan, who would have been more in touch with the physical offering of the contracts. The smell test was failed spectacularly. Tallon would pay with his job on July fourteenth.

It was unceremonious and it was underhanded, at least a lot of us thought so. Tallon had been the one to pivot the team out of their caveman ways to adjust to the new NHL and now flourish in it, though to be fair he helped put them there in the first place. It colored things a bit differently for a while.

When all of this was suggested by Josh Mora, the Hawks reporter on the local Comcast sports network (and a close family friend for full disclosure), he was fired by the network. The Hawks said they didn't have anything to do with it, but seeing as they owned a portion of the channel, once again things smelled funny. It was the first clue that not everything was rainbows and smiles in the Hawks front office.

Tallon was still in charge for the draft and the opening of free agency, and he and the rest of the team still had a taste for a big splash. The drama first centered around Havlat, who was an unrestricted free agent and whose play the previous year had most Hawks fans clamoring for his return. Tallon was eying bigger game. Soon after the window opened, the news started to filter down that the Hawks had signed Marian Hossa to his simply cartoonish twelve-year deal. This was the trend at the time, to help circumvent the salary cap. As the hit against the cap was calculated by the annual average of salary over the whole deal, you could lower that by tacking on a bunch of years at the end for a salary of one million. It was generally expected the player would retire by then anyway.

Hossa had been a focal point of the hockey world for a while. Two seasons prior, he had been the biggest prize at the trade deadline as his contract with Atlanta was running out. He went to Pittsburgh, was utterly brilliant there, but wasn't enough to overcome Detroit in the Final. In something of an unprecedented move, he then jumped to Detroit on a one year deal in the summer. In sports, there's rarely anything viewed more poorly than fucking off from your team to go play for the one who beat you. Especially when it's on a one-year deal when Hossa could have named his term and price from anyone. Hockey fans everywhere took unique joy when the Penguins turned the tables on the Wings in the Final, Hossa falling at the final hurdle again. So it wasn't like he was a conquering hero arriving at the gates. Some felt it was inviting a curse into the house.

I was a bit jaded, too. I thought I knew what an incredible player Hossa was (I didn't yet), but his signing signaled Havlat's exit. It wasn't rational, it was emotional. Havlat had saved my hockey fandom. He had showed what could be. He battled back from injuries and doubts to be the best player on the best, or at least most fun, Hawks team of my life. To be shoved aside so quickly hurt, I won't lie. I was attached to Havlat. Hossa was a Wing, a mercenary. I knew Hossa was the better player. I knew that I probably wouldn't care after a short while. This was the business, and the Hawks simply made a move to make themselves better. The sentimentality was for the fans, but that's part of being a fan.

Somewhat making up for the Tallon fiasco, the Hawks also announced a price-freeze on tickets for the season. After being punished by the organization for so long, we all had a brain bubble when they announced this. A Wirtz turning down more money? The end of the world was nigh.

As for things at *The Committed Indian* lab, they weren't running all that smoothly either. When I called my print house a couple weeks before the season started, I was informed by the owner that it had essentially burned down over the summer. Ominous, to say the least. They had directed all their clients to other places, but were going to do their best to be ready to meet my needs before the season. I'm always a sucker for symbolism, and I wasn't exactly thrilled with what I thought this meant. I was used to things I touched turning sour. I wasn't used to them turning to actual ash.

The Hawks started out 2-2 before a return to Chicago from the Flames. October games usually just blend into the scenery. You can't get too up or down about them giving how much longer there is to go. The game is different, far more open than it is a few months later, and teams are still figuring out what they are. However, it is tricky to feel sanguine about any game where your team gives up five first period goals, as the Hawks managed here.This certainly didn't help Cristobal Huet win any fans over, and every start of his at the United Center after that was greeted with unease at best and outright vitriol at worst.

John Madden, another free agent signing that summer, snuck one in before the period was over, and as we headed out for a smoke at intermission we mostly thought it was comedic. It's group therapy, where at least you're surrounded by other people who chose to spend a beautiful

October night this way. There were forty minutes left, and it would be a callback to the previous decade before everything changed.

About halfway through the second, Kane scored what became something of a patented move for him, curling from the right circle to the middle of the ice, opening up a lane for himself and picking a corner. It was 5-2. Most of us thought, "If they can get another before the period is out, at least the third could be interesting?" At that point you're just trying to justify your investment of time and money, and an interesting third period is the life preserver you'll grab onto.

Seven minutes later, Kane and Byfuglien caused a turnover at the blue line and streaked down on a 2-on-1. Kane fed Buff who deked Mikka Kiprusoff and suddenly things were interesting. Less than a minute later, Bolland shoveled home a rebound and the building was louder for an October game than it had ever been before, I'm sure. Not only were the Hawks coming back from a simply ridiculous deficit, they were making it look easy.

On the ensuing faceoff, Jarome Iginla fought Troy Brouwer, seeking to arrest the tide in any way he could. In hindsight, having your best player remove himself from action for five minutes when you're basically drowning isn't the keenest strategy. Only to hockey people does this make sense, but hockey has always had, and probably will always have, a different value system. This is what happens when the sport is governed by men from the Canadian backwoods who stopped going to school in eighth grade. Months or years later, I'm not sure, I read an interview with Brouwer about that fight. He said Iginla lined up next to him at the draw and said, "Hey kid, let's have one here." That's how easy it is in hockey at times. Brouwer tried to describe what it was like to have Jarome Iginla, hockey legend already, asking him to fight. I can't even fathom. He thought it was prudent to remove Iggy from the ice, so he went along with it. Still, I wonder what it's like to have Iggy so politely ask you to fight. I'd love to talk to Iggy one day. I also know I'd never, ever fight him.

Shortly into the third, Patrick Sharp tipped in a Duncan Keith point-shot to tie the game. The Hawks had overcome a five-goal deficit. They got the last four in the span of twenty minutes of game-time. They didn't even look all that flushed.

And they didn't. Though it took until overtime, Seabrook put one home twenty-six seconds into it. They had climbed the mountain, as John Forslund on Vs (at the time) said. We were in euphoria. For the first time, we had seen the raw power of this Hawks team. They were capable of the simply sublime. They doubled the Flames in shots. When they turned it on, they couldn't be stopped.

When you look back on seasons like this, you come up with a lot more moments in your mind where you claim you knew they were going to win it all for sure. There is always doubt until the final horn in the final game. But on that night, we knew. Who could live with a team that was capable of this?

When We All Knew
November 25, 2009
Hawks vs. Sharks

Most Hawks fans will tell you this remains one of their favorite regular season memories, if not the favorite. If the comeback against the Flames came too early to make people think destiny had arrived, then this was the one.

Most importantly, it marked the first game Hossa played as a Hawk. He had signed in the summer needing shoulder surgery, which kept him out of the season's first six weeks. The buzz about his return started weeks prior. Joel Quenneville marveled that his return to practice has sped things up, instead of slowing it down as a player returning from injury usually did. His teammates marveled at his skills and talent. Even my own ticket rep with the Hawks, who would occasionally sneak a look at practice while at work, said to me, "Wait until you see this." He was finally ready. Now the team that had already shown it was probably the best in hockey was going to unveil one of the best two-way forwards in the game.

The Hawks had methodically proceeded after that Flames win, but didn't really hit the gas until the middle of November. Huet was still struggling at times, and the Hawks had a budding goalie controversy on their hands. The power play was still a mess, an organizational curse we were going to live with until our deathbed.

Finally it all got figured out. The Hawks ripped off seven in a row before this, including the first three of the Circus Trip. That was capped off by a 1-0 shutout of the Canucks in Vancouver again, with Antii Niemi doing the honors in net. The Hawks were ten games over .500 and Thanksgiving wasn't even upon us.

Black Wednesday in San Jose had become something of a tradition, and these were the two best teams in the conference. The Wings had finally stuttered, were going through an injury crisis, and had fallen behind the Hawks in the division. With Hossa's return, this was the most anticipated game of the season. And seeing as how most didn't have to work the next day, it became more of an event.

We also tried something new for the first time, and invited our readers out to our favorite bar to watch the Hawks. In hindsight, inviting a bunch of internet commenters you'd never met to join you in drinking was a dodgy decision, but we were still naive, our community was still friendly, and we were in need of all the drinking buddies we could find. Hockey writers inhabit a lonely place, after all. Bringing together everyone only strengthened the bond we had with readers (it also caused me to meet the girl I would be with for the next five years, but we'll get to her).

The Hawks clearly sensed the occasion, and came out thundering. Things remained scoreless until late in the first, with the Hawks on the penalty kill. Keith fired a puck that had been lazily dumped into the Hawks zone up to Troy Brouwer at the red line. Brouwer came down the right wing and fired a wrister over Evgeni Nabokov's glove.

What followed is a period Hawks fans won't ever forget. Once again on the kill, Hossa poked a puck away from Dan Boyle at the blue line and just kept streaking up the ice. Toews picked it up, and without even looking up just laid out a pass for Hossa to have a breakaway. Hossa simply flicked the puck past Nabokov. It looked...so elementary. So easy. So effortless. What we had seen with Detroit the previous season…it was ours now! You know class when you see it. Toews and Hossa combining so seamlessly for this was the perfect demonstration. It was gorgeous, It was art. This was the Hawks? The creatures who had been locked in the attic for so long? Suddenly we had our own version of Montana-to-Rice.

Twenty-eight seconds later, on the same kill, Sharp got loose on a breakaway and easily faked Nabokov down and out. The Hawks had taken a 3-0 lead on three shorthanded goals simply because they felt like it. Just to see if they could? Because it sounded cool? This was madness.

The Hawks piled up twenty-one shots in the period, and would add another goal through Byfuglien. They added three more in the first half of the third, including Hossa's second where Brent Sopel threaded a pass through four Sharks to give Hossa an open net. When Sopel is doing this you're really pulling out the party tricks. This was a hockey Vegas show. All that was needed was a flying white tiger, if Hossa didn't qualify for that title.

The Hawks had walked into the building of a conference favorite and simply blew them out of the water (get it?). They had unveiled their new weapon in Hossa who scored twice after not playing a game all season. They put up three shorthanded goals just for the smell of it.

We didn't come down for weeks. Meeting our readers only heightened the excitement. We stayed out until 5:00 am, such was our buzz. We didn't say it, but we were sure the Hawks were bringing the Chalice home then. A team that could do that to the Sharks in San Jose? How could they miss? Raw power is coming for you.

This was the night we started using Van Halen's "Everybody Wants Some" as a theme whenever the Hawks blew a team out. No one said it had to be mature. For the next seven years we would have readers calling for D.L.R whenever the Hawks opened up a big lead in a game. You reap what you sow.

Hoss
December 13, 2009

Lightning vs. Hawks

We didn't get our first live look at Hossa for another week, after the Hawks had completed the Circus Trip. What was clear to me after just a couple games was that this was nothing I had ever seen before.

We had seen Hawks who could dance their way out of traffic. Savard, Havlat, Amonte, Kane: they all had speed or hands or both that allowed them to wriggle out of tight spaces. We had seen Hawks that could bull their way out of it with the puck. Roenick, Larmer, Daze, that one time from Mark Bell, they all would show off strength greater than that of their teammates.

What we hadn't seen was someone who could do both.

My father, never really a hockey fan, would remark later, "I don't know much about this game but I know good things happen when that guy has the puck." That's how obvious it was when Hossa was on the ice. It's not that the game slowed down in the same way as it did when Kane was in possession. Because defenders would go flying at him and they would just bounce off. Hossa would go wherever he wanted, and anyone trying to take the puck off of him was greeted with something along the lines of, "Do you mind?"

And then he would chase down someone on the backcheck, inhaling them like a lion chasing down a zebra that had fallen behind the pack. He would have the puck and be heading the other way before the opponent even knew what hit him. I can't tell you the amount of times an opposing player had skated a good five or six feet before he even realized that Hossa had already robbed him of possession. It was surgical.

He just looked more adult than most everyone on the ice. You kept waiting for forty kids at recess to come out and tackle him at once. There wasn't anything he couldn't do. On this night, he grabbed a puck out of the air, dropped it toward his stick and thwacked it into the net before it hit the ice like he was just hitting grounders to his little league team. And he did it at basically top speed. It was audacious.

So yeah, right after the game I called my apparel guy and begged for a #81 jersey instead of a cash payment for his ad in the program. That's the other thing about Hossa: #81 just looks cool in any setting.

Homework
December 22, 2009
Sharks vs. Hawks

Things were changing for the program as well as for the Hawks. A few weeks prior, a reader of mine got in touch to offer me a deal on my own printer. The thought of not having to drive to Elk Grove every game day certainly was appealing, and the cost benefit was off the charts.

Still, it put me in a position where I would have to explain to the owner of a print shop that had a massive fire only a couple months before that I would be taking my business away. I didn't have the ruthless streak for business, and I still don't. I nearly cried when I broke the news to them. They could not have been more understanding, which only made me feel worse. My heart is too big and soft for a capitalistic society.

But still, I had a printer in my own house. It made things incredibly easy. Except for the noise, which was only a minor drawback at this point. What I didn't realize is that if something went wrong, I was basically on my own. And the last person I wanted to trust was myself.

It was a bumpy start. First off, the printer didn't really speak to my Mac software. It took a few games to figure out. If only that had been the biggest hurdle. I should have known getting the thing secondhand was a sign of trouble. Anyone ever truly feel safe when buying a used car? And there's no CarFax.com for printers.

When it first needed a toner replacement, I couldn't get my new cartridge to fit. It just wouldn't slide into the holder. It was supposed to. I tried every angle. Eventually, it kind of slammed in. And when dealing with machinery that has hundreds of tiny, moving parts, the verb "slam" isn't one you want to be using. The whole thing was borked. I spent hours trying to figure out how to fix it, and their repair guy couldn't make it in time. I would miss my first issue due to my own incompetence.

I was in a rage. I was devastated to miss a holiday-time issue. Still, it was a Hawks-Sharks game, so I decided to make an event of it. I didn't get to pregame for Hawks games anymore, and now that the copier had robbed me of having to work, I could.

I met blog McClure and his girlfriend at a bar on Madison St. When I sat across from them they both got this bemused look. It was clear there was something they wanted to tell me but weren't sure how. I asked them a few times what it was. They were still reluctant, though their sheepish grins only got bigger. Finally they broke the news. I had toner on my scalp. I rushed to the bathroom to see. They had undersold it. From fiddling with the inner working of the printer, not only did I have toner on my scalp but in the perfect formation of my fingerprints, aligned with having my head buried in my hands in frustration, a position in which I had spent most of the afternoon (and the next few years).

I didn't care that the Sharks won the game. I had biffed an issue, possibly broken a copier I'd only had for days, and had toner embedded in places I didn't want to think about.

The perils of rock and roll decadence.

Turning The Masses
January 17, 2010
Hawks vs. Red Wings

I'm never confused as to why hockey hasn't caught on with the masses like the other three "major" sports. It's one that a lot of people didn't grow up playing. It's still something of an odd television watch, though high-definition TVs have helped. It's still horrifically marketed, as the NHL has never figured out what will break the barrier. They don't promote their stars because the culture doesn't really allow for it. It's had bad television deals and been off of ESPN for more than a decade. I could go on.

And yet, there's an odd moment here or there when I see how easily a group of people who weren't specifically watching a hockey game can get sucked in and involved. A good game that is open, fast, and has a lot of chances is simply a magnet for eyeballs. If only on a TV in the corner of the bar, you can't help but see the brightness of the ice and the speed at which the camera is panning. If there's only a couple of people focused on it, you'll see just how locked in they are. You'll want to see why. It's truly a shame that the league simply has never been able to cash in on this in any meaningful way.

I was visiting my brother Adam in New York. The Hawks had one of those annoying 12:30 pm ET starts against the Red Wings on NBC. We went to a bar he knew that made a decent Irish breakfast to enjoy it. We knew that the NFL playoffs would be starting shortly after the Hawks game, and that was what the crowd at the bar was gearing up for. All we requested was one TV in the corner. They reluctantly gave it to us, but not without a few faces from the bartender and a promise that if anyone else requested that particular TV be turned to football, we'd have to relent. This being New York, I had little doubt that anyone would request it simply to piss us off.

The Wings had improved health, and proceeded to produce something of a classic with the Hawks on this afternoon. It went back and forth, as the Hawks took a 2-0 and 3-2 lead that the Wings pegged back each time. They traded chances. Kris Versteeg and Patrick Eaves, hardly the biggest guys, had a memorable boogey-down with each throwing only haymakers meant to end each other's world. Overtime was basically one odd-man rush after another.

When I turned around for a second, half the bar had gotten ensconced in the Hawks game instead of the NFL playoff game they had come to watch. By the time the shootout arrived they were riveted. I suppose this is the crowd the NHL was aiming for when they instituted the shootout. If only they could show me evidence that it holds them, too. I certainly shot a knowing glance at the bartender who was just waiting to turn it off at any moment.

The entire bar oohed with amazement when Pavel Datsyuk essentially chipped the puck over Antti Niemi to kick it off. They roared when Sharp ended it, just as they had done when Hossa missed an open net in overtime. Hockey had grabbed them.

This is what it can do when left to its own devices. The market is there, somewhere. But I have no hope that they can seize it successfully and long-term. Shame, no sport really gets a crowd of people in a bar together the same way.

Welcome To My World, Dad
March 14, 2010
Capitals vs. Hawks

My father wasn't a hockey fan. He took me when I was a kid because he knew I loved it so. But once I got involved in it professionally (if you can call it that), he became more involved. I would catch him watching games in his room that I was watching in the living room when we were living together. He would occasionally ask questions here and there. He was a cursory fan at best, but more interested than he had ever been. It didn't hurt that his beloved Bulls at this time were boring as fuck and couldn't hold his interest much.

I don't know why it almost took two full seasons to take him to a game in my seats. I couldn't gauge his interest before. Or maybe I didn't want him to see how I was during games, even though I was claiming, at least on tax forms, that I was an adult. Finally, he asked when he could go. I felt terrible that it took him asking for me to even think of it. But hey, after all he'd done I was delighted to be the one to take him to a sporting event for once.

Knowing my father's preference for stars and performance (he could give you quite the soliloquy on Mick Jagger if you ever needed it), I chose Alex Ovechkin's visit to the United Center. This was the game's premier goal-scorer, something to not be missed. I knew this would appeal.

And twelve minutes into it, Ovechkin got ejected.

Campbell picked up a puck behind the Hawks net and was just about to curl around the other side when Ovechkin boarded him from behind, breaking his collarbone. They first sent Ovie to the box while the refs figured out what they wanted to call. When he exited the box to skate toward the bench and the tunnel to the dressing room, making it clear he was getting ejected, my father turned to me and exclaimed, half-jokingly (I hope), "THIS?! THIS IS THE FIRST GAME YOU BRING ME TO IN SEVENTEEN YEARS?! TO SEE THIS ASSHOLE?!" I sat silently the rest of the game, outright embarrassed. The Hawks ended up blowing a three-goal lead to lose in overtime as well. It was not the occasion he had been picturing, that I was sure. All I could do was laugh sheepishly.

When I saw him back at home, I tried to profusely apologize, as if I was controlling Ovechkin's movement or something. He assured me he thought it was funny in the end, and told me a story to make me feel better. Back when my brother Adam was a child and my father had Bulls season tickets, he spent a week talking up a game with the Knicks because Earl

Monroe was on the team. He regaled my brother with the treat he was in for to see Jesus live on the court. My brother apparently couldn't have been more excited, apparently buying into my father's description and thinking he was going to see something truly special.

Earl Monroe played thirteen seconds that night. So I guess I beat that? Four shifts is better than thirteen seconds.

The Greatest Moment Ever
April 24, 2010
Predators vs. Hawks (Game Five)

The Hawks went through their now regular March doldrums after Campbell's injury. After giving up eight goals in a game in Columbus at the end of March, Cristobal Huet ceded the net to Antti Raanta full-time. It was his to take, and he dropped it. Or more aptly, he let it pass by his glove hand. The Hawks snapped out of it to close the season, winning six of their last seven, the only loss on the last day of the season to the Red Wings because of course.

There couldn't have been a more anticipated opening to the playoffs. This was the best Hawks team rolling into April...well, possibly ever. They were the pick of many. Only Niemi was considered a question mark, and the team had basically spent the season taking the goalie out of the equation. We couldn't wait.

And the Hawks dropped the first game. It wasn't a disaster, but we all watched with something of a quizzical look on our faces. Like when you burn something in the kitchen. It's not the end of the world, or even the meal necessarily, it just wasn't exactly what you were planning. They bounced back with a 2-0 win in Game Two with Bolland scoring the winning goal on the power play with a full 360-backhand from the circle that floated over Pekka Rinne.

We were a little more worried come the conclusion of Game Three. The Hawks laid a steaming turd of an effort, matching the 4-1 loss they had from Game One. They gave up thirty-five shots. It's one thing to lose the opening game with the next one at home. To let the other team get halfway to the series while at home had us biting our fingernails off for two days until Game Four. Thankfully, the Hawks appeared to set things right in Game Four, a resounding 3-0 win to mark their second shutout of the series. They had been down, figured they had got it out of their system, and were going to return home to firmly put this one in a chokehold. Brian Campbell had returned from his Ovechkin-induced injury and had transformed the defense.

It was perhaps the first warmish Saturday afternoon of the spring. Still grey, as Chicago tends to be in April, but you didn't need a jacket. It buoyed the mood. This was all a procession, at least we thought, and here was the time the Hawks would take their first authoritative step on the way to fourteen more wins and a parade. Oil changed, tires rotated, let's kick this pig.

It certainly started out that way. While David Legwand scored first for the Predators, the Hawks scored the next three. Even Niklas Hjalmarsson got on the scoresheet. Tomas Kopecky capped it off, chasing down a clearance from out of the penalty box in the Predators' zone for a breakaway goal. He screamed toward the rafters as we did in celebration. To that point the Hawks had outshot the Predators 24-7. Everything was running on heavy, heavy fuel. There were only twenty-three minutes of game time to see out for a 3-2 series lead that would assuredly see a series win two days later in Music City.

A minute after Kopecky's goal, Joel Ward scored a shorthanded goal for the Preds. Well, that wasn't in the cards, but no worries. The Hawks had become experts in shutting teams down in the third period, they had a lead. This was nothing.

Barely a minute into the third, Martin Erat finished off a wonderful passing play and the game was tied. What the fuck? I was pointing at the script in my head again. They weren't really going to let this slip, were they? The Predators only had nine shots at this point. This was a farce. An unease began to spread through the crowd, the result of a lot of Hawks and Chicago sporting heartbreak muscle memory coming to the fore.

Halfway through the third, Erat scored again off a cross-ice feed from Denis Grebeshkov (your killer is always the one you'd least suspect). The Hawks were trailing. Now we were panicked. Going down 3-2 and heading on the road is exactly where you don't want to be. Still, the Hawks would find a way. We were sure. They had been outplaying the Predators all day. Merely a flesh-wound.

The minutes ticked off. Still no equalizer came. As the time became more and more scarce, suddenly I felt a real bubbling in my stomach. It wasn't just that the Hawks could lose. We had spent six months dreaming of this run, and now it was looking much in peril. Being at the very first hurdle of the playoffs, I could see all the headlines and stories from the 1991 collapse being rehashed. They spun out in front of me like some cliché TV flashback. Months and months of "Are the Hawks cursed?" awaiting if the Hawks couldn't find a comeback that was looking near impossible now.

The final minutes can be recounted by every Hawks fan from memory, but I'll do it anyway. With a minute to go, Marian Hossa, in desperation to get a puck back behind the Predators' net, sent Dan Hamhuis flying into the boards from behind. He got a major penalty for it (and probably should have gotten ejected, but we'll save that debate for another day). I felt the life drain out of me. The Hawks were down a goal and now on the kill with a minute to go. The Predators could simply play four corners and run this out.

Thirty seconds later Martin Erat lost his mind. The Hawks had sent Patrick Kane out on the penalty kill, but he never entered the Hawks zone. He was just waiting for a breakout pass to send him the other way, loitering in the neutral zone like he was waiting to be asked to play. Erat, for reasons he'll never be able to explain, tried to center a pass from behind Niemi. It clanked off the side of the net to a waiting Toews who screeched up the ice along with the waiting Kane.

The rest happened in slow motion. Toews curled at the circle and found Seabrook on the other side, who wristed a puck to the net. Keith got a tip on it that sent it ringing off the post. Sharp collected the rebound along the right boards. He sent it to the corner to Seabrook, who found Toews in the right circle to send another wrist-shot toward Rinne. It hit his right pad flush, and bounced right onto Kane's waiting stick. The whole net was gaping. He couldn't miss.

My friend Jake came in from New York to attend this game with me (he claimed he would be in town to visit family, but we have been friends since we were kids, so I knew better). I almost made sure he didn't make it back to New York, with the way I grabbed him around the neck. I wasn't screaming so much as hysterically laughing, and extremely high-pitched. I sounded like a hyena. This couldn't be happening. Down a man and a goal with a minute to go and they came up with this? This was beyond farce, beyond fantasy. It was abstract. (And having Jake there was appropriate, as when I was debating starting the program he was the one friend who was most passionate about me doing so).

Once again, my feet never felt the stairs as I sprinted out for a pre-OT smoke. McClure was out there, and all he could say was, "There's so much time left." He meant Hossa's major penalty. There were still four minutes to get through. Though the Predators' power play had been woeful, surely they could fashion a chance or two with four minutes. It felt like a desert to be crawled out of.

They did. With the teams switching ends, their power play took place right in front of me. Erat had one chance from right between the circles. As he loaded up, I went weak in the knees. When Niemi came up with the save, it was like the governor had called. Every Hawks clearance was greeted with a roar louder than that which met most goals. Every blocked shot saluted. Bolland and Sopel were everywhere. Eventually it felt like we were taunting the Predators with every ovation. Like we were saying, "If you don't get one on this, you're through," or "You're fucking this up. You'll be sorry."

Bolland and Sopel combined for one last clearance. Bolland caused a turnover at the blue line and forced the puck to center. Sopel came streaking up behind him and Bolland dropped him the puck. Sopel just steamed right into the Nashville zone. Where the fuck was he going? He ringed the puck around Rinne, and while he did so Hossa came out of the box. Hjalmarsson sent it back down low to Bolland, who got the puck back to the point to Sopel.

I can still see it so clearly, as I was standing right behind the whole thing from my seat. Sopel one-timed the puck toward the net. It hit a stick, slowing it down along the ice and in the direction of Hossa waiting right at the side of the net, with no one around him. It was all laid out in front of us. All it had to do was get there. Just continue along the path. It took long enough that there was time to consider if this was all a prank. It couldn't be this simple, could it? Surely a clown or mole was going to pop out of the ice and send the puck somewhere else.

It was that simple. It did head right to Hossa's stick, who poked it past Rinne. I saw him leap up higher than he ever had before I was mauled by my entire row. My ears actually hurt, I couldn't stop screaming, I was hoarse from smoke and yelling. I never felt better. I tackled two friends in the stairwell on the way out. When I got in the car, I'm not sure I've ever been more exhausted.

When you go back and watch the replay of Hossa's goal, and make sure you do this, as the camera pans out from the entire team celebrating along the boards near the Hawks bench, off to the right you'll see a small boy in the front row run and leap into his father's arms. It's one of my favorite moments. Because right then, we were all that boy. We were all so overtaken with elation we would just hug whomever was around. We couldn't ignore the significance of it. That was a magical moment. A moment that portended so much more. You don't pull off that comeback only to snuff it the very next game or round. Once again, we knew.

The Hockey Girlfriend
May 3, 2010
Canucks vs. Hawks (Game Two)

For pretty much my entire life, my maturation process has been behind that of my peers. There are just a lot of things I got to after they did. That includes romantic relationships. While I've always been blessed with a good number of close female friends, my dating history is pretty checkered and sparse.

So I had a lot to learn about seeing a woman regularly, especially one who was a huge Hawks fan, and had become one, in part, through our blog. This was a brave new world. When I was a kid, I became a hockey and Hawks fan partially because I knew that girls wouldn't ruin it like they had all my favorite bands (in my mind. When you're eleven, it's impossible to imagine that girls love *Appetite For Destruction* the same way you do). As I got older, I regarded my hockey fandom as a reason that no woman would ever love me. Would any one of them take me seriously after they see what a pout I could put on after a Hawks loss? Would they not be disgusted at the string of obscenities I could aim at Alex Burrows?

Was I really ready to share this huge part of my life with a girl? More worryingly, was she ready to share this with me? I met her at a blog outing, and most of our first encounters I tried to steer clear of hockey. When the subject did come up, it took me weeks before I stopped hesitating when discussing a penalty kill or a lineup decisions with her, finally realizing I didn't have to explain the elementary details. Like I said, I was slow developing. She knew. She was the same fan I was, but this can be really hard for an immature male to understand. She was patient though, lucky for me, and more than excited to share in all of it.

It probably wasn't the soundest strategy to choose a playoff game to be the one we first attended together, much less one against the Canucks, much less one where the Hawks were trailing in the series. They had dusted off the Predators, but were flat and lifeless against Vancouver in the series opener. Of course, Game One was the one I decided I would take my father to to make up for that Washington fiasco. After that was over, I told him he might not be allowed back.

Dad still got a kick of a lifetime that night, though. He stopped by my selling spot outside Gate 3 as he was heading in. He saw a line of people waiting to get programs so he thought he would just wave and leave me to it. I wasn't having it. I called him over to meet a regular reader whom I was talking to at the moment. When I introduced my father to him, everyone else in line basically climbed over each other to shake his hand. I had mentioned him once or twice in the program, but I think they just wanted to meet and thank the father of the guy writing something they had come to enjoy so much. Couldn't get the smile off his face for hours. Or mine.

Still, the Hawks were down and then they were down in Game Two very quickly. Mason Raymond scored a minute in, and then the Hawks took two consecutive delay-of-game penalties five minutes in. Giving the Sedins a two-man advantage was always death. Mikael Samuellson benefitted, and suddenly the Hawks were down one in the series and two in the game.

I tried to keep my emotions in check, even though the thought of going down 2-0 to these grotesque fuckers from B.C. turned my blood toxic. I couldn't let her see me in my true form. I nearly pulled a muscle trying to keep it all in. Seabrook was able to slam one in a couple minutes after Samuelsson's goal, so the dread didn't last. Down one there was always hope. She gave me a subtle hug after Seabrook's goal, not in celebration but in a "I know you're going through hell at the moment but it's going to be fine and you can let it out" kind of way.

The second went by too easily. The Hawks didn't muster the threat we all expected, and headed into the third needing a goal to prevent a pretty big gap in the series. Seven minutes into the third, Sharp just decided he was going to score a shorthanded goal. He broke up a play at the blue line, streaked down on a two-on-one, danced around the retreating Edler and

Luongo, and slotted home a backhand. It was unstoppable. I couldn't keep it in anymore. I let out a primal yell. When I looked over, she was yelling too. I guess I didn't have to worry. I probably should have drawn more strength from her confidence. Lesson learned.

The rest of that period was a blur. Both teams hurled everything at each other, with Hossa and Sharp missing glorious chances. With ninety seconds left, Versteeg streaked down on a 3-on-2 but stickhandled himself out of a chance, because VERSTEEG. The puck circled out back to the point, where Keith faked a shot from the middle and then slid the puck back to Versteeg waiting at the left circle. Luongo had committed to Keith, and Versteeg had at least half the net to shoot at. He buried it, and then dropped to his knees while floating out to center ice.

I turned to my left. She leapt into my arms. After a brief hug, I turned to high-five everyone else around me.

And I put her down in the row in front of us.

She was tangled in the seats, with those in that row helping her out while I was totally oblivious. She somehow decided to stay with me after that. I didn't find out for weeks after. She didn't want me to feel bad.

My vision of being a fan for as long as I could remember was having season tickets with my brother. I never saw myself leaving the house with someone else who was also in a Duncan Keith jersey. Or watching games on the couch with someone else there. Having someone in my own house swear at David Backes before I could. That's a true partner, I suppose. Let's just say a whole new world opened up because of it.

To Be Young
May 23, 2010
Sharks vs. Hawks (Game Four)

The Hawks proceeded to eviscerate the Canucks the rest of that series, clowning them in Vancouver. That included Dustin Byfuglien's "Da Fuck You Gonna Do About It?" goal celebration in Game Three to the entire Vancouver crowd and Toews's hat trick in Game Four. They had a brief hiccup in Game Five but finished the job easily in Game Six. Minutes after the final horn of that clincher, Adam sent me a text. All it said was his flight info, as he was coming home for the rest of the run. I didn't know then he had been laid off from his job or not allowed to renew his lease at his apartment. All I knew then was he was too excited and this too important for him to not be here. Work was but a trifle.

The Hawks continued their roll in San Jose, winning a tight Game One and then blowing out the Sharks in Game Two. In our mind, the series was already over. They were simply coming home for the coronation. It took overtime in Game Three, with the Sharks somehow not being able to notice the large, black man in the form of Byfuglien traipsing down their slot for Bolland to easily find from behind the net.

We showed up on the Sunday afternoon of Game Four ready to release eighteen years of frustration. The process of winning one game to get there seemed so elementary. I don't think most fans even thought of the Sharks once before the game.

The Sharks made it a little more tricky than we thought. They took a 2-0 lead halfway through the second, with Marleau scoring after a clearing attempt spilled most of Duncan Keith's teeth on the ice. But Seabrook and Bolland answered before the period was out, and Byfuglien scored from in tight on the power play with six minutes left. Versteeg would add an empty-netter to seal it. I can still hear Doc Emerick's call during the last seconds (viewed the highlights only like fifteen times when I got home): "It won't matter, Hawks to the Final!"

As my brother and I made our way around the 100 Level concourse, we spotted a young boy on his father's shoulders. He was carrying an inflatable Stanley Cup over his head, like he had just won it. Every Hawks fan who passed raised an arm to touch it or pat the boy on the leg or father on the side. The entire concourse cheered him on. It's one of my favorite images. Much like Hossa's goal, we were all that boy. Most of us were that age the last time we saw the Hawks in the Final.. It was the kind of glee only a child can feel, the kind you can get back to every so often thanks to sports. Either you were going through it for the first time like him, or you he took you back to the sweep of the Oilers in '92 and how you felt then, before Lemieux, Jagr, and Francis ruined it all.

Wanna Take A Ride?
May 29, 2010
Flyers vs. Hawks (Game One)

The wait for the Final was interminable. It started on the Saturday, a full week after the Hawks had clinched their spot. The space madness set in.

Finally, Saturday night arrived. I made sure to let all the readers know I was heading into the building early so they'd better get their programs early. Apparently everyone else had the same idea because I was out of programs with twenty minutes to go and the outside of the building barren. Thank you, NBC programming, which didn't have the puck actually drop for some twenty minutes after the stated 7:00 pm start.

I was shaking when I headed in. You dream of attending a World Series or Super Bowl with your team in it. But you rarely think it'll actually happen. This was hockey's marquee event; the Hawks were part of it for only the second time in my life, and I was there. The hottest ticket in the city can burn a hole in your hand.

The United Center edited the pregame video a bit before this one. Instead of featuring a video that showed the Hawks skating through the city, they added a wrinkle. They had various Hawks taking slapshots that saw their puck explode the logos of the three previous teams they had beaten to get there. It's silly stuff, boilerplate. But I and so many others were so charged up by the occasion, that as soon as the Sharks logo exploded I lost it. I was a frothing mess. I would have drank my own blood at that point.

The Hawks were heavily favored, as they should have been. They had been one of the league's best teams all year, whereas the Flyers had barely squeaked into the playoffs and were riding something of a Cinderella wave to get there.

For fans, everything gets wired up even more in the Final. You've come too close now to lose. You can't even fathom it. So the feelings of dread when behind are bottomless, and the trepidation when leading makes you afraid to even move. Nothing is ever safe. An opening goal in the opening game with so far to go shouldn't make you panic, but I certainly did when Antti Niemi's save off a Ville Leino shot bounced off Niklas Hjalmarsson and into the net. Even at that point, I was trying to piece back together a shattered dream. Brouwer tied it only a minute later and I think I took my first breath. Bolland stripped Braydon Coburn at the line on a penalty kill to score on a breakaway, and even though we were only halfway through the first period at the very beginning of the series, I felt like things were back on course. Adam and I hugged, this was all part of the fun of the show. Boy was I wrong, and right.

The Flyers bungled in two goals in the last four minutes of the period, including a Briere one with twenty-six seconds left, causing his beyond-annoying celebration that all Hawks fans would come to loathe very quickly. Trailing after a period? This wasn't how it was supposed to go.

Sometimes, hockey games devolve into farce. Your normal emotions to goals for and against get wiped out with exhaustion. Sharp picked up a cross-ice pass a minute into the second, came down the right wing, and blistered Michael Leighton's glove. Game tied. But then six minutes later Blair Betts did the same to Niemi's glove. Two minutes after that, Versteeg found a rebound and scored. Five minutes later Brouwer one-timed a Hossa pass by Leighton for the second time in the game. And then three minutes later Aaron Asham did the same to a Briere pass. Five goals in the second, to match the five goals in the first. There was never time to settle into any emotion. I couldn't delve into despair before the Hawks scored again, nor could I feel comfortable before the Flyers scored again. Eventually I tapped out of either. I was basically a cadaver.

Eight minutes into the third, Kopecky received a pass from the opposite corner from Versteeg. He skated around Brian Boucher, who had replaced Leighton, getting him down and out. But he was by the goal line to do so, and the angle looked too tough. He still solved it. While everyone around lost their minds as Kopecky pounded on the glass in celebration, I wasn't going to be fooled again. Surely, the Flyers were going to find another answer, because they'd found five already. Whatever reserves I had left I was not going to waste. There were four more goals to get through, right?

The Hawks saw it out, only giving up six shots in the last period. But after all that, I was just happy it was over. You don't go on the roller coaster two times in a row if you've already hurled.

The Almost Accidental Break-Up
June 4, 2010
Hawks vs. Flyers (Game Four)

The Hawks and Flyers simply had to play out a tighter Game Two, because both coaches would have pulled out machetes if they didn't.

The first was scoreless, and most of the second was too. This was somehow more tense than the cartoonish Game One, because it was starting to feel like it was going to be decided by some fluke moment. With three minutes to go in the middle period, Hossa chipped a rebound and it floated over Leighton's shoulder. He let out a scream that probably could have been heard a good distance away, as he'd taken a lot of shit for not scoring regularly during the playoffs.

A mere eighteen seconds later, somehow on a shift with Toews, right from the faceoff, Ben Eager streaked down the right wing and then fired a wrister over Leighton's glove and right under the bar. He jumped around behind the Flyers net like he'd lost his mind, which he probably had. Ben Eager doing that in the Final? Who's writing this? The Hawks saw off a pretty strong Flyers surge in the third to take a 2-0 lead. I tackled McClure in the concourse, and said to him and my brother, "It's so close now." It just felt like a matter of time.

The Hawks dropping Game Three was somewhat predictable. Philly was going to be a raucous, and probably an outright dangerous atmosphere, the Flyers would be as desperate as possible, and this was a new step. Still, they nearly pulled it off, coming back twice from a goal down and then having the lead in the third before the Flyers tied it. When Giroux scored in overtime it was disappointing, but we figured this was the one blip.

Not so much. The win emboldened the Flyers, who came out storming against the Hawks and took a 2-0 then 4-1 lead early in the third. It was the first time that playing Niemi had seemed to hurt the Hawks, as he just wasn't every good. That teeming orange mob in the arena was coming through our screen, just as vile and gross as you'd imagine any group of excited Philly residents would be. It couldn't be slipping away again, could it? Of course, all we had to remember was that the Hawks did this the previous year with Calgary, but that file was hard to locate in the cabinet of our minds at the moment.

I moved out to the patio of the bar for a postgame smoke and tried to collect myself. It really did feel like something I could have touched just four nights before had been ripped out of sight. The years it had all gone wrong flashed before me...'91, '92, '95, '96...throw in various Cubs collapses and the one Bears Super Bowl. I stood silent.

My girlfriend came out to console me but I was in full pout. This is what I was talking about earlier. Adam and I quickly returned home, as I had to get to work on Game Five's program. The lady IM'd me to see if I was ok. I was still dejected. After a few minutes of conversation, I finally realized it was time to get over it, so I wrote to her, "It's over."

This was not the best choice of words.

Suddenly she was frantically calling and texting and I couldn't figure out why. When she finally got a hold of me and demanded answers, I had to laugh at my ways. No, I assured her, I meant the pout I was feeling. That's over. Not us.

And suddenly the silliness of it hit me. I nearly scorched a relationship over one loss that didn't mean anything close to the series being over. When I saw how silly it was, I immediately began to write Game Five's "From The Editor." It stated:

> " I am fully confident that this is this season's last issue, and in the good way. I fully expect the Hawks to win tonight, and close it out Wednesday night to cue the biggest celebration of our lives. After our win tonight, I'm shutting up shop. I won't keep any change for the next night's sales, and the printer is being put in my storage room. If I feel this way, so should you. It's time to be bold, and you have it in you."

One of the few times I was right.

The Greatest Night Ever
June 9, 2010
Hawks vs. Flyers (Game Six)
The Hawks did pull out the driver for Game Five, once again shifting into, "You're not fucking winning this game, you're not fucking winning this series" mode. The Hawks came out and simply blitzed the Flyers, scoring three times in the second half of the first period. While Niemi did his best to give the Flyers a chance, every Flyers goal was met with another Hawks one, and they ran out 7-4 winners.

When the jumbotron flashed "1" after the final horn, then it became real. Really real. Really really real. We hadn't really spoken about it out loud before, but once that mark, one simple win, was put before us, the entire 300 Level chanted "WE WANT THE CUP!" It was the first time we'd ever heard it, either in the UC or the Stadium. The Hawks hadn't been this close in almost all of our lifetimes. It was possible. It was right there.

The gap between Games Five and Six was two days instead of the normal one. It might as well have been a hundred. I didn't have any work to keep myself busy with, refusing to even allow for the possibility of a Game Seven issue. I spent the two days basically imagining Game Six and how it would most like it to go. While I would have taken a 11-0 blowout just as readily, I settled on a third period goal, early in the period, to give the Hawks a lead. And then a furious stand, followed by an empty-netter with about thirty seconds to go. That seemed perfect to me. You'd get the clinching moment when you knew it was over without the absolute terror of a tie game and/or overtime.

It was so fucking humid that Wednesday. It rained in the morning, only making it worse. I ran a couple errands, and then spent the afternoon building an entire patio set for me and my father. Not because I was any good at it—I would say at most three of the five chairs I put together were usable—but just because it would take up a lot of time. I listened to The Score all afternoon too, where Dan Bernstein and Laurence Holmes were just taking calls from people, wanting to know where they'd watch the game and how they planned to celebrate. This was the night we dreamed of, and yet it would never fucking arrive.

I packed for our hockey bar two and a half hours before puck drop. I couldn't wait around any longer. I demanded any friend who had attended a game with me...well, ever, be there too. The car was full of friends and headed down, though most in the car didn't know why we had to sit in a dark bar with barely any windows for two hours waiting. But I couldn't sit any longer, and if they wanted a ride...tough. I also warned them I would be leaving the car there for the night, not anticipating being in any condition to get it home again. Safety first, kids.

The bar was full an hour before the game. I had been right. I stationed myself standing, as I always did, behind those sitting at the bar, between my two blog compatriots and behind Adam who was sitting at the bar. I would not move from here. This is my angle to the TV when it finally ends, I kept thinking. I couldn't really stop shaking. I didn't even attempt speech.

Once again, the Hawks came out rolling, determined to end this shit before it got out of hand. They outshot the Flyers 17-7, and with three minutes to go Byfuglien got one in on the power play. The way he so arrogantly slapped his stick against the glass after, taunting the Flyers fans, only made me feel better. The Hawks knew this was theirs. So should I. Sadly, Hartnell tied it with thirty seconds to go in the frame. The confidence was brief and fleeting.

Nearly halfway through the second, Briere scored what felt like hi sixty-third goal of the series to put the Flyers up 2-1. Thankfully, right after,

Patrick Sharp scored quickly enough, before I could find sharp objects, lifting his arms in relief, or in a Jesus Christ pose for you Soundgarden fans. With two minutes to go in the period, Hjalmarsson had a blast tipped in by Ladd, and the Hawks were leading heading into the third of a Cup-clinching game.

My excitement was tempered by my compatriot McClure, who strangled me while I tried to get another "WE WANT THE CUP!" chant going at the bar. He was not one for fooling around, and no risks would be taken. There were twenty minutes to go. That's all we repeated to each other outside during our intermission smoke. "Win the period, win the Cup." I probably head-butted everyone in the bar before it started.

The minutes ticked by in agonizing fashion. This is how I had wanted it, I kept trying to tell myself. Hawks protecting a one-goal lead, get the empty-netter. If I had known what it would be like, I might have opted for the 11-0 dream. Once it got down to single-digits in minutes left, it became harder and harder to breathe. We were getting there, but too slowly. It was getting closer but we couldn't look. We were surging closer and closer to the screens behind the bar, and it became more and more quiet.

Then the air got sucked out. The puck bounced around Niemi's crease with four minutes to go, before finally landing on Hartnell's stick, again, for him to deposit. We had gotten just close enough to feel it becoming reality, and then it disappeared into the ether again. The Hawks held on through the last of the period to get to overtime.

I cursed myself for dreaming of this scenario. Why would I leave it up to a one-goal lead in my mind? That was too risky. My need for drama and suspense had ruined us. Now it could all be taken away in a single moment. Others expressed their excitement over who would score the winner and make history. I just stewed in contempt for myself for having my perfect scenario fly too close to the sun. I had done this.

I know for all four minutes of that overtime I probably needed to barf. Every time the Hawks entered the Flyers' zone I thought my insides would come bursting out through my stomach. Every time the Flyers went into the Hawks zone it took every ounce of strength I had to keep watching. Maybe I'll just go outside and someone can tell me how this goes. I'm not up for it.

Then Campbell is keeping a puck in the Flyers' zone at the line. He's passing to Kane at the left circle. Then Kane is giving a head-fake, and streaking around Kimmo Timonen toward the goal line. Then he's sending a puck toward the net. Then he's skating around behind their net. There's an odd sound. Is he screaming? Then the camera pans back, as if it's searching for the puck. As it follows Kane, who is leaping and screaming toward the opposite end of the ice, I look up and see the Hawks bench has emptied. I briefly see my brother rise from his seat screaming, "GOAL!" but he's the only one. McClure, who had been standing to my right suddenly curls in front of me, his fists clenched and a look of total shock on his face.

Wait? Did he score? Is it over? IT MUST BE.

Then it's just darkness, as I'm buried in a group hug that Killion pours his beer over. Then there's Adam, with the hug we waited all our lives for. Better than I ever thought. We turn to see the replay. Yep, it had gone in. It was over. They did it. We saw them do it. 1992, you can go away now.

I hugged everyone else in the bar. We poured too many beers that we probably couldn't afford over each other. We stood outside getting passing cars to honk in celebration and high-fives out of their windows. We had cigars. My girlfriend had the torturous task of kissing me through a sweat-and beer-soaked playoff beard. The rest of the night passed more slowly than the game did, which was greatly welcomed.

We packed back into the bar to see Toews lift the Cup. A player wearing the Hawks jersey was going to lift the Cup. What the fuck sense did that make? It was something we had never seen, how could you describe it? Next time you see a unicorn, write down how that feels and see what you come up with.

I couldn't stop smiling. Some cried. My cheeks hurt by the end of it. I never wanted the night to end. I attempted to convey this by decreeing that we all should go to a 4:00 am bar. Except I stumbled getting off that stool in the middle of said proclamation, which caused my girlfriend to advise that it was best to end this night. Once again, she was right.

Two days later, I went to the parade. I usually would stay as far away as I could from a gathering like this. The Bulls parades I had seen looked so silly. But this one...no, I had to go. We got off the train and saw the masses lining Madison St. I couldn't believe it.

All those games I had seen with maybe three-thousand people in the UC. All the times I couldn't find anyone to watch to talk about hockey with. The way I was made fun of by Bulls-following grade-school mates. The way I had given up in high school, an island too far to inhabit anymore. The empty arena. The sad anthems. The beatdowns with only opposing fans cheering. The bus rides to the stadium when you were the only one going there, with fifteen minutes until puck drop. The desolate concourses and gates.

And now all of Chicago was red. It had all been washed away. Sure, it wasn't our secret, our club, our thing anymore. But who cared? Everyone now knew what we had known all along. You could sense they wished they'd known sooner, but at this time we were all there together. All of the torment and sadness was gone.

I knew it would never be the same. I didn't care.

A few days later, after things had died down a bit, on some random weekday afternoon when I wasn't up to much, my father strolled out of his room. He wasn't the most effusive man, which didn't mean I ever doubted how he felt. He just wasn't given to verbalizing. He knew what a whirlwind those days and weeks had been for me, trying to be the voice for some fans, a part of their experience, through the most memorable season we ever went through. He let me go through it on my own. I had him edit the program some in the first season. We occasionally argued over it, as he didn't approve of the more vulgar or wild sections I had put in. I explained to him in the first season of the program that if I was going to miss with something, it had to miss long and not short. Seeing as how this is exactly what he taught his students when he taught advertising part-time at Columbia College, he admitted he couldn't argue with me there. I think it might be the only argument I ever won with my father, given his brilliance and experience.

Anyway, he came out and said, "Son, I just wanted to tell you after everything you've done how proud I am of you. To create something on your own and have it be this...well, I'm just proud."

As corny and cliché as it might be, ask me what my favorite moment of the 2010 championship is, and there's only one answer. Nothing else even comes close.

Raise The Banner...With Whoever's Left
October 9, 2010
Red Wings vs. Hawks
Most recall the summer of 2010, even with the glow, and shudder. It was a true harvesting of what constituted the Hawks' depth. It was only two weeks after the celebration in Philadelphia that Dustin Byfuglien, Brent Sopel, Ben Eager, and Andrew Ladd had to be shipped to Atlanta because of the salary cap. A few days later, Kris Versteeg went to Toronto. After free agency began, the Hawks had the drama of the San Jose Sharks tendering Niklas Hjalmarsson an offer sheet, and the Hawks debating whether they could match it or not. They did, but that cost them the space to sign Antti Niemi, who went to San Jose instead of Hjalmarsson. Cristobal Huet also was farmed out to Europe. Half the team was gone, and what came in return wasn't exactly impressive.

Still, most fans tried to believe the best, which was a new leaf for Hawks fans to be sure. They still had just won a Cup for the first time in forty-nine years. Were we really going to get that upset if the team wasn't quite as good the next year?

I had to believe the best, because things in life weren't as sweet as I'd hoped. My brother's stay after getting laid off from his advertising job extended well after the Cup win, and to an indeterminate date. While my father and I were happy to help and support him, living with your entire family under one roof in a pretty small apartment was the ultimate test of one's patience. And both my father and Adam were not easiest to live with (I of course am, because I'm an elegant flower). As the season returning gave both me and my brother an excuse to at least get out of the house, I was happy to have it back no matter the state of the team.

Still, it was jarring to show up at the banner raising at the home opener for the season and see the stark changes. The Hawks first introduced their new players for the season, and that seemingly took twice as long as it did to introduce the players who remained from the championship team. The latter group was handed the Hawks' new banner by whoever was left standing from the 1961 team, and as they skated it to the other side of the ice to be hooked up to cables to be raised, my brother and I remarked that it just looked like a weekly card game in the basement. That's how few of them there were. We also wondered what the other guys thought as they just had to stand there while like eight of their teammates got to hold this banner they had nothing to do with. Did they feel like they belonged at all? Weren't they just spectators like we were?

The newcomers didn't make much of an impression that night. Viktor Stalberg was really fast, but rarely in the correct direction. A couple kids were coming up for full-time jobs, like Bryan Bickell and Jake Dowell. They looked like...well, like they took up space. This was the year that Bickell managed seventeen goals because teams never figured out that he had a really good wrist-shot if you gave him five minutes of time. And he was more than happy to settle for that, driving his coaches and fans nuts. Fernando Pisani looked lethargic, if we're being kind. Jack Skille had one move: skate really fast up the right wing and shoot from a bad angle and not score. He couldn't do anything else. We were being put through a Nick Boynton and Jassen Cullimore experience on defense.

The only bright spot was that Corey Crawford had come up from the system to back up Marty Turco, and it wasn't long before he would snap up the job himself and never give it back. But at the time, we still were seeing Turco's swashbuckling style of goaltending, and "swashbuckling" is not an adjective you ever want to associate with goaltending.

And of course, John Scott. This was the first time the Hawks employed a straight-up goon since they had become useful. Sure, they'd had Matt Walker two years before, but he could at least be trusted with ten minutes on defense. Scott couldn't do anything. This was the first sign that Joel Quenneville was getting some sort of say in roster decisions, because it was hard to fathom that forward thinkers like the Bowmans would want something like this. The theory was that Scott's presence would deter problems for Kane and Toews, except that didn't hold up to any sort of scrutiny when he played less than five minutes and the Hawks had won six of seven playoff series the previous two years without such a thing.

I was annoyed before he ever took the ice. I had gotten to the point where I realized the "enforcer" myth was just that. How was it supposed to work, exactly? If someone hits Kane or Toews, was Scott immediately going to hop over the boards? Because you can't actually do that. Was he going to join their next shift? Wouldn't he have to catch whoever he had beef with? Because he couldn't, and that would be the case if the other player was missing a leg. It was obvious already that the kind of role Scott filled was an anachronism. It was for a bygone era.

Scott was still playing defense at this point. The Hawks tied the game early in the second, and headed to the third that way. For some reason, early in the third Scott was sent out on a penalty kill. Valtteri Filppula came down the left wing with Scott waiting for him at the blue line. Filppula barely had to make a move, and Scott simply fell down. Didn't get faked out. Didn't guess wrong. He fell down merely trying to turn his hips. Filppula then had a freeway to Turco's net, and Turco wasn't much of a tollbooth on your way to a goal. It was a perfect metaphor for Scott's play and that season as a whole. The only hope was that Filppula would be laughing too hard to finish off the rush.

On a smaller level, Scott falling down to let Filppula in was a flashback to how it had been years before. The Wings had reloaded to catch the Hawks, and of course the roster purge had brought the Hawks back to the pack. The Wings and their fans were sure this would be a course-correction and on that night, they looked correct. Here were the Hawks dressing this construction horse who couldn't stay upright in a stiff breeze, and here the Wings were skating right past him to score. Hadn't we already done this for a decade or more and seen the results? On this night, when we were supposed to be celebrating the official ending of all that, here it came right back around and straight into our faces.

Wasted And Can't Find His Way Home
October 15, 2010
Hawks at Blue Jackets

At the time, it seemed just a routine game in Ohio that the Hawks won. Nothing you'd remember, as the Hawks tried to come to grips with their new teammates and lineup. Patrick Kane missed this game, and then we were told it was because of the "flu." It did not take long for the buzz to start that he'd missed the game because he was simply too fucked up to play.

The entire summer of 2010 was filled with stories about what Kane was up to in town or back home in Buffalo. You couldn't go into any bar in town where the staff didn't have a story about him being there recently or knew someone who did. Ask any three people in their twenties if they'd seen him out and about somewhere and assuredly at least one of them would say yes. He was having a summer that even rock stars would have described as "out there."

It was still in good fun, or so we thought. There weren't too many horror stories, and most reported that he was jovial if not completely incapacitated. That's when we first heard of some bars banning him, but there were more than enough to keep him entertained. He would show up to a game around this time with a black eye, and it didn't take long for everyone to find out that he'd gotten the shit kicked out of him by some bouncer somewhere. The signs were there.

Fans rarely ask their athletes to be angels. Most don't care what they get up to when off the clock, and I'm usually in that boat. The Hawks were the biggest celebrities in town now; most of them were pretty simple kids from smaller places, and you couldn't begrudge them for enjoying the benefits. But we fans wanted our athletes to actually show up to work. After all, we have to (well, everyone else does. I don't have a job). Kane failed that test, and it wouldn't be the last time either.

The Hawks kept it quiet, as they always did, and there wasn't much appetite from the press to do anything other than print what they'd been fed. Fans didn't want to hear it for sure, because most of them were newer fans and the Hawks were simply a party. We didn't want to hear it because hell, I drank a lot and I was still in my twenties and believed eventually they would all grow out of it. I just wanted to focus on hockey.

A few weeks later, after the Hawks came back from the usual Circus Trip, Kane was asked what they'd learned about themselves on the trip. The first thing he mentioned was the team's stop in Vegas. It was clear that was where his, and most of his teammates' priorities were. It should have been another loud, buzzing alarm.

Maybe if I'd raised my voice up about what Kane was doing, maybe if more joined me, the Hawks would have been forced to act sooner than they are rumored to have. More than likely though, I would have sounded like an old man clucking his tongue at "these kids." No one wanted to hear it. It certainly wouldn't be the last time we'd go down this road.

Judgement Day
April 10, 2011
Red Wings vs. Hawks

The last ten games of the season were a torture chamber for Hawks fans. The Hawks needed to win more than they lost and get help just to make the playoffs. They were without two key cogs with Patrick Sharp and Dave Bolland both out hurt. They were so desperate they tossed Marcus Kruger into the deep end right after he cleared customs coming from Sweden. And he mostly played like a kid from a different country, completely overmatched at most turns. How many times he wanted to get right back on the plane would have been an interesting study.

The Hawks just couldn't put consecutive efforts together. They beat the Panthers but then lost to the Ducks. They gutted out an OT win in Detroit, with Hossa and Kane playing over twenty-five minutes, that ended on a Hossa OT goal that Kane had drawn by outmuscling only Henrik

Zetterberg. But having the tanks emptied left them absolute cannon fodder for the Bruins the next night. They were able to strong-arm their way to a shootout win in Columbus, but then dropped the next two to Tampa and Montreal.

All of it left the Hawks having to win two of their last three games at least. In a terrifying turn, those three games were against the two teams we least wanted them against. It would start with a home game against the Blues, and while the Blues were bad it would be the stuff of their dreams to ruin the Hawks playoff chances a year after winning the Cup. The last two were against Detroit. It was being caught in a loop. One year removed from all the joy and relief, the potential to be thrown right back into our own hockey fan prison was terrifying.

Sharp returned for the game against the Blues even though he could barely walk. Even in his injured state, the Hawks needed him. They didn't play well, and went down 2-0 at the beginning of the second period. But they responded with three goals in the middle frame, basically on guts and guts alone. But with the way the season had gone, it wasn't going to be that easy.

Chris Stewart tied the game halfway through the third, as Nick Leddy and Duncan Keith once again completely lost each other as they had done for the entire time Quenneville paired them together. It was one of the many infuriating things about that season. The Hawks headed into an OT in which they had to find a goal otherwise there would be no room for error on the final weekend, while one bounce or one slip from one of their own with the reduced manpower of overtime would see curtains on the whole enterprise.

After some very dicey moments, Jonathan Toews streaked out of his own zone down the left wing and around the Blues defense. For some reason, Ty Conklin lost any definition of "angle," giving Toews an enormous amount of space on the shortside Captain Marvel had saved them, at least temporarily. The Hawks were beat up, tired, and shorthanded, but had seemingly found a way purely on know-how and "testicular fortitude," as Mean Gene Orkerlund would say.

Still, they were far from out of the woods. A home-and-home with Detroit awaited, and the Hawks needed three points out of the four on offer to clinch a playoff spot and at least save some face.

The first half of the set came too easily. We should have known. It was all a trap. The Wings were going to do this the most painful way possible, even though it meant nothing to them. That made it even more sinister. This was their way. The Hawks took a 3-0 lead in the first, added a fourth early in the second, and really weren't ever in danger. That left them only needing to get to overtime two days later on a Sunday afternoon.

Even though it was another 11:30 am start, the morning hours didn't dissolve any of the tension outside the United Center. We had been through big playoff games the previous two seasons, but at least with playoff games there's still a small sense of celebration. You got there. There was accomplishment. A loss on this day would see the defending champs not even make the playoffs. It would be an embarrassment of the highest order. While it wouldn't have washed away the joy and memory of the previous year's Cup, it would taint it just a tad. Make it seem like some sort of miracle or something. And to have the axe come down in the hands of Detroit...it was a reality we simply couldn't deal with.

And I had to miss the start of it. I had instituted a tradition of giving my tickets of the last two home games of the year to my vendors as some form of bonus, no matter how important the games were. So once selling was done, I rushed back in the car and headed home. It's helpless watching a game on TV, because you have no control. But merely listening on the radio is far worse. You have no control and you have to picture everything in your mind. You're trapped in your car, and your fellow motorists are not helping. Every red light I ran into sent me into a rage. Didn't the cosmos know where I needed to be? I needed a runway, dammit!

I got home about halfway through the first period, which remains a record. Thankfully I didn't pass any of Chicago's finest on my way. There was no scoring in the period, which only raised the tension level. I made for the bottle of Powers before the period was out, drawing a look of confusion and disappointment from my father. But these were desperate times, his opinions of day drinking be damned.

Five minutes into the second, Michael Frolik took a centering pass from Kane and rifled one past Jimmy Howard. It was elation, only for a goal. It could not have been a more tenuous lead, but it was a lead. Surely the Wings, who didn't have anything to play for, would make only a half-pass at a comeback and then worry about the playoffs.

If only.

Mike Babcock's in-game interview was chilling. He told Pierre MacGuire, "We don't have to put on a show here, they do." He knew the Hawks might punch themselves out on the pressure. He knew his wise and relaxed team would find their spot. It was clear that not having anything to play for made them only more dangerous.

The lead didn't even last two minutes. Viktor Stalberg sent a blind centering pass from the corner whizzing through the slot but no one was there. Worse yet, he couldn't know the Hawks defense was changing behind him. Because of that, the puck ricocheted out to center where Tomas Holmstrom picked it up and had nothing between him and Crawford. While Keith and Seabrook strained to catch up, Holmstrom blasted the puck over Crawford's shoulder.

Here it comes.

The Wings would pile on two more on either side of the second intermission. Seabrook would bring the Hawks within one, but Cleary would restore the two-goal lead with twelve minutes to go. It was so assured, so easy, so pleasurable for them. They were playing with their food again. The bad old days had returned. They were doing this just because they could.

Duncan Keith scored with eight minutes to go to restore hope. Even in their depleted state, the Hawks were mustering a death rattle. They threw everything at the Wings. They skated as if they were being chased by a machete-wielding maniac. They had chances. In the dying seconds, off a faceoff, the puck was put to the front of the net where Keith had hurled himself. It came right to him, and then at the very last possible moment it jumped over his stick.

The Hawks had lost.

It wasn't over yet, but it might as well have been. The Stars still needed to win hours later to confirm the kill, and they were playing a Wild team that had been finished for a while. Surely that was going to be elementary. Toews seemed shellshocked in the postgame. I watched him try to find the words, wanting to scream, "We tried to tell you!"

I didn't even want to watch the Stars-Wild game, but my brother convinced me to. In a season where basically nothing had gone right, I didn't see why this one would. Even when the Wild opened the scoring, I only viewed it as a taunt. Sure enough, the Stars scored twice before the end of the period and the Hawks were back on the last mile.

The Wild scored twice in the first half of the second to take the lead, but I still viewed it with suspicion and anger. Don't do this to me. Don't make me believe. I won't do it. You can't make me. I was almost relieved when the Stars tied it again late in the second, affirmation for my refusal to be drawn in.

Antti Miettinen scored for Minnesota seven minutes into the last period. Still I felt nothing. As the minutes ticked away, and the Stars more and more looked helpless, it began to emerge. This could happen. I could feel something. I didn't want it to, because I knew the crash would be harder. The Stars would score in the last minute and then in overtime to assure our destruction. It would have to be as painful as possible, it had to be, and that's the only way it could be more painful than Detroit being the executioner. Making it seem like you'd escaped their clutches, only to be brought down by the guys in the tower as you sprinted toward freedom.

And yet the Stars hardly mounted a stirring comeback. The desperation they should have had was nowhere to be found. The furious rush that should have been the last five minutes never materialized. They just petered out. Even just a goal down, it felt like they accepted their fate. Pierre-Marc Bouchard scored an empty-netter.

Salvation.

Our playoff tickets had arrived via FedEx weeks before, but I refused to open them until the Hawks were officially in. It was avoiding jinx, in part, and also expressing my rage at the Hawks this season. I wasn't going to show belief in them until they deserved it. After the final horn in St. Paul, I walked over to the envelope, stood in front of my brother, and made a ceremony of tearing off the opening tag. He laughed loudly. He told me, "You didn't think for one second the Wild would win until the end." He was right.

So Close, And Yet So Far
April 26, 2011
Hawks vs. Canucks (Game Seven)

Our feelings of sheepishness about tumbling drunkenly (perhaps literally) into the playoffs were not helped by the Hawks getting their doors blown off in the first two games in Vancouver. They were so outclassed. This was not much of a defense. We wondered if maybe we shouldn't have declined the playoff invitation.

The embarrassment hit the hilt when Quenneville not only dressed John Scott for Game Three, but put him on the power play. The Canucks couldn't contain their laughter when they heard. The Hawks went from champs to resorting to carnival tricks in less than a year. Of course, Scott took a penalty on a power play that the Hawks needed and the Canucks ended up scoring a couple minutes later. I think I yelled loud enough that Q would have heard me from my seat.

Selling outside Game Four was perhaps the most joyous funeral I've ever been a part of. Most of my regulars had dumped their tickets, not being able to bear the sight of the Canucks celebrating on the United Center ice. Those of us who did make it down just tried to focus on seeing one more hockey game before shop was shut up for the summer. It beat staying at home, after all.

Luckily for everyone in attendance, the Canucks had been too busy celebrating themselves, and looked like it during Game Four. The Hawks torched them, to at least save some face as it seemed at the time, and I headed out to the bar to celebrate what I thought was the beginning of summer vacation.

When your team is down in a series, you'll come up with all sorts of things to stay positive. Down 3-0, well, let's get a win just to not get swept. You get that one, and you think, "Well, the Hawks are flying home after Game Five anyway, so they might as well play a game when they get back, right?"

And the Canucks were playing right into it, as whatever fog they were in stuck around for Game Five as the Hawks smeared them into paste by a 5-0 score. Suddenly it felt real, and the air outside of Game Six didn't have any of the resignation of Game Four.

This was the first time I had seen the Hawks live when they faced direct elimination. Which only made watching even more punishment. Every rush against wouldn't just give the Canucks a lead, wouldn't just end the season, but would see them celebrate on the Hawks' ice. A fate worse than death, that.

Game Six was one of the more wild nights at the United Center I could remember. Roberto Luongo didn't start, but had to come in relief when Cory Schneider got hurt. Michael Frolik took over the third period, which is just slapstick. He tied the game on a penalty shot, which never happen in the playoffs. Ben Smith ended it in overtime when Luongo fell flat on his face, the symbolism you couldn't help but soak in.

Despite all they had going against them, the Hawks could still load up an overhand right to rock the best team in the league. In a matter of days I had gone from angry and wanting them rightly punished to not believing I could ever not believe in them. Now the Canucks were on the verge of perhaps the greatest choke in the sport's history. It would complete them.

We gathered at our hockey bar for Game Seven. I was in a bouncy mood. Not so much in my confidence in the Hawks, but my confidence in the Canucks to absolutely fuck it up in the best way possible. This was an organization that has a statue of a coach complaining about the refs outside their arena, for fuck's sake. I didn't even bat an eye when Burrows scored two minutes in. These were the Hawks, these were the Canucks. It was fine. This would only make it better.

I didn't blink when the second period passed with no goals. These were the Hawks, these were the Canucks. Fifteen shots in the period for the Canucks? Merely a tease.

As the minutes ticked off the third, I still didn't worry. These were the Hawks, these were the Canucks. Luongo wasn't going from being afraid to show his face to shutting the Hawks out in a Game Seven in the span of two days. There was no way.

When Keith took a penalty with three minutes to go, then I started to worry. And what should have been a whole night of nerves and panic got packed into the span of mere minutes. I could physically feel my chest cave in. How were they going to do this? Down a goal and shorthanded with their best d-man in the box? On the road?

Oh right, they'd done this before.

Seabrook caused a turnover right at center ice, and the retreating Toews scooped up the puck and curled right back up the ice. He then split two Canucks by sheer force, exhibiting that whole "You're not fucking winning this game" feeling by himself. He muscled the puck over to Hossa, who had a shot saved. The angle of the camera caused Toews, who was lying flat on the ice, to be concealed from view under a couple Canucks. We couldn't see him swipe his stick at the rebound. All I saw was Luongo freeze and then collapse in shock forwards. Then Toews was leaping into Seabrook's arms. I couldn't hear the broadcast over the din of the bar. Only then did I figure it out, right about the time I was in a bar-wide mosh pit celebrating.

This was it. This was the moment I was so sure was coming the whole day. The moment that would hurt Vancouver the worst.

People forget that Hossa had another glorious chance on that kill right after it that Luongo recovered to save. The Canucks had a couple themselves, but Crawford stood tall. During the intermission, all I could think about how sweet the Hawks winner was going to be. These were the Hawks, these were the Canucks.

The Canucks came out strong, and during a particularly furious shift in the Hawks zone, Burrows simply tackled Keith in the corner. Penalties were never called in OT, and I was sure this wouldn't be either and I was sure it would lead to a Canucks goal. This was the only way they could overcome who they were, obviously, by being cheating bastards. It was a relief in a way, because we could always say they couldn't do it on the up and up.

Miraculously, the ref's arm went up. Here it was. The Canucks blowing their lead in the last two minutes on the power play, and now going to be put to the sword during a Burrows penalty. It almost felt as good as the championship a year early.

I still haven't watched the replay. I probably never will. Toews picks up the puck in the corner and starts toward the net. Sharp is closing in on the other side. That passing lane is open. We'd seen this play dozens of times. Sharp never missed. Here it was. Whoever was standing next to me, I clutched their shoulder, in anticipation of another mosh pit.

Except Luongo knew. By the time the puck got to Sharp, it was clear that Luongo was already over. There was nowhere to go. Shot saved. You could hear the entire arena exhale. Was that it? That's how I would have drawn it up. It was supposed to go top corner, hear Sharp yell over the entire crowd, see the Hawks spill off the bench, see Luongo sitting still, completely stunned, shots of various Canucks crying. That all vanished.

Even with all that's happened since, there are moments where I still wonder what if the pass had been harder. What if Toews had faked that pass and tried to stuff it home? What if? It still causes me to swear quietly to myself. Sometimes in public. At least it's been quietly.

What came next happened too quickly. Like two years previous, when your season ends on an OT goal, it's too much at once. By the time I realized Chris Campoli's attempted clear off the glass had been intercepted, Burrows was skating right between the circles. Before I came to terms with that, he was winding up. Before I realized there was no one in between him and Crawford, the strobe lights around the net were flashing and fans were jumping on the TV and the bar fell silent. It would be another few seconds or minutes before I realized it was all over. You're waiting for some kind of intervention, even though you can't possibly fathom what it would be. Act of God? But then you know it's not coming. How could it end this way? Seeing it end that was is like getting blindly doused with something. First you have to figure out why you're wet. Then you have to figure out what's been poured on you. Then you have to figure out where it came from. Then who did it.

It fit in with the profile of the curse being a Hawks fan had been for almost all of my life. While the championship had lifted a lot of it, it hadn't lifted all of it.

In perfect melody, the next day was my thirtieth birthday. That was how I entered my thirties. I doubt I've forgiven them since.

Of course, the Canucks went on to lose in the most agonizing way possible, a Game Seven at home. Which was a consolation, to be sure. Schadenfreude can be therapeutic.

The Slow Build
October 8, 2011
Stars vs. Hawks

The Hawks headed into the summer with some flexibility and would gain more.

The offseason kicked off with the trade of Brian Campbell. I was out for a close friend's bachelor party when I got the news. And I felt more deflated than I had any right to be or had anticipated. I had spent longer arguing for Campbell than I had any other player. His signing had signified a different era for the Hawks, one in which they would be major players in the free agent market. We hadn't seen that before. As more and more fans got knives out for him, including the broadcast team for reasons I still can't understand, I only appreciated him more. We felt like a cult, those who could understand what he brought to the team. For most of my life as a fan, there had only been a handful of players who could do what Campbell could. Doug Wilson, Gary Suter, there were about four minutes where Eric Weinrich got into the good stuff and played like a cyborg, and Duncan Keith. There were a couple others who pit-stopped in Chicago before heading onto bigger things, but this was it for players who remained Hawks for multiple years.

His trade didn't just feel like the removal of a player, but a loss on some other front. That the Hawks themselves had bought into a meatball way of thinking. That they were still shitting on Dale Tallon by getting rid of his first big free agent, and better yet sending him back to Tallon in Florida. In reality they needed the cap space and thought Nick Leddy was ready to take over that spot. But I couldn't see that at the time. I felt like I was being repudiated. Once again, I felt like I was on the losing side.

That wasn't the end of the Hawks summer though, not by a longshot. Troy Brouwer was also moved along for draft picks, causing some of the same feelings as Campbell's departure though not nearly to the same extent. It was hard to believe that there was no so little left from the 2010 team.

The Hawks used their newfound financial flexibility in something of a scattergun fashion. They signed Andrew Brunette, Jamal Mayers, Sean O'Donnell, Steve Montador, and perhaps most controversially, Daniel Carcillo. All of them would go on to have either bewildering or simply non-existent careers as Hawks. In fact, all of them save Carcillo would never play for anyone else in the NHL. And Carcillo came close. Usually when your free agent signings shuffle off into the abyss after one season, you haven't really had a successful offseason. The Hawks were something of a hockey hospice.

Another dagger in the heart of any progressive thinker was the introductory press conference for all of them in July. It wasn't three minutes in before all of them would be asked about fighting by what was a still underdeveloped media. The perception was that the Hawks got beat up by the Canucks in the playoffs, instead of just being overmatched talent-wise like they were. Who the fuck gave the least amount of shit about whether Andrew Brunette, who could barely move at this point, was willing to drop the gloves? But they all had to answer as the meatheaded press corps sought its chum. It was a solid indication of where greater Hawks and hockey thinking was at that point in this town.

It's chilling to look back on now, considering that Montador's career, and a few years later his life, ended due to his concussion problems. Here were the frothing press corps seeking some sort of bloodlust in the middle of the summer from a guy who, though he couldn't have known at the time, was in no shape to be doing such a thing. Did he feel that pressure from the press? From the team? Who was taking cues from whom?

Carcillo of course ate it up, and baited basically the unwashed section of the fanbase with his answers about the Canucks, even though he'd been in the Eastern Conference the previous three years. It's almost impossible to describe the idiocy of this whole day. Here was the team's media base basically: "Hey, don't you really hate the Canucks? Everyone here hates the Canucks. You should, too!" and then giggling at their handiwork.

Another repressed memory for many out of this offseason was the training camp experiment of Patrick Kane playing center. It came out of nowhere, though its roots were planted in Patrick Sharp deciding he didn't want to play center anymore. Sharp had moved out of the center role the previous season for the most part, but when things got tense toward the end of the season he moved back to the middle. Apparently that was it for him, because as the Hawks showed up with only Toews, the never-healthy Bolland, and the unproven Kruger as centers, it was Kane that was first foisted into the gap. That was after a season during which the Hawks tried Michael Frolik and Tomas Kopecky there, so clearly Sharp was a break-glass-in-case option then, and not even that at this time. It was just the latest chapter in the multi-year search for a center to slot between Toews and Bolland.

Joel Quenneville still had a fair amount of glow from the Cup a season previous, so we didn't really view this as the whacked-out hunch that it really was. There was no basis to try it other than "What the fuck?" And "What the fuck?" is rarely something you get away with at the top level. Lord knows it wouldn't be the last time Q would reach into the big bag o' tricks.

The Statues
October 22· 2011
Avalanche vs. Hawks

On this night, the Hawks unveiled the statues of Stan Mikita and Bobby Hull. It was a big event, even though the statues look a bit odd with their painted red jerseys on the bronze.

Much like the original "Heritage Night" they received when Rocky and McDonough first took over, we didn't think much at the time of the message they were sending by bronzing Hull forever. It was just yet another marker of the Hawks trying to honor their past that they hadn't before. No one at the time mentioned that there was now a statue outside the UC of a wife-beating, nazi-sympathizing shithead. And anyone who might have mentioned it at the time would have been shouted down.

It was the first time that my emotions started to turn cold to the whole thing. Considering the newness of the fanbase, the Hawks really gained nothing by honoring Hull over and over again. It certainly would cost them nothing to quietly separate themselves from him. Having him around only insults and enrages whatever fanbase that pays attention to what he was and is. At best, it's simply lazy and ignorant. At worst it's outright malice.

Sometimes I wonder how long that statue will last. It could be forever. Everyone is pretty clear on what Hull is and was, and there still hasn't been much of an appetite to take it down. I've never heard anyone suggest it. As long as Rocky is around it'll probably be there. I wonder if it won't be when the Hawks have to change their name and logo and want to cleanse the whole image. You'd think it would happen at some point. Maybe one day, when anyone who actually saw Hull play has spun off their mortal coil, the Hawks could do it. But then the memories of what he did off the ice will have probably faded, too.

They could put it next to Paterno's statue, wherever that is.

Rubix Q

The Hawks were a wonky outfit, though they had somehow stumbled to the top of the division early in the season. They had done that even though the first real cracks in the working relationship between their coach and GM began to really show.

We hadn't really seen it before. The 2010 roster was so loaded that there couldn't have been any problems. The salary cap restrictions that handcuffed the 2011 roster didn't leave any room for maneuvering from Joel Quenneville or Stan Bowman.

But this was different. Bowman had his first offseason where he could add some pieces, and had added a few of them. And yet none of them, over a month into the season, were being used as envisioned. Steve Montador, probably the big prize, was in and out of the lineup and sometimes at forward. Andrew Brunette was on the fourth line. Sean O'Donnell and Sami Lepisto were sitting behind John Scott. And why was John Scott playing ahead of Mayers and Carcillo who were, in theory, brought in to do the same things? Wasn't Mayers Q's guy from St. Louis?

It was active shitting on all of the GM's offseason moves, a coach trying to flex all the muscles he had. But wasn't Q in on all the meetings when they planned to sign these guys? And if he wasn't, why not? He's the one who has to play these guys and he should at least know what's going on in the front office. Nothing was working how it was seemingly designed to. The dedicated Hawks fans had a lot of questions, and there weren't a lot of answers forthcoming.

This was when our Twitter war with the beat writers really went into overdrive. It started with the following from Tim Sassone from the Daily Herald: "Don't know why Q keeps using John Scott but he must have his reasons." A reporter, speculating on whether or not the coach he covers *every single day* has reasons or not for a decision. Geez, maybe, and I know this is coming out of left field and is revolutionary, ask him? Why weren't these questions getting asked? What was going on between coach and GM?

And yet, no one asked. Every time we wondered why, we were basically patted on the head by the mainstream media and told how adorable our confusion, curiosity, and anger was. We were assured that there was no way the Hawks would answer any question in that mold, even though we never saw anyone try. They hinted at some sort of Langley-like lockdown on information, yet no one even wanted to test it. Would the Hawks really strip someone of their credentials?

It was about this time that more and more of our readers were wondering why we didn't seek out press passes. Now, we knew this was fruitless. The Hawks had no relationship with bloggers, which was to their detriment. Blogs had long surpassed the beat writers as the go-to for for serious fans, and we were covering the game the way they wanted. Other teams in the league had given bloggers full access, and even hired some. The Hawks had no interest.

But I'd be lying if I said we had any interest either. We were offered credentials once, before the 2010 Final. But seeing as how I had season tickets and was going to every game anyway, I didn't see the point. Once Killion found out you couldn't drink in the press box, he lost any interest as well.

I'd never really seen the point. I was no journalist, just a glorified commenter. I needed the beat writers to get the info I would never be allowed to pursue. And if by some miracle the Hawks had given us credentials, it would have lasted no longer than a press conference or two. Because after asking one or two questions that might have threatened probing, I'm sure the Hawks would have had no problem stripping these silly kids of them.

These issues only got worse as the season went on. And it wouldn't be the last time there was a disconnect between upstairs and downstairs. Things were not all right in Mudville.

Kruger's Brain
December 20, 2011
Hawks vs. Penguins

The NHL had something of a concussion crisis at this time, if it doesn't constantly. It certainly was caught standing still when it came home to roost. Sidney Crosby missed this game, and he would miss most of the season with his concussion problems. A week prior, Chris Pronger played his last game in the NHL thanks to a concussion. Players were dropping and the league knew it had a problem. Soon a lawsuit similar to the one the NFL was scrambling to cover would arrive at the NHL's doorstep as well.

The Hawks couldn't escape it forever. Their handling of brain injuries before didn't inspire a lot of confidence. There was sending Martin Havlat back out for the next game after he got completely trucked by Niklas Kronwall in the 2009 playoffs, to the point that his eyes rolled back in his head. Dave Bolland had missed most of the end of the 2011 campaign and the first three games of that series against Vancouver, and the Hawks weren't too hesitant to let it be known to the media that they thought he was taking too long. There were other players in the organization that had it not so quietly suggested were taking too long to come back from head injuries. All of it spoke to a somewhat dismissive attitude to head injuries.

During this loss to the Penguins, Marcus Kruger was turned into plaster by a Penguin defender, and returned to the bench. He didn't make it out for a couple shifts before the Hawks declared him out for the game. He should have been immediately removed.

And he played the next game, where Rick Nash would send him out with two punches to the back of his head. It would be the second time that season, and not the last, that Kruger would suffer a head injury only to miss a period or two. The Hawks weren't compelled to administer any kind of test as they and every other team is now. They basically let Kruger say he was fine, and they went on that to reinsert him. Who knows how much worse they made it, and it's not even worth thinking about what could have happened.

The Hawks went on to learn some harsh lessons about this during this season and beyond. Steve Montador ended up missing most of the second half of the season due to a concussion. He came back for one game (where he was played at forward), suffered another head injury, and was never heard from again. Three years later Montador passed away with massive damage to his brain due to CTE (chronic traumatic encephalopathy).

That's not to claim the Hawks are responsible for Montador's death, and they ducked the family's lawsuit of the NHL (if you want to speculate on how their financial compensation to the family previous influenced their avoidance of being sued, I'm not going to stop you).

Hockey has the same problems as football and all sports really, in that everyone is encouraged to play through pain and injury. Hockey especially glorifies what these guys put themselves through in the playoffs. There are countless stories of guys playing with broken feet, punctured lungs, broken ribs, busted knees and wrists. For so long, brain injuries were just categorized as just another malady. There are decades of attitudes to undo, and the people who carried those attitudes are still coaching and managing teams at every level. Until they are removed, there is going to be a problem.

There is no way to make hockey totally safe, just as there is no way to make football totally safe. We're getting to a point where all players realize what the dangers are and can make informed decisions for themselves. Total information of course is going to lead to less participation, though I doubt hockey will go the way of boxing, the way football very well might.

The Hawks have followed the rest of the NHL, maybe just by force, in taking special care with head injuries. But the way they got there was not pretty.

Into The Tank
February 10, 2012
Hawks vs. Sharks
Never had things completely fallen apart on the Hawks in the Quenneville era like they did after the All-Star break. They doubled up a loss to the Preds in Nashville with all of us barely conscious in the stands by

losing to them again at home two days later. The post-break schedule started with a West Coast swing. They lost in overtime to the Canucks. They then had perhaps the strangest loss of the decade in Edmonton.

What made it more strange is that the Hawks' previous visit to Edmonton in November saw them surrender nine goals. At the time it was just one of those nights where everything that could go wrong did, but the Hawks were flying high (get it?) at the time and it was brushed off.

Except their second trip there saw them surrender eight goals, and on every goal Sam Gagner had a hand. He scored four of them, and assisted on the other four. He put up eight points in one night against the Hawks. No one has scored four goals against them since. No one has come anywhere near eight points. They had given up seventeen goals in two games to the Oilers who were definitely the NHL's remedial class. Most Hawks fans can still clearly hear in their heads Pat Foley's exclamation after the eighth goal of, "EIGHT POINTS!!!" Maybe it was, "EIGHT POINTS?!!!," like he couldn't quite believe it was happening. This was a farce. It was a dumb show. It was bad magic. Eight points in a game was something you might see in the '80s. In 2012, this was seeing a white whale.

Most can tell you where they were for signature games. Where they were when the Hawks won the Cup each time. Those wins over the Sharks or Wings or various playoff games. The night Sam Gagner scored eight points is another. If you're like me, you just stared at your screen, trying to make sense of the colors and shapes in front of you but failing terribly. Over and over in my head I kept reviewing the definition of "eight points" and "Sam Gagner" and "one game." Separately they all made sense. Combined was fucking word salad.

We kept wondering where bottom was. We were actively reaching for it. It didn't come the next night in Calgary, where the Hawks lost again. Four nights later it still wouldn't arrive as the Hawks lost to Colorado.

Ok, I would put myself on the case and take care of this in person. I headed out to see some friends in San Francisco, with the trip revolving around seeing the Hawks in San Jose. Surely they couldn't lose seven in a row.

It ended up being a surreal trip. My first night there I discovered the hard way that Racer 5, though delicious, was about 10% ABV. When writing the manual on how to stay with friends, you wouldn't put "leave the key to his apartment he just gave you hours before in the door when you come home at 3:00 am" near the top of the list. Early the next morning, my friend found out he had passed his EMT exam and we spent the whole day celebrating, which included breakfast sandwiches and Budweisers in some third-shift bar at 10:00 am and champagne by 11:00 am.

We got to our seats in The Tank later that day, with plenty of time for puck drop. The arena in San Jose feels smaller than most of the newer buildings, which is a refreshing change. The Sharks took the ice to

Metallica, skating out of a shark head. Loud music, intimate feeling building, goofy sideshow…it touched the child within me for sure.

Any joy I was feeling lasted about two minutes. Corey Crawford went swimming on a Hawks power play, leaving Justin Braun an entire net to aim for. It happened again halfway through the period, and though the Hawks would manage a couple comebacks Crawford would eventually surrender the winner in the third.

This was the game where it became official that Crawford was having his PROBLEMS, at least to me. The clue should have been the EIGHT POINTS, but I could delude myself for longer than most imagine possible. He looked awful in this game, and based on the expense and time to get to San Jose I was watching him with a little more anger in my eyes. He was flying out of his net, always off his angles, and unconfident to the point you could feel it in the seats.

That two hour train ride back to San Francisco is a lot harder when you're out of beer and the Hawks have just lost their seventh in a row. You're hungover in every way no more than halfway through it. And of course the Sharks fans on the train are in a boisterous mood. It's about as low as you can get when you're being taunted by a bro wearing sunglasses at night. Silicon Valley, yo.

Thanks Crow.

The Hawks would go on to lose two more, making for a nine-game losing streak. Worse yet, during that Sharks game Toews took a hit from Thornton that would eventually see him leave a few games later and not return for the rest of the season. We couldn't come to grips with a nine-game losing streak. That didn't happen to good teams. That didn't happen to teams that wanted to go somewhere. We hadn't seen anything like it in years.

When a streak like that is going, the crashes are hard. Three games you shrug off as just the way the ball bounces sometimes. But once you get to four or five, you start to worry that something has infested. It's not just luck. After every loss you build up to the next game, sure that'll be the one to snap it. When they lose that one, you crash farther than where you started. And to build back up with hope for the next one you have to work harder. Get to eight or nine, and you're absolutely exhausted. At least Sisyphus only had to roll the boulder from the same point every time. Hawks fans had to keep finding a new bottom. I even went clean-shaven for the first time in five or six years to try to reverse the mojo. "How long is it going to take to grow back?" my girlfriend asked upon first seeing my bare "chin" for the first time. Point made.

The losing streak fried the synapses of a large swath of the fanbase and media. This was when the calls to trade Patrick Kane for Ryan Miller became popular, which was just beyond belief. What was this? Everyone was losing their mud.

What a way to run a railroad.

This Is Your Public
March 18, 2012
Capitals vs. Hawks

One of the beauties of the job I held as program writer was getting to meet so many readers in person. It gave me a good sense of what people wanted, how much they were enjoying it or weren't, and how to make it a little more personal of an experience for them. But sometimes, that sort of thing would get weird, though adorable.

It was a relatively warm night for March. For once I got to my spot on time, which was a real struggle thanks to my loose grasp of time and Chicago traffic. I got the vendors all set up, myself set up, and started selling programs to those waiting in line to get into the arena before the doors opened.

Shortly after, an adorable little girl came up to me, three dollars in hand. This would happen from time to time, as parents would give their children the thrill of holding money and purchasing the program for them. But clearly this was more than that. She had something she wanted to say. She was so nervous talking to an adult (or rather this person who was at least adult-sized) she didn't know, but I tried to make it as easy as I could for her, even though to this day I have no idea how to talk to kids. I asked her what her name was and how long she'd been reading the program. Finally I asked her if there was something she wanted to ask me.

She looked up, nervous and excited, and with a shaky voice so sweetly said to me, "No. But...I just...I just wanted to say...that my favorite part...is...is…when you call Detroit 'Assbutts!'" Then she sprinted away, mission accomplished but wanting to get the terrifying experience over.

I couldn't stop laughing. I was poisoning the youth, the way I had been poisoned.

When I went into the arena and joined my father inside—I was making my second attempt at showing him Ovechkin, because the first one had gone oh so well—he couldn't ignore the odd smile on my face. He inquired and I relayed the story to him, and I still don't know how to describe his reaction. He chuckled, but his shoulders also sank. He laughed while simultaneously slapping his hand to his head. He couldn't admit to being proud that his son was teaching small children to swear, and yet he couldn't hide the fact that he was. I don't know what my father dreamed I would become or what he wanted for me. I highly doubt writing a publication that caused little girls to delight in the term "assbutts" ever entered into it. And yet he had to know something that unique would be a result. I was his son, after all. We didn't follow anyone else's path.. I guess he was lamenting what he'd helped me become, while simultaneously being delighted that it couldn't end any other way.

Most Peculiar, Mama

April 19, 2012

Coyotes vs. Hawks (Game Four)

Even though Toews missed the rest of the season, even though Duncan Keith found himself suspended for the last five games of the year for dropping a People's Elbow on Daniel Sedin, the Hawks finished the season relatively strong.

Though the Hawks finished the season 16-5-4 after their nine games from hell, thanks to the way the NHL does its standings, they couldn't really make up any ground on any team above them. They finished in sixth in the Conference, which lined them up with the Phoenix (now Arizona) Coyotes. Most fans were delighted by this, because they seemed to be the easiest matchup. We all basically ignored how well their goalie Mike Smith was playing, and how solid defensively they had been. Merely a statistical outlier, of course. No question some of the dismissing of the Coyotes from Hawks fans had to do with their locale. It's a blindspot for hockey fans to this day, as if a team in Arizona has to employ players only from Arizona or something.

What ensued was just about the strangest playoff series you'll ever see. Toews returned for Game One, and ended up scoring on his second shift. At the time, we all thought it was just a harbinger of the Hawks getting ready to hit fifth gear. But the Coyotes found two goals in the second period. Both Crawford and Niklas Hjalmarsson were simply awful, as they had been for most of the season. They both played in such a panicked fashion. The Hawks trailed until there was fifteen seconds left, when Brent Seabrook was able to finally blast one past Smith. Surely this would turn to the Hawks now.

It wasn't to be, as Martin Hanzal scored off a draw halfway through the first overtime. Eh, big deal, we thought. Smith can't play that way the whole series. Lucky punch.

Two nights later, once again the Hawks emptied the chamber at Smith. They had twenty-one shots in the last two periods, but nothing would get by him. They decided to up the degree of difficulty, and this time Sharp tipped in a point shot with only six seconds left to tie the game. The image of Smith burying his face into the ice after looking behind him would sustain me, or so I thought.

Halfway through overtime, Viktor Stalberg picked off an Adrian Aucoin pass, fed Bryan Bickell in the circle, and he got to enact his finisher of snapping an open wrister past a goalie. There. The Hawks had recovered from the sucker punch of Game One and now everything was in order. Come home, clean this up, move on.

Game Three obviously got off to a less than ideal start. Not quite halfway through the opening period, Raffi Torres attempted to decapitate Marian Hossa at center ice about ten seconds after Hossa had passed the puck. It was one of the rare times per season a stretcher came out on the ice, and whenever that happens there's a hush and fear throughout the building. When the fear of a permanent injury is right in front of you, you can't help but wonder what you've asked of these guys and what you've become. Was it worth all this? You shut out the danger these guys are in because they almost always get through it. When one doesn't without major damage, your illusions get dimmed.

Torres was the exact type of player that fighting doesn't stop from being a scumbag, and one the NHL has to do a better job of getting out of the game. He actively tries to hurt people, and having to answer to a fight never deterred him. I couldn't believe how there could be such an absence of respect for a fellow professional. All these guys are performing the same job. All these guys are making a living, and most of them have families. No matter what your role is, no matter how competitive you are, no matter how much it means to you, I still find it impossible to fathom of how a player could be so unhinged as to lose sight of all this and to think it's acceptable and even demanded that he try to injure another player specifically. He was a workplace hazard, and where else would that be accepted?

The Hawks took the lead twice, but in the middle of the third Johnny Oduya and Nick Leddy lost use of their legs and arms for a brief period of time during a four-on-four and simply gifted an equalizer to Ray Whitney.

In overtime, the Hawks were once again all over the Coyotes but couldn't crack the code of Mike Smith. The UC faithful had been all over Smith thanks to his "Toast Of Croyden" antics that had gotten Shaw suspended for three games. And yet it felt like the more "Mike Smith Sucks!" chants that came raining down, the better he got. This asshole was feeding on this. They had fucking Doomsday in net.

Halfway into the overtime, the Coyotes dumped the puck into the left corner of the Hawks' zone, and it was their first entry there for what seemed like hours. Mikkel Boedker found the puck in the corner and just flung it from the goal-line at Crawford. It hit Crow's stick and directed behind him. It was a terrible goal, and even worse in overtime. And it basically broke Crawford. It was the first time since Sandis Ozolinch had shattered my heart (and the whole organization) in '96 that I was in the building for a playoff OT goal against the Hawks. I had to once again come to terms with the initial small groan, and the silence that follows it that allows everyone in the building to hear the players' celebration on the ice. The way the mind tries to recoil for a few seconds in a bid to not accept what you've just seen and try and avoid the dread that follows, and the deflation when you the dread unavoidably descends.

Game Four was another slog. There was no scoring in the first two periods, which only raised the tension level to unbearable. The Coyotes scored twice in a minute in the third, and doom seemed to be ringing the doorbell. Brendan Morrison, yes he was a Hawk there for a minute, scored in the middle of the period, and the Hawks once again entered, "You're not fucking winning this game, you're not fucking winning this series" mode. They never let the Coyotes out of their own zone, but again kept running up a wall.

Once again, it was up to Michael Frolik to save the day.

The Hawks had found it once again when they absolutely had to find it. They were all balls. They came close to falling on the mat but summoned a punch to get back to the stool. Ok, here we go. Market correction, here it comes. Tie the series, go back to Arizona and set up a shell-shocked Coyotes team for the kill back here. This was the quickly written script in our heads.

Yeah, no.

Barely into the overtime, Boedker took advantage of Leddy fumbling the puck at the offensive blue line and went the other way on a partial breakaway. Leddy and Oduya were able to hassle him enough that he never got off a shot. And yet the puck still slid under Crawford. I watched Crow skate back to the bench, and he was clearly emoting the feeling of being the loneliest man in the world. The Hawks had been the far better team in both these home games, and he had given them away. Now the danger felt real. They had just blown the "You're not fucking winning this game" game. That was their finisher. When they pulled that out, the game and series always went the Hawks way. The Flames, the Canucks (twice) the Predators, the Flyers, all had felt its power. And the Yotes kicked out of it before the ref counted three.

The Hawks would manage a death rattle in Game Five, tying the game late and Toews winning it in overtime, the first time a series had gone to overtime in the first five games. The stress of all the overtimes was causing all of us to lose weight.

We had seen the previous season the Hawks come back from 3-0 down to tie it, so coming back from 3-1 would be easy, we thought. Get this one at home, and then Game Seven would just fall to the Hawks.

The first period of that Game Six is still one of the best I've ever seen the Hawks play. They were dangerous on every shift. It looked like they had seven skaters out there. They were creating chances every few seconds. The building was roaring. They outshot the Coyotes 16-2 in the period. Every entry into the Arizona zone looked like a wave of red crashing over the storm barriers.

But they didn't score. Smith was heroic. He stopped at least three odd-man rushes that looked for all the world like goals. There was just no way past him. When the horn went for the end of the period, there was a feeling that the Hawks had missed their chance. They didn't get the knockout, the Coyotes made it to the bell and now would get to rest.

There was one last chance. Sadly it fell to Brendan Morrison. Kane had found the trailing Keith after pulling up on the boards as he always did. Keith had all the time in the world, and just about the time we were going to beseech him to shoot, he slid it over to a wide open Morrison. But we could see Smith follow the pass, and his pad was there before Morrison got the shot off.

Oliver Ekman-Larsson would score from the point on the power play a few minutes later, and though it was only one goal we knew it was over. They had outshot the Coyotes 28-8 through the first forty minutes, but now it was clear the window had shut.

First rule of bear-hunting: You can't miss the bear.

The third played out in some sort of weird, kabuki style snuff film. The Coyotes scored three more times, but I felt nothing. You can't kill what is already dead. We watched the season tick off on the clock, watched the bad side of the handshakes in front of us for the first time in this era. The Hawks lingered until after the Coyotes had left the ice to salute the crowd, but the feeling of nobody getting what they want was palpable from team and crowd.

The Hawks had their second consecutive first-round exit, and the memories of the parade and champagne from two years previous were getting more and more in the rearview mirror. Had it all been a mirage? Was it really this hard?

Dear Patrick Kane, Please Stop Drinking Because You Suck At It
May 10, 2012

It was hardly the first time that Patrick Kane had ended up on Deadspin. Up until that point, it was just the most seen. He had been spotted earlier in the season out at a bar the night before he missed a game due to illness, and though he half-heartedly protested the whole thing it was obvious he had been caught. It was actually the first time the local media pressed him at all about it. His response was, "I guess that's the reputation I have."

Of course, no one bothered to ask him if he thought that reputation was earned or not, though everyone knew he had clearly brought it on himself. The stories of Kane out on the town were multiplying, and some were getting uglier though there was never any way to confirm them. They were just whispers you heard in the Chicago grapevine, a guy who knows a guy or girl and such.

After the season, Kane got caught acting like a jackass in Madison, WI, which admittedly is hard not to do. Most of his behaviour while unpleasant wasn't anything that someone who had spent a night out in Lincoln Park hadn't seen. Being boorish, being unbalanced, surrounded by assholes, demeaning to women, etc.

There were more sinister views and whispers this time, though. Some claimed he had choked a girl at a frat party for turning him down. Some said he was walking around to every girl and then exclaiming, "Not good enough!" Again, nothing I and many others hadn't seen plenty of douchebags do in awful bars, but certainly the mark of a raging asshole.

Still, we all viewed it on the comedic side. Maybe this was a small part of the problem. Maybe it was larger than that. I wrote a post titled what you see the title of this chapter being, mostly because I was offended as a drunk. He was just bad at drinking, like the guy who slips to the dark side after one too many and thus can't have that many. But again, should I and others been taking a more quizzical eye? Looking back on it now, it seems so clear where this was all headed.

It was also the first time the Hawks showed real impatience with him, though it was probably all for show. They had their own press conference expressing their anger, which made you think there had been other warnings and meetings (and the rumors ran rampant that there had been, and they mostly had to do with habits beyond drinking). For the first time there was a real sense that Kane could actually party himself out of Chicago. The Hawks had an image they definitely wanted to maintain, and players in the future who ran afoul of it would see the consequences, and stumbling down State St. didn't fit in with it.

It was just tiresome to most. The same mistakes being made but ultimately chalked up to a misspent youth. While some of the unwashed objected to Kane being photographed partying so soon after an agonizing playoff exit, most were just weary of these stories. Why was this fun anymore? How did he keep ending up on Deadspin? Why couldn't he keep it private as most every other celebrity could?

Probably not the questions we should have been asking.

The Lockout II
September 15, 2012

Much like the one that had preceded it by eight years, hockey fans couldn't say they didn't see the storm coming. Warnings of a lockout had been sprinkled throughout the previous season, and the Players' Union didn't hire Donald Fehr merely to roll over and have their belly rubbed. Or at least not immediately. Once again, the owners were crying poor, even though they had canceled a whole season to get his very economic system. The cap had shot up at a rate that was unforeseen, thanks to new TV deals and sold out buildings and some other factors. But once the NBA got a deal that ensured the players and owners split all revenues down the middle 50-50, you knew the NHL was going to do its best to follow suit.

We held out hope they could avert this, but then we soon learned that would have meant everyone acting like an adult. Which is something that

Gary Bettman and Donald Fehr were not all that interested in. On the eve of training camp, or what would have been training camp, the owners made their first proposal, which went about as far as Ron Obvious trying to jump the English Channel on Monty Python. Whereas players in the previous deal earned roughly 57% of league revenue, the owners first offer gave them 43%. However, simple math told you that the players had earned 7% above 50% before and this was for 7% below, so it was obvious to everyone what the endgame was here. Except you couldn't just get there at the first jump, because everything in hockey CBA negotiations had to go down to the last minute.

Whereas the previous lockout I could let take place outside my sphere and distract myself with other things, now I was involved. I had to watch the updates on negotiations intently, which was just about the most infuriating thing in the world. When they were talking there were so many false dawns and crashes that I simply couldn't feel much of anything by the time it was all over (which didn't stop me from yelling at Bobby Ryan on Twitter). Whenever the sides got together there would be incremental progress, and the hope would rise that everyone could figure it out. A day or two later one side or both would leave in a huff and the crash was absolute. Whereas I dealt with this emotion before while watching hockey, the fact that my livelihood was in the balance made the rises and falls more violent and more harrowing. When the two sides would simply freeze each other out, the feeling was beyond hopelessness. I can only compare it to being stuck on a deserted island, and in the distance seeing a ship that could provide salvation, but it never moves. It just sits there staring you in the face while you continue to be surrounded by nothing. They could afford to go weeks without speaking together, but those were weeks where I had to piece together how to pay the bills.

I tried everything I could to fill the time. I attempted to do a spoof of the program about every Bears game during the lockout, though it failed terribly. What I aimed for was a publication that sounded like a bunch of hockey fans talking about football because they had nothing else to do, no matter how clueless and confused they were on the subject. What I got was far short of that. It was the joke I couldn't quite pull off. I attempted to do a weekly program about the Hawks' minor league team, the Rockford IceHogs. The problem was that the online feed for every Hogs game was just taken from the scoreboard of whatever arena they were playing in, and the quality was Zapruder-like. And when you're watching blurry images of AHL hockey in your living room, it doesn't make you feel to positive about where you are in life.

Allowances were made for me by everyone around, which I appreciated but didn't necessarily make me feel better. I had to skip out on a family function of my girlfriend's as I couldn't afford the flight. My local bartenders wouldn't allow me to tip them. I delivered fruit baskets around downtown Chicago for a couple weeks. I took whatever assignment NBC could throw at me, which wasn't much. Said girlfriend had to see me through several temper tantrums at the situation, and witnessed more than a few chairs get flung against a wall out of frustration whenever the latest negotiation broke down.

It took a toll on my family as well. As my brother was also still unemployed, my father went from his sons riding high to both being listless in the span of a year or so. He provided us all the help he could and most he couldn't, but I know the stress was taking a huge toll on him. We did our best to stay positive, but it was getting farther and farther from us. You always promise you'll make it up to your parents, and then time comes and you've run out of chances. The best we can do is live as well as they always hoped we would. When you're not, it's torture for them.

I learned the true cost of all this. There were so many near-agreements. There was one before Thanksgiving. There was one in early December. There was one in late December. And every time things collapsed, I would see Bettman's smarmy face on my screen trying to explain it all away as if the very fate of billionaires and millionaires were riding on it. No Gary, my ability to live was riding on it. Same with every vendor and stadium employee across two nations. But we were the littlest community, and no one was speaking for us. Every time the sense was they were close, when negotiations broke off it felt as if my organs were sucked through the bottom of my feet. I could handle losing my dream job through my own incompetence. If it just wasn't good enough, or I had done something to ruin it all, at least I would have taken my swing. This wasn't even allowing me to get to the plate.

The nadir came before Christmas, at least personally. Desperate to find more paths to income, as every job application I filled out made it somewhat clear that when the NHL season started I would be going back to my job, I went to apply for a delivery position at a pizza place near my house. They had their own takeout section in the back of the restaurant, and I headed in and inquired with the woman at the window about an application. She handed me one and I realized I had forgotten my pen in the car. When I politely asked her if she had an extra as I had left mine behind, she simply berated me about not having a pen when applying for a job in front of everyone in the room. Here I was, getting mocked by applying for a job I didn't even want by a woman I would never have wanted to work for and wouldn't need to in a couple weeks. Thanks, Gary and Don. I dreamed that the lockout would get resolved in the next day or two so I could return with a bag of pens and tell her to take that delivery job and stick it in an uncomfortable place, and here's a bunch of pens so that when the next desperate soul comes looking for a job she wouldn't feel the need to rub their nose in it and rob them of whatever dignity they might have had left. Sadly, that didn't come through. Whatever. She's still answering that phone and I'm not taking her orders.

The combination of anger and helplessness is a strange one. Though the rage positively boiled within me and every other fan that millionaires and billionaires couldn't figure this out far sooner to not deprive us, those whose money had made them said millionaires and billionaires, of our hockey season, we knew that there was nothing to be done. Major sports leagues are not a normal industry. If a certain restaurant or theater decides to go dark, you can go to another one down the street. But there is no other top sports league for whatever game is your favorite. My brother and I attended a few Wolves games during the lockout, but it was so clearly not the same. The quality wasn't there. The play was choppy and disjointed. Three consecutive passes completed was some sort of lost treasure. I wasn't a Wolves fan, and even when they played the Hawks minor league team I didn't feel invested. It all took place in front of me, not with me.

Because of how I felt, and I knew how other fans felt, I knew that fans would go flocking back as soon as the doors were opened. That's how they got away with this. Where baseball did have to recover a lost section of fans after 1994, hockey fans' bond is that much harder to break. They weren't going anywhere, because for too long they had to cling to it on the outer edges of the landscape. There was nowhere else to go. They would have our money and our attention in short order, just as soon as they allowed us to go spilling it out again. Baseball also takes place in the summer when every activity is open to you. What the fuck else were we going to do when it was four degrees in February?

Right after Christmas, it was looking like they were going to get a deal done. They would drag it to the last minute, but everyone agreed they were too close now to blow it. Shortly after New Year's, they did. My father told me when he heard the news on the radio in the car he let out a huge bellow that surely would have blown the eardrum of anyone else in the car, which thankfully there wasn't. He wasn't excited that hockey was back, but that he would get one son back on his feet. A few days later, my brother would get a job, though sadly in Columbus, but at least we were both functioning human beings. And I quickly tried to make up all my girlfriend had to put up with whatever meals out and professional massages I could afford.

There would be a week-long training camp, and the season would start on Saturday, January 19. The Hawks would be the guest for the Kings as they raised their banner from the previous season.

I couldn't bring myself to go back into the building that quickly though. It didn't feel right. I didn't want to be angry anymore, as that's a shitty way to go through the day. I knew hockey and sports were unique, and heading back in wasn't some statement on my willpower or principles. But I couldn't do it. Even if my statement was only to myself, I wasn't going to just roll over as soon as they opened the doors on the twenty-second.

I was blown away by the reaction of most of the readers Most of them handed over far too much cash for their program and told me to keep the change, as that's what they would have been spending on programs for games that never happened. I was nearly brought to tears. It's amazing the bond you can forge when you simply are honest and provide a product people like. I was sure delighted to be among hockey fans again. It didn't matter that night the air hurt my face.

For Our Next Trick
February 2, 2013
Hawks vs. Flames

My boycott lasted five days. Though I had planned to skip the first two home games of the season and return after the Ice Show trip, my tickets didn't sell for the second home game of the year and I didn't have much else to do on that Sunday night. Eating the cost of the ticket wasn't going to teach anyone anything, and it certainly wasn't going to make me feel better. So I called my friend Ashely, and she couldn't hold out either, and off we went to see the first game of the last season the Hawks and Wings were in the same division.

The Hawks had won the first five games of the season, but other than the season opener against the Kings they hadn't looked particularly good doing it. They were sloppy in a revenge win over the Coyotes. They nearly blew a three-goal lead to the Blues. They had squeaked by the Stars and Jackets. They weren't much better than that against the Wings.

But there was Duncan Keith blasting one home from the circle on the power play two minutes into the game, and there I was involuntarily leaping out of my seat. It was reflex, and it felt comfortable. This was how things were supposed to be. Whatever protest I wanted to put forth, if only to appease myself, melted away. It felt good, and I was happier when I had this in my life. Why fight it? What pyrrhic victory was I really going to attain?

The Hawks headed out on the road, and this is where the debate over their "record" start would begin. They would lose the next two games in shootouts, clouding the claims that they would go undefeated to start the year. You would always have to amend it to "regulation loss." To me, who had abhorred the shootout since its inception, it was basically considered a tie. If the Hawks had lost either of the games in Vancouver or Minnesota in overtime, I too would have derided this "regulation loss-less" streak. But they didn't, and I'll hold onto that forever. Call it whatever you want, because believe me I've heard it before.

The night after dropping a shootout to Vancouver, the Hawks were in Calgary. And they were awful. They were second-best all over the ice, with the crunch of the schedule and road trip making its presence known.

They were outshot 20-12 through two periods. Four minutes into the third, Kane gave them an undeserved lead. The Flames would equalize ten minutes later, and with thirty-five seconds to go Jay Bouwmeester would give the Flames the lead. Ray Emery had been heroic in trying to steal his team a point or two, but even he couldn't suppress all twenty-four shots the Hawks gave up in the third period alone. You can't stop a tidal wave.

Or so went any rational thinking. This was our first clue that things were not going to be rational this season..

The Hawks immediately invaded the Flames zone after the faceoff following Bouwmeester's goal. Hossa fought off an attempt to strip him at the line. Toews, Kane, Leddy, and Keith all searched for a shooting lane. Finally, Kane sent a cross-ice pass to Keith, who got the puck to the net. The rebound landed on Hossa's stick perfectly with three seconds left. Before we knew what happened he was wildly pumping his fists, like Butthead trying to dance. The Hawks had answered a goal with thirty-five seconds left with one with three seconds left. It obviously wouldn't be the last time creatures from the land of the unheard of would come to say hello.

Emery had to turn away a couple more chances in overtime. He then stopped every attempt in the shootout.. Kane scored for the Hawks, and that's all they would need.

It was a true miracle. Emery had been at best choppy the previous season as backup, and here he was simply winning a game on his own. He had no help. He turned away forty-six Calgary shots, where the Hawks only managed nineteen. They gave up forty-six shots to a collection of hobos called the Calgary Flames, and still won.

A goalie win from Emery? Just what was going on here?

Kickstart My Heart
February 22, 2013
Sharks vs. Hawks

The Hawks would continue to pile up the wins, shrouded around one more shootout loss to Anaheim. They had tied the NHL record for most games unbeaten to start a season at sixteen, and could break the record on this night.

Of course, we couldn't simply enjoy it. Sports fandom doesn't work that way. For one, there was a great fear that the Hawks had simply peaked too early. To us, going seventeen undefeated to start the season meant it was less likely they could successfully manage four out of every seven games for four rounds. It was simply counting, at least in a fan's eyes. There were a requisite amount of losses every team would gather, and the Hawks weren't picking them up at all. That meant they had to be coming later.

People berate Alabama football coach Nick Saban for his complaints about how winning national championships had actually gotten in the way of his recruiting and made his job harder somehow. But deep down, every sports fan knows exactly what he's talking about. There simply has to be a bargain for everything good you get. That's how it works. The better it got, the worse the price that was going to be exacted. Seventeen games unbeaten to start the season? That meant something truly awful waited down the road. No matter how sturdy the ice seemed as you walked out on it, one always fears the cracking sound.

Secondly, the Hawks' start had made them the story of the NHL, and really sports. Along with the Hawks' streak, this is when the Miami Heat were piling up a twenty-seven-game winning streak in the NBA. The two stories became conjoined in a way. This only sent a section of both Hawks and hockey fans into apoplexy. One side of it is that there is no one hockey fans loathe and love to deride more than LeBron James, who has come to represent the NBA and lord over hockey fans' inferiority complex. To have a hockey team linked with him in any way made the Hawks the Sith of the league.

For Hawks fans being the center of attention of every other team and fan in the league was something to be feared. Being the center of the hockey universe only meant that everyone else wanted to see them fail more than they already did. We could envision every fan of every other team huddled in front of their TVs, wolfing through the popcorn, excitedly smiling through sharpening teeth just what the end of the streak would be and how the Hawks would pay for this. Suddenly every game against the Hawks was a true test for every team, and their fans would take extra glee in the demise of the Hawks. The only thing fans love more than a hero is to see a hero fail, so says The Green Goblin.

And you wonder why we're so miserable.

The Hawks set the record anyway. Jerks.

Not Here, Not Now
March 3, 2013
Hawks vs. Red Wings

The Hawks continued to roll. With every game they added to the record, it felt more and more like seeing the Jesse White Tumblers. For those not from the area, the Tumblers are this group of young kids, mostly pulled from poorer areas, who entertain at high schools and halftimes around town with a pretty impressive acrobatic/gymnastic act. The finale is always a succession of jumpers trampolining over a certain amount of people. When the next guy clears twelve you're immediately relieved some small child didn't get crushed. But you immediately begin anticipating whether the next guy could get to thirteen. With each successive win the relief and anticipation would grow. As soon as the Hawks wrapped up a win we immediately looked to the schedule to see what was next. It was only a day or two later thanks to the compressed schedule, but that excitement for the next one made it seem endless. The Hawks were the best roadshow going, and you couldn't miss one game. You wanted to know how far the ride would go.

You'd look ahead on the schedule, and you'd make little deals with yourself about where you'd be ok for it to end. "Ok, they could lose to that team and it would be ok." "Well, if they lost that game I don't know any fans on that team so I could deal with that." And so on.

What everyone agreed to was that having the streak broken by Detroit was going to be unacceptable.

Even with a Cup in tow, there was still a little brother complex for Hawks fans when it came to Detroit. They had finished ahead of the Hawks the next two years after that championship, and it was still very hard to argue there had been a shift in the relationship between the teams and fans. This is when the Wings really began to fade, and the Hawks had something truly special in hand.

Which is what made the dread worse. Here the Hawks were, the story of the season, the story that actually got hockey to transcend its usual audience, a place in the record books, and we just knew it would be so in character for it all to come undone on the shores of the Detroit River. It just felt like something that would happen, because that's what always happened.

Though this was hardly a vintage Wings team, you could sense they felt a duty to carry on what that team had held over the Hawks for over a decade. They threw everything at the Hawks. Jimmy Howard was brilliant in net. It was as back and forth, and as fast as any regular season NHL game could get. Somehow, there was no scoring in the first forty minutes, though hardly for a lack of chances. Of course these fucking assholes would play their best game of the season against the Hawks. It's like they planned it.

Three minutes into the third, Tomas Tatar would poke home one after a scramble in front of the sturdy Crawford. The Wings and their fans celebrated the goal as if it had clinched a conference championship or more. We could hear the taunts that would follow for years ringing around our heads already.

With just over two minutes left, the Hawks were on the power play. Patrick Sharp would send a shot from the point that would be blocked by Niklas Kronwall. But before Kronwall could get his stick on the puck after it had dropped to the ice, Viktor Stalberg stripped it away and sent it right to Patrick Kane waiting at the right circle. He viciously ripped a wrist-shot over Jimmy Howard in an instant.

Not only did it feel like the whole game changed, it felt like the whole feeling about this Hawks team, and the Hawks against the Red Wings changed. The streak had come close to ending before this. But this was the Wings, who had a supernatural ability to take things away from us. Suddenly, the Hawks got the power play they needed to tie a game late.

They got the turnover the Wings always got to set them up. They scored the goal at the worst possible time for their opponents to avoid defeat. Wasn't that what the Wings always did? Suddenly we went from fearing the ice would crack under us every game to believing this would never end.

With that one goal, suddenly it felt like the Hawks would always have an answer. They would find a way.

Kane would go on to score the only goal of the shootout, and he would have an arrogant, dismissive look on his face as he looked toward the Detroit crowd, assuring them there was nothing they or their team could do to stop the Hawks. We all took on that bravado from there out. The Hawks always knew. The Hawks were always better. Whatever you could do, they would do faster and more assuredly. The fuck were you going to do about it?

Nothing, that's what Kane's sneer said. We sneered right along with him.

The streak would last twenty-four games, and would be capped off with a last-minute winner from Dan Carcillo, to fully cement that we had entered the surreal. You couldn't ignore the randomness, or silliness of it. To go that long without losing, there has to be a huge element of luck. After all, the 2010 team, that was certainly a more solid outfit, could only manage eight in a row. The best of the best, the Edmonton Oilers, only managed a fifteen-game unbeaten streak throughout the '80s. To go twenty-four, it was a supernova. It burns to brightly and powerfully to happen all that often. It's an anomaly. It's the break in the code. Of course it would be topped off by a last minute winner from Car Bomb. What else could it be?

Back Into Hell
March 20, 2013
Hawks vs. Ducks

After surviving the lockout, and the crush of the condensed schedule, my family and friends insisted that I take the first break of the season—the Hawks didn't have a home game for eleven days—and go somewhere. I decided to return to L.A. for the first time since I moved away, centering the trip around the Hawks' trip to Anaheim.

It was not without trepidation. Two previous trips had images and horrors of being yelled at by Orange County teenagers, of course in four syllables. Stuck in traffic on the I-5. That fucking duck horn. But wrongs of the past had to be righted. I would not rest peacefully without victory in Anaheim.

I flew out, spent a couple days catching up with old friends, drinking in favorite spots, and of course, eating In-N-Out. But then the time came to cast ourselves back into the void, to collect what had avoided us before.

We stopped at a Mexican place that had been recommended, and couldn't avoid obnoxious Ducks fans there. Even citing our more recent Cup and league's best record wouldn't seem to calm them. So of course came the natural barbs about the Cubs, because that's the salvation for anyone trying to get one over on Chicago (at least it was). We were in the belly of the beast.

The game was about as anticipated as any that season. Even though the Hawks had gone half the season without losing, the Ducks were not far behind them. They were only five points behind in the standings, and it was the first time in NHL history that teams with these kinds of records were meeting this late in a season. This was the pivot point in the NHL universe, even if it was a godforsaken, tourist created, hellscape that is Anaheim, CA.

We got to our seats early, and quickly noticed that Hawks fans had taken over the building. This was not something I'd gotten the first two trips to Honda Center. I was not an odd piece of garbage floating in a dark sea of Ducks gear. We had taken the field. Of course, right before puck drop when the Hawks fans behind us kept asking each other who various Hawks players were, I quickly realized these weren't exactly the cream of the crop of our kind. Anaheim had even poisoned those I claimed to be amongst.

Much like my first trip there, the Ducks scored within the first two minutes of the game. The nightmares of previous trip quickly began to fill my mind. Now I hadn't just driven down, I had flown out for this. But there was always Jonathan Toews.

Toews came down on a shorthanded break, one-on-one with Cam Fowler. He went to Fowler's outside, and then simply dusted around him to the net. He got around Jonas Hiller too, and easily slotted the puck past him. The horrors of the past were quickly erased.

Leddy scored on the power play in the second, and the Hawks headed to the intermission with us feeling assured. The Hawks didn't blow third period leads. Vengeance would be mine. You cannot break me, Orange County.

Right before the third I headed for one last beer (which out there were twelve bucks, for fuck's sake). But I discovered that the Honda Center cut off sales at the third period. What fresh outrage was this? These lame fuckers couldn't drink during the final frame? I should have known then. It was a clue. Get out now. You don't have to see this.

Early in the period, Brandon Bollig appeared to score what would have been a clinching goal. He slammed home a centering pass from about eight inches out. My second mistake, after trying to get that last beer, was ever believing that Bollig would score an important goal. Replays would quickly show he kicked the puck into the net. I couldn't ignore the signs now. I braced for what was coming, as if the brakes had stopped working and a hairpin turn quickly approached.

Of course, this being Anaheim, they had to wait until belief has just about trickled in. Bobby Ryan got on the end of a centering pass and scored.

I couldn't see past the dark cloud my mind had projected before my eyes. I knew what was next. It would only take a minute.

Did it have to be Teemu? No, it didn't. It didn't have to be any of it. But the things that cut deepest are the ones that seem excessive. Teemu was already on his decline, the world-class speed that set him apart deserting him. But he channeled young Teemu, for just one shift. Oduya recklessly flung a puck into center ice, which he hadn't done all season. Getzlaf was the only one there. He and Selanne streaked in with only Oduya between them. I didn't even bother watching when the puck slid over to Selanne It was all so obvious.

I still see one Ducks fan, who was sitting one section over, running up and down the stairs and doing some bow-and-arrow celebration to taunt all the Hawks fans around. There is no victory in Anaheim. There is no honor.

Prime Time
May 3, 2013
Wild vs. Hawks (Game Two)

The playoffs opened to a feeling of celebration more than they ever had. There wasn't the manic pressure like 2010, everyone feeling genuine expectation for the first time in a long while, if not the first time entirely. When these playoffs began, the only thing I can compare it to is when the '90's Bulls began their playoff runs. It was a feeling as if the practice runs were over, the preamble through with, and now it was time for the real games to begin. After two first-round exits, Hawks fans were going to enjoy being overwhelming favorites again.

And the Hawks had the stage to themselves. Thanks to the delayed start, by the time the Hawks got to the playoffs the Bulls, who were incredibly beat up and this is where the Derrick Rose drama began, were being ritually killed by the Heat. The Cubs and Sox were a month into already-lost seasons. The entire city was ready from the beginning for the Hawks and the NHL playoffs.

Game One was a little trickier than you would have thought, going to overtime merely at 1-1. But there was never any air of panic. It felt like everyone in the crowd knew that even if the Hawks dropped the opener, they were going to be too much for the Wild. Thanks to Stalberg and Bickell on a 2-on-1, we didn't have to worry much.

The rest of the series didn't provide much drama. The Hawks clubbed the Wild in Game Two, dropped Game Three in overtime, and then clubbed them again in Game Four.

Game Five also proved rudimentary, but came with some personal tension. Three days after Game Five there was a wedding in my girlfriend's family. If the Hawks wrapped it up in five games or less, I was headed to

Pennsylvania to meet a whole family I had already spurned once due the lockout. It's bad enough meeting the whole family without the baggage. Inspections were clearly going to be thorough.

So even as the Hawks stomped to a 5-1 win in Game Five to clinch it, there was a growing sense of dread. Couldn't you guys have helped me out a bit? As soon as the final horn went, my phone vibrated. I inspected it to see the following message, all caps, "SEE YOU TOMORROW."

No victories are ever completely sweet.

For us, the series was basically highlighted by the Hawks firing CSN reporter Susannah Collins. During an intermission she had a slip of the tongue which caused her to say, "The Hawks have had a lot of sex," instead of "The Hawks have had a lot of success." The Hawks apparently weren't concerned that both statements were factually true.

The gaffe caused some more attention to be paid to Collins, and some comedic, ever so slightly blue online videos she had done in her past came to light. The Hawks basically fired her right after they did, claiming that she didn't represent the organization in a way that they wanted, as she worked for a station they partially owned.

Of course, the whole thing was ridiculous and it was hard not to point out the fault in their logic. After all, a wife-beating, Nazi-sympathizing drunk roamed the concourses for them every home game glad-handing the bigwigs in Bobby Hull. Where was the standard? It should have been yet another sign of what was to come.

Shall Sound In The Deep, One Last Time

May 15, 2013
Wings vs. Hawks (Game One)

A few days after the Hawks put the Wild to the sword, the Wings and Ducks had a Game Seven. If the Ducks won, the Hawks would face San Jose. If the Wings won, the Hawks and Wings would meet for the final time as conference and division opponents, as the league's realignment the following season would see the Wings move to the East.

Perhaps for the only time, Hawks fans wanted to see Detroit. First, it felt right. These were the only two Original Six teams in the West, and if this was their last season together then their should be one more playoff matchup. Second, it was the first time that Hawks fans viewed the Wings not just as equals, but as a decided underdog. For every other playoff series of our lives against them, they were something to be feared. No more. The Hawks were the best team in the league by some distance. They had the most recent Cup. Third, there was something intoxicating about punting the Wings off to the Eastern Conference with a loss to us as their final act in the West. It should end by our hand.

But mostly, everything the Hawks had become and accomplished needed one last seal of approval. The Hawks hadn't beat the Wings in a playoff series since 1992. The last one saw them easily outclassed in five games in 2009. There was still a feeling of, "You never went through us." It was the last barrier to be broken. We wanted to leave them and their fans with no outs.

So when the Wings beat Anaheim, there was genuine excitement about what was to come.

That party atmosphere of the previous round was only heightened for the second round. This being the last series these two teams would have, at least as members of the same conference and division, whatever happened it would be remembered.

It felt like an occasion that my father should see as well. I had brought him to several games over the years by that point, but he had yet to see a playoff win. Normally I would hesitate to bring him to a game against the Wings, the atmosphere always teetering on toxic and my own behavior not being something I'd want him to know was within me. But this being the last one, and my confidence about the series got me past all of that.

Game One was tight. The Hawks and Wings traded goals two minutes apart in halfway through the first though Hossa and Helm. There was no scoring in the second or in the opening exchanges in the third. Just about the time my father, who had sensed and read my assuredness about how the series would go, turned to me and said, "I'm sorry son, but I don't see what the Hawks do so much better," Sharp and Kane caused the overmatched Wings blue line to turn the puck over to Oduya who was able to blast home from the circle. I turned to my father and said, "That."

Kruger and Carcillo would cause similar problems a few minutes later that Kruger would cash, and Sharp would add an empty-netter. My father got his playoff win, everything was on course, nothing was out of order. Surely it was smooth-sailing from here.

Whoops.

It spiraled so quickly we barely had time to comprehend. Game Two took place on a Saturday afternoon, which is always a bit weird. Regular season games in the afternoon are one thing, but a playoff game, especially one between these two, needed a full day of anticipation. Hawks and Wings games don't take place in brilliant sunshine. They're supposed to be in the dark corners after the kids go to bed.

It started smoothly too, making the turnaround even more stunning. The Hawks took the lead in the first through Kane finishing off a wonderful passing play. It was the kind of panache the Wings used to show against the Hawks. The period finished that way.

And then it fell apart, and wouldn't come back together for three games. The Wings were all over the Hawks. Babcock was dancing all over Quenneville as this was a rare time that Q wasn't chasing matchups every shift. The Hawks became shaky and turned pucks over left and right. The

Wings scored two in the second, two in the third, and it looked routine.

All right, no big deal. One blip was more than allowed. This was never going to be a sweep, no matter how badly we desired that sort of authoritative conquest. The Hawks would surely quell this mini-resistance.

Game Three felt like the Hawks kept trying to get to a sprint but were were spinning their legs on an oil patch in cartoon fashion. The Hawks were really good in the first period but couldn't score, and had a perfectly good goal ruled out because Andrew Shaw's aura interfered with Jimmy Howard or something. The Wings took a 2-0 lead in the second on some poor defensive play from a few people. Kane brought the Hawks within one early in the third, but then Pavel Datsyuk did Pavel Datsyuk things and found a spot in the net you couldn't throw it into from five feet away if you had ten chances.

Suddenly, creepily, it felt like Inigo Montoya running against the locked door, screaming for the help of Fezzik as the six-fingered man was getting away. We'd waited so long for this, it couldn't slip away this easily, could it?

Unfortunately for all of us, Jonathan Toews felt the same sense of panic and frustration we shared. It's the only time it happened before or since, but he lost the plot. He took three minors in the second period alone. At the end of his second, the Wings scored. Fifty seconds later he was in the box again. How the Joe Louis crowd roared and gloated. Here were the Hawks again, just like in 2009, when the chips were really down, and they were coming apart at the seams.

Really, looking back on it, the difference in the game was Jakub Kindl and Nick Leddy both hit a post with a shot on power plays. Kindl's went in. Leddy's did not. That's what these massive occasions are decided on a lot of the time, which makes you wonder why anyone bothers at all. But at the time, it looked like the Hawks were simply solved. It felt like their coach lost his mind. He pulled Leddy off the power play for Rozsival. The Hawks insisted on trying to stretch pass their way through a trapping Wings team, Q unable to unwilling to recognize that Detroit coach Mike Babcock had changed up his plan. Toews's penalties, turnovers, and throw in six shots in a third period where the Hawks trailed to try and avoid going down 3-1...THE FEAR arrived.

Not only did it look like the Hawks would lose to Detroit again, but then the Wings would go skipping off to the other conference, giggling all the way. There would be no chance for retribution or revenge. This would be the final statement on the whole relationship. That we could never measure up, even when it looked for all the world the Hawks finally did. It would be permanently etched on our foreheads.

I couldn't eat or sleep. I wasn't alone.

Now You Have Permission To Leave
May 29, 2013
Wings vs. Hawks (Game Seven)

The two days between Games Four and Five were interminable, while also going by in a flash, if you'll allow me to delve into cliché juxtaposition of phrases. There was just enough time for everyone to convince themselves there was a way. Surely the Hawks were not going to lose four games in a row, and were not going to lose the series at home. So that's one. Then it just came down to Game Six in Detroit, because the Hawks weren't going to lose a Game Seven at home, either. Or so went our thinking in our time of need. I must've repeated this mantra to myself 109,000 times in the time in between games.

Before Game Five from my post, I was alarmed at how many Red Wings fans there were. There weren't nearly that many for Games One and Two. Had my fellow fans of the four feathers given up hope and dumped their tickets? Could they just not bear the thought and shed them out of terror? Either way, these grinning, evil gremlins were now in our midst and in numbers. When I got to my seats, I was surrounded. This was getting worse.

The Hawks controlled the opening of the game fairly comfortably, even if I was watching through all of my fingers. Finally, the dam broke with six minutes left in the frame as a puck squirted right out in front to Bryan Bickell who didn't miss the open cage. I leapt out of my seat and made sure to yell in the direction of the four Red Wings fans to my right. I'm not a confrontational guy, but I didn't want to convey my fear inside outward. We had this, or at least that's what I wanted them to think.

The Wings equalized in the second, causing my Adam's apple to house my heart for a little while. But Shaw tipped in a Keith point shot on the power play a few minutes later, and then a couple minutes after that Toews also scored on the power play with his patented roof job from the side of the net. It was the ultimate symbol of defiance. Here he had been seen melting down a game before, his team going with him, and now he was answering with a clinching goal. Shaw added another in the third, and we all breathed again. The Wings fans had come for a party, and at least we had ducked witnessing that.

I've seen many classic Hawks games. I can remember them all. Sometimes I watch the highlights just for a smile. There is one that I wouldn't go through again if given the chance. That would be Game Six.

We knew if the Hawks got it, they would suddenly be favored again. Things would tip in their favor. They'd have Game Seven at home, they'd have won the last two, things would be corrected. But we knew getting it was going to be a real trick. By the time the octopus was thrown on the ice at the end of the anthem, I was fairly sure I would be the first human on record to throw up so hard he gave himself a seizure.

I didn't feel much better when Hossa simply powered one through on a power play four minutes in. Every Hawks fan was just making deals with whatever higher being they could get in touch with. Just get us to the intermission up one. That's all we ask.

No such luck. With about a minute remaining, Eaves got hold of a rebound and got around Crawford. We would have an intermission where I couldn't even sit down in my own apartment.

Halfway through the second period. I was sure it was all over. The Hawks weren't very good in that frame, and the Wings came for the kill. Joakim Andersson floated a soft wrister from the blue line toward Crawford. It eluded his glove and in.

I accepted my fate. That kind of goal, after everything we had seen before—all the posts the Hawks hit, the penalties they got, the calls they didn't get, the chances they missed, added to our years of experience—was simply the death knell. My chest sank. No way could they be beaten. They just had something. This was how they wanted it. We were forever in their shadow. I could barely hold my head up to watch. I cursed my luck that I had grown up rooting against the Wings, and Packers, and Cardinals, who had clearly been ordained to always win. That if they didn't win, a cardinal law of the universe would be broken and there would be a rip in the sky or something.

The Hawks barely hung on the rest of the period, though I almost wanted Detroit to score. Just end this so I can get accustomed to my new reality as quickly as possible. You're just toying with me, universe, and I won't have it.

The Hawks, thankfully, were not the fatalists I was.

Not even a minute in, a pinching Hjalmarsson got the puck to Handzus in front who had no one around him. He took his time to find the corner above Howard. We were tied. Five minutes later Toews was digging a puck out of the corner and sending to the net. Howard couldn't handle it, and Bickell didn't miss the rebound. Four minutes after that Frolik was blocking a point shot and then streaking away, only to be slashed and get a penalty shot.

We knew this was pivotal. Score and the Hawks would have a two goal lead we knew they wouldn't cough up that late. Miss and the Wings would have a pivot point to come back. Waiting for him to take it I felt my organs sink into my feet and bounce up through my throat at least three times. Fro came down, pivoted his feet to make it look like he would go to his forehand, but then flipped his backhand to the shortside. It was so easy. I still see Howard going immediately to yell at the ref for awarding it in the first place.

In the span of twenty game minutes, a half an hour real-time or so, I'd gone from having my ribcage scraping my spine out of pure deflation to screaming so loud I'm sure the neighbors called the cops on me. We had it.

We brought them back to us. They had brought out their voodoo, and for the first time the Hawks merely swatted it away.

I was heartened to see that not nearly as many Wings fans were outside the UC before Game Seven. I don't know if Hawks fans bucked up and decided to not dump these tickets, or Wings fans feared what was coming, or some combination thereof, but they were scarce.

I walked into the arena just praying the Hawks would finally burst for three goals in the first and calm the nerves. This was my first Game Seven in attendance anywhere. Baseball, hockey, anything else, this would be a new experience after five years as a season ticket holder. Of course it had to come against the team they absolutely could not lose it to.

I'd tell you Game Sevens in person feel different, and they do until the puck drops. But then it's just like watching any other playoff game. It moves too fast to really try and figure out what everything means. Sure, you're chain-smoking at the intermission, not knowing if this is going to be your last intermission or not. But you can't conceive of the context when you're in it.

The Hawks did not burst out for three goals in the first. They didn't burst for any. We had to wait until a minute into the second, when Hossa, Handzus, and Sharp combined on a beautiful passing play for Sharp to score. Ok, this is it. The Hawks had finally outlasted the Wings and this was the beginning of the close out. I even thought about exhaling for a minute there. But the second goal never came. They huffed, and they puffed, but the house was still very much standing.

Game Seven feels different when you get to the second intermission. You know when you return to your seat from wherever you went—smoke, piss, beer run, corner to cry—that when you leave it again things will be very different. You'll either be heartbroken or elated. It feels like being led into a fighting pit.

Thirty seconds in, Nyquist and Zetterberg caused a turnover and Z scored to tie the game. Tie game, whole third period to go and the opponent was only the team that had been our scourge for our entire lives. Kill me now.

I watched that third period trying to keep my eyes from rolling in the back of my head. It was dread, it was hope, it was more dread. Couldn't escape the sense of "the horde is coming." They're going to do it to me again. Why did you bother having dreams anyway? Didn't you know better?

Most playoff games, once you get to the last five minutes tied, you're fairly sure you're headed to overtime. Both teams are canceling each other out, and you're in essentially overtime anyway. Goals are a rarity.

So my heart stopped when Andrew Shaw pulled up along the right boards, and found Hjalmarsson in acres of space with a pass. What the hell was Hjalmarsson doing there? Where the hell did he find this space? It was in slow motion. I imagine it's what like finding love at first sight is.

Everything but what you're focused on just stops. You can't hear anything. All I could see was Hammer in the slot, no one around, winding up. You never got the time for a full blast from that close. And Hjalmarsson was the one getting it?

At the point of contact, time did stop. And then the puck was hurling past Jimmy Howard's glove. Right into the top corner. It was so authoritative. It was so definite. Not just a goal. A thunderbolt. A final act of defiance. A final plunge of the sword into the great beast. It was over. They were conquered. We went nuts. Everyone was jumping. We climbed all over each other. I couldn't stop screaming.

And for the second time, after she'd leapt into my arms, I put my girlfriend down in the wrong row. Three years hadn't taught me much.

But then the music stopped suddenly. The crowd slowly sank into a confused hush. What was going on? Why weren't the players celebrating?

They had waved it off.

The ref had seen some infraction in front of the Wings bench, and didn't have the balls to call only one penalty on Kyle Quincey, which is what was warranted. Had he, the goal would have stood as the Wings never touched the puck. But no, he called one on Brandon Saad as well for being tackled. He blew the whistle. No one heard it.

The air came out of me at such a rate I'm surprised I didn't sound like a Whoopee cushion. When we saw the replay on the TVs above us, I felt robbed. It was so Wings. They always got the call to bail them out. It always went their way. And now, in the biggest moment between these teams of my lifetime, right after the most dramatic way to finally turn the tide, they got this. They were stealing it from us. And most of all, we had to sit there and watch them do it because there was an overtime to come.

During the intermission before OT, I walked down to the smoking pit in a daze. I stood there like a zombie. I accepted my fate again. They had taken it from us, and now I was sentenced to watch them dance off with it when I re-entered the building. This was the way things were. The natural order. I trudged up the stairs like a kid to a booster shot. Charlie Brown had nothing on me.

For the few minutes of overtime, I wasn't even tense. I didn't just think it was over, I knew it. I just wanted to dive into the sweet embrace of the darkness, like falling backward into a pool. It's fine. It won't even hurt now. Don't dare to hope, you'll only have the knife plunged deeper.

I didn't really get excited when Bolland cleared out Gustav Nyquist along the boards in the neutral zone. Didn't really even have a pulse fluctuation when Seabrook picked up the puck and moved forward. But he kept moving forward. No one came to meet him. He just kept going. And then suddenly he was right in the heart of the Detroit zone. Still no one within reach. Hey, mayb....

Then the puck was off his stick. And Howard was flailing his glove hand. And then the puck was in the net behind him. It was all so clear, and yet it didn't make any sense. Seabrook was streaking into the corner. Zetterberg passed in front of me, stick on his knees and head down. I know these movements, but they didn't add up. Everyone next to me was shaking me. I was watching myself jump up and down, but I couldn't match what I felt.

Was it over? Had they done it?

They had. Finally, we got one over them. Finally, we had the upper hand. They would shuffle off, knowing their last act as our division opponent was to lose to us. That would be the lasting memory. Run off now, Wings. We finally had rearranged things. You had your way. You got the call. You got the breaks. You got the brain-lock from the Hawks. And it wasn't enough. Finally, your magic ran out.

It was almost as good as a Cup.

Marathon
June 12, 2013
Bruins vs Hawks (Game One)

The Hawks saw off the Kings in the conference final surprisingly easily. It all ended with Toews and Kane on a 2-on-1 in double OT. It's amazing what you remember about certain moments. How certain images stick out. Eight minutes into the second overtime Bickell stripped Slava Voynov at the Hawks blue line and sent Toews and Kane away on a 2-on-1 with Voynov stretching every sinew to get back. Toews easily found Kane on the other side to end the series. I don't really remember the puck hitting the net. I do remember Joanthan Quick sprawled out on his face, having failed to get over to save the shot, as Voynov went spiraling into the corner like a downed helicopter. I know my brother and I hugged, but I can't see it. I can see Voynov spinning into the boards whenever I want, though.

The 2013 Final did not come without a fair amount of personal dread. Boston was the opponent, and I knew there were a legion of college friends rubbing their hands together over it. A permanent wedge in our relationships was hanging over the whole thing. The Bruins also came in a hulking threat, as big and nasty as they could be, and having won a Cup even more recently than the Hawks had. I guess it had a feel of which team was going to certify theirs as more real. I promised to enjoy it as much as I could. The 2010 version we were all too focused on a first championship in forty-nine years, on endings, on firsts. This time, I said I would appreciate the event. Or at least try.

At least I got a story out of it. Standing outside Gate Three, my post for selling the program, I was soaking in the atmosphere. The Hawks had set up a beer-tent thing across the street, and I was enjoying the tunes. A recent addition to our outdoor carnival were a group of Jesus freaks protesting...well, life in general I guess. A fair few readers got a huge kick out of seeing me standing amongst those with signs like "Repent your sins." I couldn't help but smile at the juxtaposition, that's for sure. I also learned to never try to talk to someone holding one of those signs. Generally they are glassy-eyed and incapable of conversation, and those that are capable don't have anything to say you want to hear.

A few moments later, I saw Billy Corgan walk right by me. That's cool, I thought. Would have been nice if he bought a program. But then about ten feet away from me he stopped and turned around to come back. He asked me if this was that "independent program." I told him it was and he asked for one, while I tried and failed to find the nicest way possible to say that the Smashing Pumpkins' first two albums are two of my favorites, while not mentioning any other. He said thanks anyway, and walked off.

Five seconds later, I froze. I realized that right in the middle of Game One's issue, I had written a joke digging on Smashing Pumpkins. It was a comedic piece comparing the cities of Boston and Chicago, as I had lived in both. There was one category, "Local Bands To Have Completely Ruined Their Reputation Lately." Of course, Boston's was Aerosmith. I could have left Chicago's at Liz Phair. But I was never one to stop short. So Smashing Pumpkins were listed too.

You'll be shocked to hear Billy never bought a program again.

If only that was the end of the night's surreality. The Bruins proved every bit the threat we had feared in the first, taking the lead through the line of Lucic-Krejci-Horton which was simply unplayable. They would take leads of 2-0 and 3-1, but the Hawks fought back with two goals in four minutes in the third through Bolland and Oduya to tie it. So for the second straight game, the Hawks headed into overtime.

And it didn't stop.

The first overtime even had the rare penalty call, but no goals. The Bruins threatened more than the Hawks, and toward the end it felt like the Hawks were just hanging on. A second overtime for the second game in a row? I mean I liked being at the United Center but this was getting a tad silly.

The second overtime saw Zdeno Chara hit the post and other close calls, but still no goals. We were headed for a third OT. And when you get that far, you really worry how long it might go. Players are basically out on their feet. If there isn't a goal in the first five minutes, things tend to settle into a punch-drunk rhythm and not much happens. An additional overtime goes from possibility to likely

If you're in the crowd, it's a strange haze as well. You haven't had a beer in hours, so you're already starting a hangover. The adrenaline from watching a playoff game still flows, but it's pumping into a rapidly tiring body. Whatever is keeping your eyes wide open isn't really something that belongs to you. You begin to feel a little like a puppet being played from above.

The third OT dragged on, and not too much happened. There weren't too many chances either way. Generally goals this late spring out of nothing, and this one did too. Rozsival picked a puck off the boards on the left, skated toward the middle, and let go an awkward looking wrister toward the net while off-balance. We could hear it hit Andrew Shaw's shin pad, and there it was bolting for the padding in the bottom of the back of the net. After this long, you weren't sure if you were hallucinating.

The scream you let out after this long is more relief than exclamation. Finally you can go home, and even better the Hawks won! You're almost too tired to put in the right celebration, and soon you worry the bar might close before you even get there.

At the bar, our compatriots kept asking my friend Ted how he enjoyed his first ever NHL playoff game. He kept answering, "Um, I hugged a stranger?" He wanted to know if that was ok. Of course, everything is fair during the playoffs.

I brought my father to Game Two. Right before the puck dropped he said to no one in particular, "Alright assholes, I want three periods and no more." I told him he just doomed us. He agreed. And he did. He should have known better.

Affirmation...In 17 Seconds
June 24, 2013
Hawks vs. Bruins (Game Six)

Of course it rained that day. And of course it rained as I was walking to our hockey bar. Thankfully, the burrito that I had purchased for sustenance didn't get soaked.

It had been a crazy Final. The Hawks dropped Game Two in OT (because my father had forced an OT) when Brandon Bollig just handed the puck to Tyler Seguin to find Daniel Paille wide open. Game Three was as weird as you could get, with Marian Hossa not able to make the bell, Ben Smith replacing him without a warm-up, Joel Quenneville losing his mind with lineup decisions and turning Jonathan Toews into a fourth-line center which left Patrice Bergeron free to run wild. Most Hawks fans blacked out during Game Four, the turbulence of which probably usurped 2010's Game One as the Hawks blew 1-0, 3-1, 4-2, and 5-4 leads before Seabrook won it in overtime. It was the game that cost Corey Crawford his Conn Smythe, which he more than deserved, simply because Pierre McGuire decided to pick on his glove during the coverage. However, surviving that game on the road to tie the series did feel like the entire tide had turned. Patrick Kane scored twice in Game Give to put the Hawks on the brink of a second Cup. A second one...six years previous we just longed for a playoff game. Now this.

It was stupid humid leading to that rain, because thanks to the lockout the season had extended to the point at which even the baseball season begins to drag. The clouds opened up about 5:00 pm, which of course is when I was arriving at the bar because what was I going to do, sit around the house some more?

Puck drop never seemed like it would come. Thanks to the crush of customers there three years before, the bar had reserved all the seating for its regulars. I didn't need one, I had to stand the whole time anyway. Killion joined me, but everyone else we had three years prior decided they had to be home alone for this one. I understood. I needed strength in numbers, however.

Ask most fans about games this consequential and they can't recall most of them. It's mostly a blur to me, I know that. I can recall black flashes going one way and white ones going the other. I remember Chris Kelly's goal early in the first where he fooled Crawford. I remember the flashes of whatever can I was drinking toward my mouth, but no matter how many beers you stress drink you don't even really get buzzed. Too focused.

I can see Toews firing one through Rask in the second, the puck bouncing into the net after squeaking through. I remember wondering how the bar's floors didn't crack with everyone jumping. I can't tell you much about the time between then and when Lucic scored in the third. I'm sure it was torture.

Right after Lucic scored I turned to Killion and said, "They'll score with the goalie pulled and go to overtime. That's just how they're going to do it." Was I joking? Probably not. Was I serious? Probably not either. I was probably just emitting sounds. There was certainly a part of me that believed it. But then there's always a part of you that believes aliens are going to show up any moment now.

The minutes ticked by, but that part still held on tight to the Hawks scoring with the goalie pulled. It had to happen. And just about the time Doc Emerick was informing us the Hawks were in fact calling Crawford to the bench, Keith poked a puck to the corner to Toews, who came toward the net. He slipped it to a waiting Bickell, who slammed it home with the same force as a LeBron dunk. It happened too fast to comprehend on TV. The puck had hit the back of the net and slipped back under Rask before we knew what happened. But every Hawk had his arms raised, and then I was covered in everyone at the bar's arms. Overtime, here we come. Faith rewarded, or at least that's what I told myself despite the percentages within me that actually believed hardly being a majority.

The ensuing faceoff took place, and suddenly the Hawks were streaking back toward the B's zone again. I said to Killion, "My god, they're going to score again." This time I'm fairly sure I was joking, though the alien part of me probably wasn't. Oduya slapped one from the point, Frolik deflected it, and it hit the post. For that brief second I thought, "That was the chance I was joking they'd get. They almost did it." If I even had time to complete that thought.

The puck rebounded off the boards, and there was Bolland waiting. He was smothered from the camera though by Johnny Boychuk. Or more to the point, the open net was. We didn't see the puck go in, but we saw Bolland strip off his gloves and turn around in utter shock. It was as if he'd scored the clinching goal and was flinging off his equipment as was tradition. But this wasn't overtime. And he was weird, he could just decide to take his gloves off with less than a minute to go in the Stanley Cup Final. But no, Boychuk bending over in despair told us.

Normally, when you're celebrating a goal, you scream but you're at least attempting a word. It's either "YEAHHHH!!!" or "YESSSS!!!!" or "GOOALLLLLL!" That wasn't this time. I was just screaming. It was just noise. It was the war cry Sergeant Hartman would have demanded. It came from my feet. There wasn't a word. Just an utterance. I was leaning on a stranger at the bar, back-to-back, screaming at the ceiling, perhaps admonishing the lord for putting through all this or thanking him or both.

The last fifty seconds took forever. Toews dumped the puck into the B's zone one last time and with eight seconds to go we knew it was over. They were already pouring off the bench. We were in ecstasy. It was so fast. You don't even know how you got there, much less trying to comprehend the ride. We hugged and yelled but we still didn't really know why. A friend poured a full beer over my head. I just yelled. It would take hours before we could come to terms..

I got a text from my close friend Erin in Boston, a huge B's fan: "That sucked. Congratulations." My girlfriend arrived to celebrate. She had quit smoking a year earlier. Before even a hello she asked for a cigarette. We had our cigars later. We drank into the morning.

I'm still not sure I know what happened. I don't think I want to. It's better this way.

Swagger
October 1, 2013
Capitals vs. Hawks

A second banner-raising in four years. Most of the 20,000 that entered the building probably pinched themselves upon getting inside. It wasn't real.

But this one was so different from the first one. While the first one remained a celebration, it almost felt like it was an ending. The roster had been gutted after the first Cup, and once the banner was raised it felt like we were letting go of something. That once it had ascended to the rafters, something was over. We didn't know when we'd get back.

This time, the roster was brought back. Basically the whole thing.

Bolland and Frolik had to be moved along for cap reasons, but everyone else was back. Even Handzus and Rozsival, which seemed strange. The Hawks were clearly getting off on not having to jettison anything that was nailed down this time. Maybe they went overboard.

This time, it wasn't an ending. It felt like a beginning. A second Cup meant this was the Hawks Era. They were the premier team now. It felt like possibility. And with that, we were free to be as arrogant and obnoxious as we wanted. No more could they label our one win a fluke, or our turn. We had done it again, and they could in the future too. We were the pivot point, the center of hockey. And we were going to let everyone know about it.

It also helped that thanks to the delayed season before and this one being bumped up for the Olympics, it felt like the season started about eight minutes after the last one ended. The Hawks won an entertaining 6-4 contest over Washington, and we left the dock into a sea of something we never knew before. Confidence, swagger, assuredness.

Take that, Old Man Wirtz.

Sequestered
December 30, 2013
Kings vs. Hawks

This was the only game in my eight-year run doing the gameday program that I selectively just didn't do one. I tried. I spent two days trying to write one. But every time I opened up the laptop, I couldn't focus. My fingers would move across the keyboard but I didn't follow what they were doing. I was simply too distracted. My father lay in a hospital bed not a mile away, and quite frankly that's all I was thinking about.

He had a heart attack three days before. My brother, who came home from Ohio for the holidays, called me while I was printing that night's issue. "Bad news, Dad's had a heart attack."

There are some sentences that come through your ear canal and then collapse your chest. This is one of them. Dad's health had been...well, I won't say deteriorating because that's a bit strong, but it had definitely been slipping for a while. There had been a couple hospital visits in the previous year, though he wouldn't convey what was bothering him to us beyond, "just feel off." There was an irregular heartbeat, that's as much diagnosis as he would sit still for. Even with things internally going haywire, he still insisted on his two hot dogs per day. When Dad was entrenched in his seventies, most of his attitude was that he was on house money at this point and he was going to do what he wanted all the time, diet be damned. But still, I couldn't see this coming.

I raced over to the hospital. Adam met me there. We waited forever in a separate room, like the other people in the waiting room couldn't be allowed to see us. Whatever info we got added up to the worst ending. They told us he was stable but not conscious. They told us he would be that way for days as they tried something of a deep-freeze treatment, where the body temperature is lowered to try to slow or even halt the damage to the brain from the heart being stopped. But when you hear about the heart being stopped for any length of time, you know where this is going.

My brother and I punted our tickets and sat together in my apartment to watch the Hawks. We barely spoke, but when we did it was to joke about the game in front of us. We didn't talk about Dad. There wasn't a need and this is how we dealt with everything. We were together, that was enough. Thanks to the holiday schedule our days consisted of visiting Dad in the hospital and then going back home to watch the Hawks. One to balance the other, I guess.

Still, our visits to him made it clear what was going to happen. You always hope for a miracle but have to deal with what you see. As they brought him out of the freeze there was little sign of life. We listened to what the doctors had to say, and all the possibilities, but we knew. And we knew what had to be done. Dad was always very clear how he wanted it to work if something like this came up.

Shortly after this game, my father had a seizure. That caused them to do a series of tests on his brain, and they called us to tell us what we already knew. He had suffered massive damage to his brain while his heart was stopped. There was no debate for us now. If we'd kept Dad on life-support for any length of time, he would have come back to life merely to kick the ever-loving shit out of us before walking outside and calling his own number. The last thing a proud man like my father ever wanted to be was a burden to anyone. As hard as it was, I'm forever grateful that my father made that decision so easy.

We took him off the respirator the next night. And as much as I could, I felt ok. My father wasn't just my father, but my inspiration, my best friend, and so much more. But once you lose one parent, as I had when I was fifteen, you know that you might have to go through it again at some point. You're never prepared, but you can have a structure in place to brace. And with my brother now back on his feet, and me where I was, if Dad had to go then this was the time. We could take it now. My last words to him were, "We've got it from here." We would be ok. He didn't have to prop us up anymore. He had launched us, though maybe it took longer with more fits and stops than it took others. We take our time, we Felses.

We headed back to the United Center a few days later, on a viciously cold night yet somehow still in a blizzard for a game against the Sharks. Just as we had done when we lost Mom, Adam and I sat together at the United Center, healing in one of the only two places we could, the other being Wrigley. Some knew what had been going on and came to give their condolences. We were grateful, but mostly we just wanted to be back watching hockey. We didn't need that, we just needed fans to be fans and provide what we always loved. And they did that.

My brother stayed for weeks after, as we had an apartment and estate to clean up. We went to every game together. It was our escape from cleaning out a closet or chasing paper trails in our father's convoluted finances (example: Dad didn't have a will because, not knowing what the process would be without one and not caring to find out, figured everything would just pass seamlessly to us and more importantly, he didn't want to bother to find parking downtown to go to whatever office he would need to visit to have a will). It's as close as we got to what I'd always dreamed of; the two of us as season ticket holders, both successful, meeting up for every game. Never got that exactly, and I'll have to settle for hockey simply being some sort of medication for grief.

I sincerely thought we would be ok. I thought we had it from here. I was ready, and I thought my brother was, too. We had done this before, and we knew that death is not a break up. There isn't a certain amount of time and then you feel better. We knew that it's something that you carry forever, that you are forever changed, and you have to adjust to life through those new sights. And I could do that. I knew it would be hard but I knew I could do it. I thought Adam could too. We had done it before.

Never will I be haunted more by being wrong.

Last
January 19, 2014
Bruins vs. Hawks

The thing about "lasts" is that you either A) don't know they'll be the last time you do something with someone and hence can't make them the event you think they should have been after the fact or B) you know they're the last and you simply are too sad or angry or both or whatever else to truly enjoy them. Because they should be enjoyed. They should be cherished, and chances are you always miss out on that for one of those two reasons.

This was the last game my brother and I attended together. We couldn't know it then. We had spent the past weeks cleaning out Dad's apartment, donating his clothes where I hope hipsters are utterly delighted at the selection we provided (so much tweed, so much plaid, so much style). We had figured out all the financial crap, which takes forever. We had the service, and we decided that I would carry out one of Dad's more out-there fantasies for the dispersal of his remains: to be spread out the back of a convertible in the desert around Las Vegas. He had only mentioned it once or twice, but the shit-eating grin on his face when he did made it clear that's what he wanted. I guess I shouldn't say we decided, but my best friend Kristy booking a trip to Vegas and renting a convertible in anticipation of being the driver was the main impetus. All the chores were done, and Adam was going to take dad's car and dog back to Ohio (insert Pretenders joke here).

For a last game, there could have been worse. It was a rematch between the previous year's finalists. Neither the Hawks or Bruins were playing particularly well at this point, but were also prime contenders to get back to the Final as well. It was close, and a little more tense than a January game would normally be given the recent history between the two. It ended in a shootout, with Kane faking his normal 100-dekes move and cutting it off short to fire one past Tuukka Rask to win it. Shootouts are still the worst, but a display of skill like that will always make you take notice.

Adam headed out the next day. I didn't know I'd never see him again. I didn't know how deep in the hole he was in was. He never would let me know. He would never want me to worry until it was too late. I thought we were ready to be the only representatives of the family together. I told him if the chance came up, I wanted him to find a job back in Chicago. I thought it would be best for both of us to have each other in proximity. He agreed and hoped that opportunity would come up. I was feeling...ready, that's the best I can say. Certainly not excited, but not full of dread either. This was the way the road bent, and I could navigate it.

Still, the look on his face when I saw him drive off...something was off. Maybe I should have known then. There was fear, though I guess I just assumed it was fear that Dad's nineteen-year-old Infiniti wouldn't make it to Columbus (a genuine one, to be fair). It didn't look right. I shouldn't have waved it off so casually. Just a man in grief, I thought.

Should have done a lot of things.

Plaid
May 28th-June 1st, 2014
Kings vs. Hawks (Games Five-Seven)

It's best to group these together, because they feel like one game in my mind. After all the years of watching the Hawks, the numerous playoff series I had seen them partake in, this is the pinnacle as far as the quality of the hockey on offer. And sadly, we'll probably never see it again.

The fact that it was a rematch from the previous spring's conference final gave it an Ali-Frazier feel. These were now holders of three of the last four Cups, and clearly the class of the league. The Kings had loaded up at the deadline to make up the gap the Hawks had established the previous season, while the Hawks figured their exact same team from the previous year was enough. Still, the collection of talent between the two teams is as high as we'd seen in several years.

The Kings had already won two previous series in seven games each, both on the road, including coming back from 3-0 down against the Sharks.

They had dispatched the Ducks in Anaheim only mere hours before they had to show up in Chicago, and the Hawks got the jump on them, winning Game One relatively easily. But once the Kings got settled, they were all over the Hawks. They exploded in the third period of Game Two for five goals to turn a 2-1 deficit into a 6-2 win at a canter. They scored three straight goals in Game Three to coast out to a 4-2 lead that would end 4-3. They scored the first four goals of Game Four to blow out the Hawks, and for the first time in the latest era of Hawks hockey it looked like the Hawks simply didn't have any answers. They had only been outclassed once since becoming championship level, and even then they were able to look Vancouver in the eye in '11. But this...this was wasn't supposed to go this way, and the Hawks were simply getting blown out of the water. At least those Vancouver games were close. The Hawks were on a standing eight count in all of these games.

They returned home, for what seemed like one desperate lunge to avoid defeat at home before running out of gas in Los Angeles. They scored twice within the first four minutes, but just couldn't shake the Kings. Jarret Stoll would pull one back. Brandon Saad would extend the lead to 3-1, but only for two minutes before Marian Gaborik would get them back within one. The Kings would take the lead with both goals in the second period, but Ben Smith would tie it early in the third.

And then everything went plaid. The pace of play was kicked up to something that was hard to watch, let alone describe. It felt like the TV camera had a hard time keeping up. The play bounced from one end to the other like souped-up pong. The teams traded chances seemingly a few times a minute. They emptied the chambers on each other. It stopped resembling hockey and became more like Smash TV or Running Man. All of us were exhausted from watching it. It was dizzying.

Finally, in the second overtime, after what seemed like an hour long battle scene from *Braveheart*, Saad found Handzus open streaking toward the Kings net. Handzus faked Quick out and roofed a backhand. At the bar, I sank to my knees in surprise and fatigue. My friend John burst out laughing at the sight. I don't know how the players got through it, because merely being a TV spectator as soon as I didn't have to lock in anymore I was simply drained of all feeling as soon as it was over.

Game Six didn't slow down at all, and this is just about when Patrick Kane and Brandon Saad went nuclear. Again, both teams were throwing haymakers at each other all games. It was Hagler-Hearns on ice, if I can mix boxing metaphors. The Hawks took a 2-1 lead into the third but the Kings poured in two goals in two minutes to take the lead, and it looked like the scythe was being brought out. Halfway through the period, Kane found Keith with a blind, through-the-legs pass that I still can't really fathom. With four minutes left, Kane circled in the offensive zone until finding a lane through the middle and labeled on top corner. He was basically doing it himself. The Hawks somehow held on through the end, even though the Kings fired everything at Crawford. They had pulled even, and were bringing the Kings back to Chicago for a Game Seven.

It's probably the best game I've ever attended, but I didn't feel that way at the time. It would take me a long time to come to that feeling and to appreciate it. It wasn't torture at the time, because it was too fast and tense in the building to feel any emotion whatsoever. There wasn't time. Emotions were stripped to service focus. There were only so many resources a body has. Someone was getting a chance every time you blinked. Our throats were raw by the second period.

And the Hawk couldn't shake the Kings. They scored first, with Kane finding Saad on the other side of the net in a way only he could. Toews got a lucky bounce off the glass to score into an empty net when Quick was fooled. But again, with two goals in less than two minutes the Kings were tied. Twelve seconds after that, Sharp bounced one past Quick on an incredibly weak shot.

But the Kings got their own bounce off a skate for Toffoli to tie it in the second. Sharp would score a power play goal with less than two to go in the second. We headed outside for the intermission. It felt like the entire crowd was out there, and they were all chain-smoking. It was all too much. We nervously talked at each other instead of with each other, trying to calm our frayed nerves. Heading back inside felt like going into some weird science experiment.

The Hawks made it nearly thirteen minutes before Gaborik would put home a rebound. From there we knew it was overtime, and repeating everything that took place before the third.

Overtime...well, it was basically involuntarily being thrown onto a roller coaster. You were thrown from one side to the other, pitched up and down, all the while just kind of hoping it would all end soon. The Hawks had their chances, and whenever they didn't go in you felt it physically, as in your stomach creeping closer to your throat.

I still see it right before I fall asleep sometimes. After an icing call on the Kings, Quenneville sent out Versteeg, Handzus, and Bollig, three forwards who had been barely used due to their own incompetence all series. He was trying to steal one shift to rest everyone else. But as soon as I saw them, there was a sense of dread. You could barely blink before they'd lost the draw and the puck was in the Hawks' zone. These three? Trapped in the defensive zone? I'm surprised I didn't crack every tooth I have, grinding them as I was.

The puck didn't get out. Alec Martinez grabbed it off the boards and sent a wrister toward the net, but nowhere near on target. Leddy emerged from behind the net to have it hit him in the chest right at the side of the goal. And then it's just a flash. The puck behind Crawford, but it couldn't have gone in like that, could it? The Kings pouring off the bench, right under us. Crawford in shock. And then it was over. Trying to comprehend losing that series in that instant, and unable to come to grips. Every time I tried to think, "The series is over" it would short out in my mind, like a neon sign. I could almost hear the buzzing.

For the longest time, I wished I hadn't seen it. I would have happily settled for the Hawks to win Game Seven 5-0, or to just have lost it in five games. I didn't care it was a classic. My brain still couldn't come to terms with the ending.

But now I do. I see it for what it was, and see that we might not get it again. This is what the NHL is missing out on with their hard salary cap. Teams will not be able to amass and build these kinds of teams. You can't buy it anymore, and if you develop this many players you won't be able to keep them together. The NHL won't get two teams of this quality in a playoff series again, or very rarely. They won't get this quality of hockey again. They won't get a series played at a pace that was so ridiculous.

And how does it expect to grip the casual or non-fan without it? Everyone was talking about those games after they were over. Has it happened since? I doubt it. The NHL won't get two marquee teams in its biggest markets like that for a long time, if ever. The Hawks and Kings both had to strip down soon after. The league may get one team this good, but for things to align for them to get one along with that just seems too hard. Most teams look the same. The differences between them now shrinks every year. It may make it competitive, but the level of play won't rise. To have had that, to have been there, now I'm glad I was.

But geez Leds, get out of the way.

A New Anthem
October 11, 2014
Sabres vs. Hawks

I generally hate it when people say sports don't matter. It's almost always one of two things: 1) it's a rationalization to try to come to grips with some massive happening, usually disaster, that we simply can't understand; 2) it's an attempt from someone who doesn't follow sports to feel superior about something they're simply just left out of. I've seen far too many people come together, made far too many friends, and have far too many memories around sports to ever think they don't matter. No, we don't have control over them. Yes, sometimes we let them affect us too much because we don't have control over them. In that sense, no, they don't matter because they're something affecting us over which we have no say. But that doesn't mean they don't matter at all. Far from it.

There are times when you know what is important, what shapes you, and what will alter your life forever. I was pretty depressed after the Hawks lost that Game Seven to the Kings. They had lost out on their best chance to repeat as champions. They were so close to yet another comeback. And the offseason seemed like it would be miserable until we could get to the new season.

Then I found out what true depression is.

Seven weeks after that loss, seven months after I lost my father, I lost my brother. His health had simply fallen apart over the summer, but I only found out through what he would tell me. He kept telling me it was insomnia problems. But he wasn't going to work, he was seeing doctors all the time, and complaining all the time of symptoms that sounded strange and beyond simply not sleeping. He kept assuring me things were going to be fine, and I had no reason to not believe him. But things kept getting worse. I could hear it over the phone, which is how one knows something is truly wrong. His voice was different. His attitude was different. I could hear genuine worry coming through the phone.

On a Saturday afternoon, when I could sense things were simply getting no better, I told him that if he didn't feel any better during the day I wanted him to go to a hospital. Even an urgent care center. I told him to call me if he did and I would be on my way to Ohio instantly. I knew it had gotten to that point. I hoped this would lead us to the start of getting through it.

The next morning, he called to ask me to come to Ohio to look after him. He said he had been prescribed something, I can't remember what, and had a doctor's appointment the following Tuesday but needed some help until then. I heard outright panic in his voice. He sounded on the verge of tears, which I hadn't heard before about his own worries. He asked if I wanted to fly out, but I said after finding a flight and getting to the airport and all that I wouldn't save that much time instead of driving, and having the car around would probably be a good idea anyway. Within fifteen minutes I was on the road.

It was hellish getting out of the city, summer Sunday afternoon and all. Maybe if I'd found a different route. He kept checking in to see where I was. I thought he was just being an older brother. Now I think he was just desperate for me to get there.

I got to Columbus around dinnertime, maybe a touch before. I pulled into his building's parking lot, but went around to the wrong door. I called him to find out where I was supposed to go. He told me to walk around the building to the main entrance, not where I was. He sounded tired but he was joking with me. We laughed about something silly. He was glad I was there, I could tell. I told him to wait for the buzzer and hung up the phone. I headed around to the right entrance.

It was the last time we spoke. I headed back around the building, stopping by my car to clear out some trash. I got to the right entrance, but there was no answer to the building's buzzer. I kept trying that and calling him on my phone. Then I looked over to a balcony down a little bit from the entrance. Between the time we joked on the phone with me at the wrong door, to my getting to the entrance, he had collapsed.

I spent the next month, maybe the next two, maybe still, as if I'd just had a bomb go off five feet from me. I could see everything around me, I could hear noises and sounds, but I couldn't process any of it. Things went on around me, but not with me. It was as if a divider was between me and the rest of the world. There were moments, maybe more than I want to think about, where I wondered why I was even bothering anymore. What was the point? Who was I doing this for? A major motivation in life for me was to find the happiness my family so desperately wanted for me, and sacrificed a great deal for. And now what?

Soon the season came around, and it was time to start writing again. And I couldn't. My whole reason for being a fan, the genesis of everything I'd experienced through being a Hawks fan was gone. Could it be the same? Could it even be enjoyable? What I always knew...was it gone now?

Eventually I came to the conclusion that my brother would have been sick if he thought he, even in absence, was depriving me of something I had loved so much. He loved the program, and I had to keep writing it, even though my mind would wander and there were a lot of nights when my heart just wasn't in it.

Again, I can't stand it when I hear sports don't matter. What I came to learn over that summer is that the last few years of my brother's life were not kind to him. I knew about some of it—the job loss, the job search, the feelings of falling behind—but couldn't fathom the depth. They took a toll far beyond anything I knew. He kept so much from me so I wouldn't be scared. Or maybe he thought I couldn't handle it or wouldn't understand. I don't know. I'll never know. What I do know is that in that time, when we were sitting in our seats together, or just watching a game on my couch together, he was happy. Whatever was eating at him, and in fact killing him, disappeared for a few hours. He had hockey, he had his brother, and he probably had a beer; what else did he need? Try to tell me that doesn't matter and I'll stab you in the throat. If only I could have found more that made him feel that way.

So I showed up to my usual post for the home opener. Thanks to Adam's contributions to the program, his presence on our blog and Twitter, it wasn't much of a secret. Scores of readers stopped to express their condolences, and it was a bigger lift than I thought it could be. Maybe if he could have seen how many people he touched even through just his silly writing on hockey. Maybe.

I headed inside, but froze in the 300 concourse. The anthem was minutes away, but I honestly didn't know if I could do it. All I could think about was the first one, back across the street. How worried he was that I couldn't handle the noise even as he taught me about the tradition. How his smile grew as mine did when I first experienced it. How lucky he felt that his shithead little brother wasn't just handling the noise of the anthem, but was relishing it. It was the first of so many, but now that number had a cap. Was I really ready for the first one of the rest of my life?

I made it up. The anthem started. I didn't clap. I didn't cheer. I just kept staring at the rafters. I didn't cry, like I was sure I would. I guess I felt thankful. Thankful that he had given me this, and I could still enjoy it with him gone. Maybe in some way trying to signal to him that I could take it from here, just as I had months before with my father. Or at least that I would be able to in time.

The anthem ended. I smiled. The game started. It felt familiar, but not entirely so. The Hawks won easily. I enjoyed watching them. I knew that I would every time, but that it would be different. On that night, I knew there was a long road of adjustment to be traversed. But for the first time in months, it felt possible. I could get there.

I got in the car after the game. The phone didn't ring. It always rang after home games he wasn't attending with me. He wanted to talk about that game, the Hawks, hockey. It would take many more home games before it didn't hurt that my phone didn't ring in the car. Actually, it still does. That's the thing about loss. Every day, sometimes multiple times a day, something happens, or doesn't happen, and you think to yourself, "That's never going to happen again. This is how this is now." I stared at my phone in my parking spot for a few minutes. It was never going to ring after a game again. You can't wrap your arms around what that means at first, if ever. You just keep saying to yourself that it's never going to ring again, trying to make the words have meaning. But they don't. Not for a long while.

The phone still doesn't ring. Maybe noticing that it doesn't ring helps me feel like he's around in some way. I don't know. Sitting in the UC is different. Watching hockey at all is different, because the phone doesn't ring.

What's In A Name?
February 9, 2015
Coyotes vs. Hawks
I had heard the complaints even when I first started. Back then though, they were one or two a season. So it was easy to dismiss claims that the name of the blog and program, *The Committed Indian*, was inappropriate, racist, and/or ableist. When you rarely hear something, it's easy to dismiss. And I knew that I didn't mean any harm, as it was a joke from a Denis Savard quote. I thought that fact gave it street cred that was necessary to appeal to longtime Hawks fans, including ones who read *The Blue Line*. I thought my intent was enough.

As the years went on, the calls got a little more numerous. I would see them once a month, sometimes more. And generally my reaction was to recoil and lash out. After all, I meant well. Who were these people to comment? They didn't understand the quote, they weren't Hawks fans, they didn't have any frame of reference. On Twitter and via email I would send snide responses, which certainly didn't help matters.

But the complaints didn't go away, and ever so slowly I began to listen. I'm slow, but I get there eventually. And eventually it came time to have the discussion. We put the question up on our blog, and in the following program.

The discussion was actually much more cordial than I had deserved after previous responses. The majority seemed to suggest that the logo was much more offensive than the name. At first I thought it was just a cute cartoon of a looney-tunes-like Native American with a hockey stick in a straight-jacket (typing it out now, it's pretty easy to see the problem). So within weeks, I changed it, and was excited to use the opportunity to honor my brother with a logo in his image.

But I still should have gone further. I took far too much solace in reading the emails and the comments of those I just simply wanted to see and read. You can't learn anything like that. There were enough of them to make me think I could "get away" with not changing the name, even though everyone close to me in life was urging me to do so. I felt attacked, which was silly. This was something I created after all, I didn't mean to hurt anyone, so why was I getting tossed into the same boat as Dan Snyder and actual racists? I would learn what it truly meant to be attacked a few months later, of course.

All of it of course leads to a discussion of whether the Hawks are going to have to change their name and logo. The answer is of course they will, someday. And it really won't hurt a bit. People will act like it will, but they won't go anywhere. It won't cost the Hawks anything. Whatever money it costs to rebrand a professional sports organization will be quickly made up by those people complaining the loudest immediately running out to by the new jersey with the new logo on it.

It just isn't worth it, or eventually they won't feel it is, to upset anyone in this way. The payoff isn't worth it. The Hawks do a lot of work with local groups from First Nations' people, and that's nice, but it won't be enough. But the Hawks fear that backlash from their hardcore fans.. I'm sure it's more infuriating for others than myself knowing the right thing won't cost anything and still isn't the road taken. We shall see.

Now You See
May 21ˢᵗ, 2015
Ducks vs. Hawks (Game Three)

Sometimes, people join you in shouting at the rain. It had been a strange playoff run for the Hawks, in that it didn't really involve a lot of drama. The closest was a small goalie controversy in the first round, where Corey Crawford was pulled for Scott Darling in Game One, then Darling started Games 3-6, only to see Crawford relieve him in Game Six for the win and never give the net back. The Hawks never trailed in the series, and then they swept the Wild in the second round. It was all rather clean. None of the drama of previous years. So something clearly had to give.

While I refused to risk flying out to Anaheim to get the fan vengeance I so craved, I figured a Conference Final win over them would satisfy enough. I doubt there was anyone in Chicago to whom a victory over Anaheim meant more to.

This wasn't so easy. The Hawks dropped Game One, and then took three overtimes to get a win in Game Two. The length of that game ruined the dinner and post-dinner plans my girlfriend and I had for that night. It nearly passed closing time, which would have been a real debate for our hockey bar. Thankfully, Marcus Kruger spared them that.

The Hawks returned home for Game Three, and I returned to my post outside Gate 3. As I was selling, there began a buzz that started on Twitter from the beat writers and then filtered to discussion outside. The rumor was that Joel Quenneville was going to scratch Teuvo Teravainen and Antoine Vermette from the lineup for the game to dress Joakim Nordstrom and Bryan Bickell. And everyone was stupefied.

For years, we had questioned some of Joel Quenneville's moves. He had favorite players we couldn't figure, detested some others without seeming reason, constant lineup changes, and other moves. Most of the time, we were met with howls from fans along the ever so cultured argument of "TWO CUPZ!" It was as if we weren't just wrong simply because we weren't Q, we didn't have the right to even question him.

Finally, on this night, it felt like people got what we had been saying. While Quenneville is unquestionably a great coach, that doesn't mean he was perfect. As I stood at my spot, and when I headed into the arena, I watched as more and more fans either checked their phone or heard from their companion the news, and they all reacted the same way. "THE FUCK?!"

It was personal affirmation. Now you see what I see. It felt like the fanbase was learning and evolving. It was fleeting, but at least we gotten there for a brief time.

The Hawks would lose that night, and it felt like what they deserved. Both Teravainen and Vermette would return the next game. Vermette would score the OT winner, and then two game-winning goals in the Final. All of them assisted by Teuvo. Perhaps Q could point to "motivating" them to this level. But most fans, finally, knew that would be bullshit.

Being There

June 15, 2015
Lightning vs. Hawks (Game Six)

The tears started right after Game Five. Shortly after the Hawks went up 3-2 in Tampa, I had to take myself outside our hockey bar to collect myself. Every fan dreams of not just seeing their team win a championship, but actually being there. At least those who can, but to most it is beyond reach or comprehension. Suddenly it was on my doorstep, except I couldn't avoid that I wouldn't be there with the companion who was always in my dreams and visions of it. It was too much to take.

The Hawks had seen off the Ducks in seven games, Game Seven being a night-long party for me given the opponent. There was never any doubt that the Ducks and Bruce Boudreau were going to cough up yet another Game Seven at home, and I treated the whole thing like a parade. And that's how it played out.

The series with the Lightning wouldn't be called a classic. It was low-scoring aside from Game Two, but was tight with each game being a one-goal decision. The Hawks barely squeaked out Game Four to tie the series, and then took another 2-1 decision in Game Five to set up the first possible clincher in Chicago since 1971, which the Hawks never actually clinched.

Like the previous two championship days, it was hot and silly humid. It rained early in the morning, which only exacerbated the humidity, and made the approaching storm in the afternoon all the more vicious. I got in the car with all the programs I thought I would need somewhere before 4:00 pm. As I headed down Western Avenue I looked to the west, and all I saw was doom. There's storm clouds, and then there's clouds that look like they were spawned straight from the mind of Lucifer, and might actually come to life and descend upon the Earth to simply wipe out life as we know it. These were the latter.

They moved in rapidly, and unleashed their angry burden upon the city before I reached the bar I always dropped programs off at before the game. I wouldn't get back in the car, that's how hard it was raining, because even that twelve-foot journey would have left me soaked. I waited, because normally when it rains that hard it only lasts for a few minutes. There just can't be that much water. But this demon spawn of a storm didn't adhere to the normal rules. It just kept going. It even got harder. Just sticking your hand out in it could see it bruised. For the first time I could ever remember, tornado sirens went off downtown. It was that heinous.

Finally I couldn't wait anymore, and dashed for the car. I figured I would drive/float over to the UC, and by the time I got to my usual parking spot the rain would have stopped just enough to get to my spot without drowning.

But it didn't stop.

I parked where I usually did, and just sat in the car. After a few minutes, I opened the door just to see. I couldn't see the street, the water was that deep. There was no delineation from the street to the sidewalk. It was all pond. And it just kept raining.

I tweeted out to try and let every reader know that I would be there as soon as the rain would let me. I texted my fellow vendors that I was coming and to hold on somewhere dry. There was enough of a break, from hellish fury to simply a raging downpour, where I felt I could get to my spot. As soon as I did, the fury broke again, and I huddled with everyone else under the awning of the ticket windows. We couldn't get to our spots. Some readers found us under there, but most just sprinted for the gates. I couldn't blame them.

So at 7:00 pm, I headed in, with hundreds of extra programs. It's ok, I thought, still going to be magical night. The sight of the Cubs' Anthony Rizzo running by me inside and giving me a thumbs up as he went by was only more sign of that.

The tears started again as I got on the escalator. Thankfully, most everyone was already inside so no one saw me. My brother was supposed to be here. I thought by wearing his Secord jersey (two sizes too big, at least) I would feel like he was. But it didn't work. I composed myself before heading to my seat, but I needed the game to start quickly so I could stop thinking.

The game did start. While the United Center couldn't ever match what the Old Stadium sounded like in full-throat, this was as close as it could get. It felt like the demonstration of the THX sound system in movie theaters, except it was for three hours. It seemed like everyone was at the end of their rope when the puck dropped for the first time.

The Hawks sensed it, too, and came out firing. They couldn't find a way past Ben Bishop though. But the anticipation never turned to impatience, which was surprising. The crowd just kept getting louder and more positive. This was our night, nothing was going to stop it. Even a scoreless first period didn't break the spirit.

The second carried on much in the same way as the first, with the Hawks trying to force the door down but finding no luck. Tampa came more into it, with Stamkos being stopped on a breakaway and the rebound as well. The UC faithful cheered those saves louder than most goals I had seen there. But still not breakthrough. Christmas morning was dragging on, and yet we weren't allowed to unwrap our present yet. Some tension started to mix in.

And then it burst. With three minutes to go in the period, Duncan Keith sent a shot from the blue line toward Ben Bishop. Cedric Pacquette had come out to try and close the lane, turned around to see where the shot went, and stopped. But Keith didn't. He never stopped moving, maneuvering around Pacquette and right to the front of the net. Bishop dropped the puck right to him. To this day I don't know if Keith meant to chip the puck up and over Bishop's shoulder or he just shanked it and it did that anyway. I know he didn't care, and I know I didn't either. I saw the puck flutter over Bishop, took a second to consider if I was actually seeing it, and then was buried in a wall of sound. It took my chest in.

That intermission was surreal. None of us could quite come to grips with being twenty minutes away from seeing the Cup on our ice. We kind of didn't want to talk about it. We walked back in. Even though we had just purchased beers, Killion suggested we get two more so we would be assured of not being without at any point during what we knew was going to be a torturous ride. Smart kid.

Every time I checked the clock, it felt like it was moving the wrong way. How could only forty-eight seconds have ticked off? When I checked during stoppages and actual minutes had ticked off, I could almost feel just a little more nervousness physically fall off. But man did it move slow.

And yet this is always how I pictured it. A one-goal lead late into the third. A definitive empty-net goal to torch off a wild celebration. We were heading toward it, and yet all I could do was curse myself for envisioning it that way. Anything could go wrong here to let the Lightning tie it up, and then overtime where it was always dicey, and then it could be a Game Seven on the road. They could still take this from you, Sam.

The Hawks didn't take it down to the last minute, as I had always envisioned it, and I'm glad they didn't. With five minutes left, Saad, Richards, and Kane came down on a 3-on-2. Saad dropped it to Richards, who just kept gliding toward the net. No one got in his way. It kept going slower and slower. He could have reached out and touched Bishop. He had sucked him out just enough. Right about the time me and about 20,000 others were going to yell, "SHOOT THE FUCKING THING," he slid it to his right where Kane was waiting. He couldn't miss.

I grabbed...well, someone's shirt. I'm not sure whose. Someone grabbed mine, not sure who. There was still five minutes left, but the roar that filled the building at that moment was assured. It was joyous. It was over. Silver would be on the ice soon.

My entire row were arm-in-arm for the last minute. Sure, teams had scored two goals in the last minute before, and we tried to pretend that we were tense. But we weren't. We counted down the last seconds together. I saw Keith fling his stick and gloves in the air with seconds to go. I saw Stamkos skate across his blue line, stick on his knees and head buried. And then it was just hugs.

A friend who sits a few rows in front of me came up moments later, stepping on the armrests of the row in front of us. He offered Killion and me champagne that he had gotten... well, let's not think about it. There are some times where you don't ask questions.

The Cup was delayed thanks to the storm before the game flooding many routes from the airport to the arena. No one cared. We would have stayed there for hours. Finally, it emerged from the Zamboni entrance.

When you're there, it's actually kind of hard to see past the shine and gleam. All you see for a while is glare. Bettman handed it to Toews, and the roar that greeted his raising of it probably lifted it a couple inches beyond Toews's arm-length.

When he handed it to Kimmo Timonen, it was just a touch more than I could take. That would have been Adam's favorite moment. I took a seat, put my hat over my face and took a moment for myself. This wasn't what I had always pictured, but I wouldn't be having this without him. I found appreciation and thankfulness out of the sorrow.

We watched every player skate it, every coach, every trainer. We saw the picture. And then we headed out. Killion and I discovered the store already had the championship hats, and we nearly got into a fistfight over who would get to pay for the other's. I think I won out. I'm sure it doesn't matter.

I had a cigar at my selling spot, greeting whatever regular reader I saw. I got in the car and headed to the bar. We were there until close, just remarking how this kind of thing never got old. I was doused in rain and beer, and some of my own tears.

It'll never get better. And in a lot of ways, that's where it ended.

And Then It All Ended
October 7, 2015
Rangers vs. Hawks

Most people don't believe it, but some I've told experience the same thing. On the rare nights I get solid sleep, I have these dreams where I see something in the future. It's never something useful, of course. I never see the lottery numbers or who's going to win the Kentucky Derby or the next big thing in the tech world. It's always something random and small. Like I'll dream I'm sitting on a bus, listening to a certain song, and someone next to me will say something out loud that will stick in my mind. And then days or weeks later that will actually happen, with that person saying exactly the same words I had in my dream. I know it sounds crazy, but it happens. And it's always something that negligible.

Only once did I see the future lay out in front of me perfectly in a meaningful way. Sadly, I wasn't asleep.

It had already been something of a rough summer for Hawks fans. Brandon Saad was traded because the Hawks couldn't meet his contract demands. Patrick Sharp was traded because he wasn't affordable anymore, and maybe because of whatever off-ice issues he brought (still debatable). Johnny Oduya left for greener pastures. These were three key members of two Cup teams, three in Sharp's case, players fans had become very attached to. In Sharp's case, he had been with the team ten years. We had watched him grow as a player along with the team. He was an identifier to the beginning.

If only that had been the biggest problem.

I woke up on August first of that summer, walked the dog, and before heading to the gym checked the Twitter feed. It was the first thing I saw. "Patrick Kane in police investigation." I tweeted out "Oh goodie." That's all. Even before it became known what he was being investigated for, I kind of knew. It was not that hard to get to. When it became official that it was a rape investigation, it all splayed out in front of me.

I, and the others on the blog, took our stance that he shouldn't be given any benefit of the doubt. He had his history already, the one we had mostly laughed off. He had the rumors around town, which were getting harder and harder to laugh off. We also knew that most cases of this kind are rarely falsely reported, but also rarely even get to court. It's even worse when the accused is a celebrity. And I had people close to me who had seen it from the inside, let's say. It was personal. I knew we would stand apart from most fans and writers, too. I knew it was going to get ugly in a hurry, that the woman involved in this would be called all kinds of names and anyone who sought to support her would too. I knew it would get more and more polarized, that it would become a sporting event itself. It would have teams, it would have winners and losers, and it was far too serious of a matter for that, and that would sicken me. I knew that it was highly likely no charges would be filed, because that's how these things almost always went. I knew that fans would take this as some sort of "victory," and I would feel ill at the sight of it. And I knew the fun of all of it would be sucked out, and I knew that it was fairly likely it would see me stop writing about the Hawks.

I saw all of it in the hours following the news breaking. And that's essentially what happened.

I tried to be as diplomatic as I could about it, and very few cared. I tried to lay out just how difficult these cases are on everyone, and via email or social media or whatever else everyone basically told me that I was calling him guilty. I couldn't fathom how everyone rushed to his defense. Everyone knew what he was and is. The stories about him were not hard to find. I didn't go looking for them, they just found me. This was the dark side of the Hawks trying to turn every player into a family member of their fans. People felt protective of Kane, even if he couldn't really give a shit about them. They thought he was a friend.

If he was, he wouldn't have been one you'd hang out with. We knew about the cab driver, the party in Madison, and the stories from that of putting his hands around a girl's neck. You didn't have to strive all that hard to find stories of him acting in boorish and obnoxious ways in all kinds of venues around town. These were in the bloodstream.

Hawks fans and Kane's fans only got more vitriolic. Our comments were filled not with just disagreements but insults and sometimes threats.

We closed them, never to be reopened. There were people who if they saw some things that were written would have terrible wounds opened again.

I wrote how I never wanted to see Kane on the United Center ice again, not so much because of him, or not entirely, but because I didn't want to be amongst his most dedicated fans who saw him as some sort of idol for bro culture. How could people be so callous about something like this?

What I was most surprised by was that everything being said to me sounded an awful lot like what I said defensively to those who had questioned or protested the name of the blog and program. A refusal to listen, to see it any other way but their own, to shut out any disagreement of held opinions and feelings. People holding dear to opinions about things that they didn't really understand. That didn't affect them directly. It only made me more sick about the way I had been.

The Hawks of course didn't have a clue what to do. I hoped they wouldn't have him at the opening of training camp, but realized there wasn't much they could do to prevent him. I sat in shock when it was announced they would let him talk. Here he would get an entire media bullhorn, another chance to whip the fans into a frenzy, while the victim got the contents of her underwear leaked to the press. The press conference remains one of the strangest happenings we have ever seen. Kane couldn't answer any questions, merely responding that he "appreciated" everything being asked. John McDonough completely froze and revealed himself to be a total fraud. He started off the conference reciting the Hawks' accomplishments, as if that made everything before and after ok. Then he claimed he wasn't tone-deaf. And it went on like this.

I should have suspected. While McDonough and the Hawks loved to cite how large of a percentage of their fans were women, they didn't do anything for them. Two previous summers, a female fan and blogger at the convention asked the Hawks' brass about the Ice Girls: why they were decked out in such revealing outfits but the male members weren't. Why were the feelings of the female fans ignored in such a way? The following season, the Ice Crew were put in pants and sometimes coats. The organist stopped playing "The Stripper" whenever the female contestant of the shoot-the-puck intermission entertainment. Those were good steps. But the following season, the Ice Crew were back in the short skirts, now that it wasn't top of mind. This came after Susannah Collins's firing for a couple blue jokes years before, while Bobby Hull stumbled around the concourses behind the skyboxes.

Kane took the ice for the first practice to a standing ovation. I knew it was coming, we all did, but it still made me nauseated. Did these people know what they were cheering? More to the point, what against? To those who cheered, what would they say to someone who was a victim of rape? To someone close to one? Did they know they likely knew one? Toews would say after the practice how great it was. I don't blame him. He didn't know better. He should have never been allowed to speak about it. The Hawks couldn't get out of their way.

It all went so predictably. I was removed from the fandom I had been a part of my whole life. I seriously considered quitting right then and there. I decided to carry on, to try and go out on my own terms.

I rode down on Opening Night, Banner-Raising Night, to drop off programs. I had long ago sold my tickets to that game and many after it, unsure when I'd feel I could return. Also, the Cubs had their wildcard playoff game that night, so I wanted to watch that anyway. Still, just dropping off programs I felt ill being down there for even minutes. How could everyone just be as normal? Who among these people had openly cheered or screamed at us? This wasn't where I was supposed to be.

That's not to label every Hawks fan a rape-apologist. Many of them are good people who just want to enjoy what they've always enjoyed. Even if we wanted massive changes, how do we go about effecting them? Giving up our tickets would only see them snatched up by someone else in an instance. There would never be enough eyeballs taken away from screens to affect ratings. This is how sports and society works.

But isn't that the attitude that lets these things fester? That resignation that this is just how things are? Isn't that just culpability?

I rooted against the Hawks that night, and a lot of games that season. I didn't want Kane, McDonough, or Rocky, or any of the more virulent fans to defend Kane to have any sense of satisfaction. They didn't deserve joy, even though I knew they would get it and my feelings wouldn't matter.

I don't know what happened that night in Buffalo any more than anyone else. That cloud of uncertainty acts as a shelter for most to watch the Hawks as they always have, and I don't blame them. For me, that cloud still makes it uncomfortable, because I suspect what Kane was and still might be. And what his biggest fans said and feel.

What I did learn, and I think what a lot of people learned, was that the Hawks' brass was a bunch of frauds. For years they had gotten credit for the biggest turnaround in a sports franchise...well, possibly ever. But when you began to look at it, you realized they didn't have any original ideas. They put the home games on TV? They treated their players and fans well? They tried to win? Was this so revolutionary? Their game presentation was lifted from arenas around the league. Their charity work is hardly new, though greatly welcomed. What they were really good at was telling you how they were really good at stuff.

But faced with an actual crisis? When they actually had to negotiate some very choppy waters and try to ease the discomfort of a lot of fans? They were announcing a bobblehead night for Kane two days after training camp started. Months later they would welcome back Garret Ross to their minor league team even though he only got off his revenge porn case due to a technicality. When it came to tough decisions, they didn't have a clue.

This Is Not My Beautiful House

December 8, 2015
Predators vs. Hawks

      I didn't attend any home game for the season's first two months. Part of it was being distracted by the Cubs. Mostly, I just couldn't bring myself to. I didn't want to be in there. I didn't want to be surrounded by people who not only didn't understand mine and others' trepidation, but thought we were blatantly wrong for having it. I didn't know who in the seats had been amongst the many to call us every name under the sun, who had shit on any survivor that might have been reading what they were writing or hearing what they were saying. I didn't know if I was headed for some confrontation.

      After a while, I figured it was time to go, at least for work purposes. The Predators had Seth Jones, and I figured that was enough.

      It was awkward, but not outwardly unpleasant. What struck me most was that I just didn't feel anything. I didn't really care when the Hawks scored. I didn't really care when the Predators scored. It felt like I was just watching from a different angle on a TV. For the first time, I was just watching a hockey game live. None of what had drawn me to the game lo those many years ago across the street, aside from watching the best live sport, was present. I couldn't bring myself to root for an organization I now felt was evil. But I couldn't go back on all the years and root against them either. It was stasis.

      In the second intermission, someone recognized me as I conversed with a friend at a concourse bar. Thankfully, it's the only kind of confrontation I've ever had. And even this was cordial. He wanted to know why I was in the arena when I had written I never wanted Kane on the UC ice again. I told him it was my job and I wanted to watch hockey. He wondered if the lack of charges changed my mind at all, and I told him no, because of how rape cases, especially against celebrities, are handled, and what I knew Kane to be. I told him I was still uncomfortable with it but didn't begrudge him for not caring. We all have our lives to lead.

      I didn't really get the feeling back all season. Kane would go on to have his best season, a ridiculous performance given the shackles the game has now on scoring. He would set a team record for games in a row with a point. Soon, the organization was pumping stories in the press about how "he'd overcome so many obstacles." This only sickened us more. Human beings are not obstacles and should not be reduced to such. It was a lessening of what had really gone on. But most fans ate it up. There was a section of fans, and I don't know how big it is, that took Kane's MVP performance as a victory over whiny feminists. That this was a step against women who were trying to ruin sports because they actually wanted to be treated well and have their concerns addressed. I just couldn't take it.

I attended a few more games, but still felt nothing. It sucked in some ways, because any other season I would have been eating up the surprise performance of Artemi Panarin, one of the most exciting players to come to the Hawks in years. But because of who he was on a line with, I just couldn't. It was gone. I kept reaching for it at times, and I couldn't find it.

Bottom
April 19, 2016
Blues vs. Hawks (Game Four)

The season felt interminable. The Hawks surged to the top of the division, and then spent two months dropping out of it in February and March. They didn't really have a defense, as Keith could only do so much, but the absence of Oduya was simply too much to overcome with the likes of Trevor van Riemsdyk, Rob Scuderi, Trevor Daley, Christian Ehrhoff, and whatever other goofus they could scrounge up from Rockford. When they were winning, though it felt like a thumb in the eye of those who were already questioning their fandom, they were at least entertaining. When they weren't, whatever satisfaction I might have gleaned from the Hawks suffering was rubbed out by actually having to watch them.

The playoffs began, and I hoped that the vicious ballet that is the NHL playoffs would rekindle some passion within me. After all, it was another tilt with the Blues, and I still had a fair amount of distaste for them.

I didn't know there was one more vault into the bottom of the barrel waiting. The Hawks dropped both games Three and Four at home to go down 3-1. They twice coughed up leads in the third period, which they simply never did. And then at the end of the Game Four, when the series seemed lost, they completely melted down, beyond anything we'd seen.

And it centered on Andrew Shaw. Shaw had become a fan favorite, because he played the way we all imagined we would if given the chance. Just face first into everything, he never stopped moving or yapping. His act was already wearing thin, and then he torched it. At the end of Game Four, while trying to fight every Blue he could find after the game was lost, he was caught by the TV cameras clearly calling the ref a "faggot."

It was one last indignity for any fan with a conscience. The Hawks had already become the most hated team in the league for all the things that had gone on with Kane and Ross previously outside of Chicago, and here was another thing we simply couldn't defend. I hoped that the Hawks would suspend Shaw themselves, but they waited for the NHL to do it. I just wanted to believe that the organization itself had some line that couldn't be crossed, some level of decency that they upheld. They did send Shaw out to apologize in front of the media, and to his credit he did seem truly remorseful. But it still felt like the Hawks were trying to duck a suspension from the league, and it was hard to tell if they and Shaw were sorry he said it or just sorry he got caught.

After calling for his suspension, I got more emails telling me that I was too sensitive and this was a word tossed around various hockey rinks and men's leagues everywhere. Taking the time to explain that that was the exact problem was simply more shouting at the rain. Old white men didn't want to hear it because it's so fucking hard to change one's vocabulary. Nevermind that these guys have already cheered on a gay player on the Hawks, because the percentages tell you there's been one, and probably several.

After that, I just wanted it all to be over.

A Reminder
April 23, 2016
Blues vs. Hawks (Game Six)

And then just a few days later, I was reminded why I bothered at all. The Hawks had pulled out Game Five in double-overtime to bring the series back to Chicago. The thought of the Blues blowing a 3-1 lead, I couldn't suppress the smile that brought. I tried, but I couldn't. The blog guys got together one last time to watch the Hawks at one of our favorite bars.

The Blues scored three goals in five minutes in the first to cancel out Shaw's opener, and it looked like Game Five had merely been a blip on the way to the demise this Hawks team was destined for and probably deserved. So I was happy to Irish wake the rest of the game, and bid adieu to a season from hell that I didn't want to bother with anymore.

But from nowhere, or from that place only the Hawks could find, they erupted for three goals in the second. The bar was going nuts. It was one last stand, the kind we'd seen before. And I couldn't help but get swept up in the excitement. Here they were taking it away from the Blues again. Here they were showing their championship class one more time, what had seen them out of so many jams. Here they were coming out from the undertow to find more oxygen.

And there I was high-fiving and cheering along with everyone else. Surrounded by close friends in a raucous bar watching the most entertaining thing in the world, playoff hockey. It was still there, I wasn't completely dead inside. And being around those people, I knew why I bothered. That kind of camaraderie, that feeling, you only get it through sports (and maybe a really good concert). During some of the rougher times of my life, there have been friends who rush to buy a beer or dinner and want to talk everything out. I enjoy and appreciate that. And then there are times when you sit with a buddy and watch a game without saying a word. That's just as therapeutic. And it works during the happy times too. I found that nerve, for at least one night.

Of course, the Hawks would go on to lose Game Seven in St. Louis, and though now that I had found some semblance of the emotion again, I wasn't upset that the season ended. It needed to. The defining image of that game is Brent Seabrook hitting both posts with a shot that would have tied the game, and the Hawks couldn't find another chance. After my life as a hockey fan, I can't think of a better metaphor than that for what I've learned and seen.

After eight years of covering the sport and scouring all the analytics and trying to understand a game I never played all that much, after a lifetime of being a fan whose daily mood could be swung so wildly by it, I learned that at least at the NHL level so much came down to luck. Especially in the playoffs where things become so tight and space so scarce, there was only so much that coaches and GMs could control. The NHL playoffs, which consume our time and emotions and basically torture them for a couple months, really come down to nothing more than a game of pitch and toss. You can construct the roster in any way you'd like, deploy your lineup in any way possible with every theory behind it, you can have all the best players, and you're still banking on the winds to blow your way. Coaches and players say it without even realizing they're saying it. You'll hear all about "traffic," "net front presence," "greasy goals," and other ways to describe what they have to do to get the goals to win the game to win the series to win the Cup. But what they're really saying is that they need to increase the number of times per game that a puck might hit someone in the ass. Because the more times a puck hits someone in the ass in front of the net, the more times it might bounce off that ass and either into the net or onto a teammate's stick to find an open net while the goalie is wrong-footed. And that's not even including the ways the puck can bounce funny off the glass or boards. or how an opponent can have a pass bounce off his stick. Or how a wonky ice-surfaces or refs having a bad day or all the other things that no one has really any control over.

As folly as it can be to be a sports fan at all, seeking a dopamine release in an activity we have no control over that sucks up so much of our time and money, it seems patently ridiculous that anyone is a hockey fan at all. How many times have we watched one superior team batter another over a series and yet be the one going home because the other goalie drank virgin's blood or something and strung together they best six or seven games of his life? We watched the Hawks lose a chance at a fourth Cup (third at the time) because a puck hit Nick Leddy in the chest and went into the net. How do you plan for that? (And some would tell you it's what got Leddy traded. Imagine that. Having to uproot your entire life because some piece of frozen rubber hit you in the chest and bounced in a certain direction?) How many times have we watched a gifted sniper go scoreless in series and be labeled a "choker," even though he was playing the same game he always had and just watched a couple puck bounce off the post? What kind of deranged people invest so much of their lives in this activity? Surely there are thousands of better ways to enhance our lives and to feel something resembling emotion than this sadistic experiment on our blood pressure, our sanity, many of our relationships, and the aerodynamic tests we conduct on our remote controls when we invariably fling them across the room.

But you know what? So much of life comes down to luck too. And we never want to admit that because we like to feel we determine our fates, our futures, our consequences. Much like hockey teams, we can make a series of smart and responsible decisions to put ourselves in the best position to achieve what we want and avoid what we don't. But there's still so much that has to happen that is out of our control. You want that dream job? Sure, you can work hard through school and one or two jobs out of it and gather all the references and skills you need. But then that job has to be open, you have to see that's it's open through whatever avenue you use, you have to be in the right town for it, you have to send your application at the right time, and you have to hope whoever is interviewing you on that day didn't get his or her car dinged by some moving van in the morning or someone didn't spill coffee on them on the train into the office that morning. Then you have to hope they don't find someone else who's either more qualified, or is the CEO's offspring, or will work for 60% of the salary you want. And then you might get the job and the guy in the cubicle next to you always has cheetos on his fingers and wants to constantly tell you why Han shot first. Not so much of a dream job now, is it?

That dream girl or guy? You have to be in the same place at the same time, either physically or digitally. You both have to be looking at the same time. You have to be wearing the right shirt on the right day. No matter how good of a person you are or how you take care of yourself, you need a lot of fortune to find your romantic counterpoint in the world.

I don't know that hockey is any more of a microcosm or alternate reality to life than any other sport. But we invest our happiness in this kind of crapshoot pretty much every day. We value our self-worth in things that we really can't force to happen no matter how many motivational Facebook posts we believe in. I suppose that makes it seem that life is meaningless and you should break out all the Joy Division records you have (you should do that regularly anyway), but I don't think that's what I'm getting at. Because sometimes it does work out and the work you've done does get rewarded with the bounce or break that you need. And all the times it doesn't is what makes that one time more rewarding than it would have been. Sure, maybe the bad breaks pile up and it feels like the good one will never come, and then you're basically a Leafs fan and you're one of the most miserable people on Earth. But we keep plugging away, believing that one time the puck will land on our stick with the goalie down and out. Otherwise, what's the point?

Hockey is a series of building things together and watching it not work almost all the time. Baseball is considered a sport of failure, because if you don't get a hit just seven out of ten times you're an All-Star player and do that for long enough you'll be in the Hall of Fame. Well, hockey is collective failure. Instead of just you at the plate, you have four teammates out there trying to string together passes and movement and shots to score. And on almost all of your shifts, you don't. Every possession in the offensive zone is so fragile and is undone by a puck bouncing over a stick or a defensemen being right where he needs to be or a shot being saved. It's a Sisyphean task. You roll that rock up the hill and watch it roll back down and have to start over every time the puck isn't in the net. And it rarely is.

But sometimes it all comes together. Sometimes everything goes tape-to-tape. Sometimes a d-man falls down or doesn't see the guy behind him or simply whiffs. Sometimes the goalie doesn't get to the other post quickly enough or leaves the top part open. Sometimes it all comes together. Sometimes all the strategy and work and yes, luck, all combine and you break through. Pile enough of those moments together, and who knows where you can go.

That's not such a bad lesson, is it?

Made in the USA
Columbia, SC
20 June 2017